MILWAUKEE
Rock and Roll
1950-2000:
A Reflective History

MILWAUKEE
Rock and Roll
1950–2000
A Reflective History

**Featuring Marquette University's
Jean Cujé Milwaukee Music Collection**

Edited by

Bruce Cole

Curator, Jean Cujé Milwaukee Music Collection
Marquette Raynor Memorial Libraries

David Luhrssen

Managing Editor, *Shepherd Express*

Phillip Naylor

Professor, Department of History, Marquette University

Art Editor

Dan Johnson

Chief Photographer, Marquette University

MARQUETTE
UNIVERSITY
PRESS

©2019
Marquette University Press
Milwaukee WI 53201-3141
All rights reserved.
www.marquette.edu/mupress/
Founded 1916

Library of Congress Cataloging-in-Publication Data

Names: Cole, Bruce (Drummer), author. | Luhrssen, David, author. |
  Naylor, Phillip Chiviges, author.
Title: Milwaukee rock and roll, 1950-2000 : a reflective history / by Bruce
  Rogers Cole, David Luhrssen, Phillip C. Naylor.
Description: Milwaukee : Marquette University Press, 2019. | Includes
  bibliographical references and index. | Summary: "This book takes you
  from the beginning of Milwaukee rock in the 1950s to the turn of the
  century. A fascinating era of rock and roll influenced by the city's
  rich musical heritage and lingering Germanic-Polish cultural legacies"--
  Provided by publisher.
Identifiers: LCCN 2019025317 | ISBN 9781626000544 (hardcover)
Subjects: LCSH: Rock music--Wisconsin--Milwaukee--History and criticism.
Classification: LCC ML3534.3 .C65 2019 | DDC 781.6609775/95--dc23
LC record available at https://lccn.loc.gov/2019025317

Conscientious efforts were made to secure copyright consent.
The editors and publisher gratefully acknowledge the permissions
granted to reproduce copyright material in this book.

Book Design by Shawn Biner

Manufactured in the United States of America
∞ The paper used in this publication meets the minimum requirements
of the American National Standard for Information Sciences—Permanence
of Paper for Printed Library Materials, ANSI Z39.48-1992.

ASSOCIATION
of UNIVERSITY
PRESSES

Contents

About the Cover Image

The Royal Lancers cruise Wisconsin Avenue (*Milwaukee Journal*, 21 October 1962) (Left to right: Roy Malvitz, bass; Paul Stefan, vocals; Lee Breest, drums; Doug Tank, guitar; John Pavlik, guitar) (photo courtesy of the *Milwaukee Journal Sentinel*).

If you grew up in the early 1960s in Milwaukee and liked local rock music, you would remember the "Royal Lancers" and their local/regional hit "I Fought the Law." The guy on the far right of that picture, guitar player John Pavlik, is still out there performing with his group the "Green Men."*

In his book *Do You Hear That Beat: Wisconsin Pop/Rock in the 50's and 60's* (1994; see Selective and Suggested Bibliography), Gary Myers mentions Pavlik's "mind for business." I remember sitting near Jimmy Sessody (drummer of the Legends, Milwaukee's biggest 1960s band) at "Crazy Jim's Demo Derby" at the Hales Corners Speedway (a dirt track oval). Sessody told me to look out for the Royal Lancers' car. Sure enough, there was John Pavlik driving—no, smashing—steel and chrome in a jalopy with a big Royal Lancers band logo on its side careening all over the muddy infield. Great publicity stunt. For those who have never been to a demolition derby, the deal is this: crash into all the other cars until you are the only moving car left. If I remember right, Pavlik actually lasted pretty long, maybe one of the last three or four cars left. I thought that group promotion was terrific, I wanted really bad to be in a demo derby with my band's name on the side of the car.

Never happened.

Bruce Cole

---

* The "Green Men" (dyed their hair green) met the Beatles, the Rolling Stones, and Jimi Hendrix (see Bibliography, Starks 2006). They also had a Hollywood career appearing in the *Batman* television series. See an autobiographical interview with John Pavlik/Johnny Green: http://www.batmania.com.ar/paginas/johnny_green_interview.htm

To those who played and play...

Acknowledgements

Thanks to all who directly and indirectly assisted in this project including Alexandra and Adele Topping, Dennis Higgins, Jim Higgins, Sherman Williams, Nick Contorno, Bill Stace, Stephanie Kilen, Lil Rev, Barry Ollman, Guy Hoffman, Francis Ford, Ron Seymour, Clancy Carroll, Jim Eannelli, James Brozek, Rich Zimmermann, Guy Porter, Erol Reyal, James Middleton, Dennis Darmek as well as Marquette undergraduate and graduate students (particularly Professor Naylor's graduate research assistants and department of philosophy graduate student, Sterling Knox). Dr. Andrew Tallon, the retired Director of Marquette University Press, expressed an early interest in a book on Milwaukee rock. Marquette University's Richard (Rick) Holz, Dean of the College of Arts & Sciences, James South, Associate Dean of Arts & Sciences, and Janice Welburn, Dean of the Libraries, supported the project. Maureen Kondrick, the Manager of Marquette University Press, enthusiastically engaged and constantly encouraged the enterprise. Without her persistent support (and sense of humor) this book could not have been achieved.

We also appreciate the assistance provided by the Milwaukee Public Library, the University of Wisconsin-Milwaukee's Golda Meir Library, the Milwaukee County Historical Society, the *Milwaukee Journal Sentinel*, and particularly, Marquette University's Raynor Memorial Library's Jean Cujé Milwaukee Music Collection.

Thank you all for recognizing the significance of Milwaukee rock and roll.

Bruce Cole
David Luhrssen
Phillip Naylor

Introductions

by Bruce Cole

The Milwaukee rock story up until the turn of the century is really three basic stories representing three eras: before the Beatles, the Beatles, and after the Beatles (with the emergence of punk rock pioneers). Everything else stems from those periods. Bands with car names like the "Electras," "Starfires," "De Villes," "Impalas" (nope, not the animal), matching sweaters, and a little hair swept over the ears began things here. Then it was "whoa, the Beatles" with different "do's" and attitudes followed by punk rockers' irreverent takes on living in Beertown.

After fifty-plus years drumming for about a hundred groups after playing my first gig at Lane Junior High School (Highway 100 near Greenfield Avenue) in West Allis, I'm still out there enjoying it. Over the decades I've played with or known many of the musicians included in this book. I'm *still* working with many of them and reminiscing, of course, between sets.

Over the past 25 years, I have had the privilege of curating Marquette University's Jean Cujé Milwaukee Music Collection. Featured in this book, the Collection has particularly preserved and archived Milwaukee's rich rock legacy.

This book takes you from the beginning of Milwaukee rock in the 1950s to the turn of the century. It is an introduction to a fascinating era. I'm proud and happy to be part of this history as well as this project.

Bruce Cole
Curator
Jean Cujé Milwaukee Music Collection
Raynor Memorial Library
Marquette University

by David Luhrssen

From the beginning, one of the impulses driving rock and roll, and what separated it so-ciologically from country and western or rhythm and blues, was the creation of a separate generational space. Rock and roll arrived in Milwaukee, as it did in many other places, on the first night Elvis Presley materialized on the *Ed Sullivan Show*, 9 September 1956. Within the next few years young Milwaukeeans began playing the new music, sometimes with residual influences from the city's rich musical heritage (see Corenthal 1992).[1] By some accounts, the earliest wave of rock and roll combos sometimes included accordion in the lineup and were able to toss out a polka if called upon. However, the audience was primarily people of the musicians' own age, their generation, seeking markers to differ-entiate themselves from their parents.

As the years ticked by new generational cohorts rebelled against their predecessors; innovations pushed rock music forward through the end of the twentieth century, yet there was always a pull in the opposite direction, the magnetic attraction of roots. Mil-waukee was no different from anywhere else in that respect as the city's young musicians responded to the Beatles, Bob Dylan, the blues (usually discovered via British rock acts), psychedelia, the birth pangs of heavy metal, and the rock and roll revival of the early 1970s whose most popular local exponent, Truc, scored a hit on Milwaukee radio (and coverage on hometown TV) with their doo-wop cover (originally by the Capris), "There's a Moon Out Tonight."

By the mid-1970s, when I was old enough to begin searching out the music of my hometown, Milwaukee had already nurtured creative musicians with a claim on original-ity as opposed to imitation. Shag[2] would be belatedly recognized for recording one of the greatest 1960s garage-punk classics, the psychedelic anti-drug song "Stop and Listen." The Messengers' "That's the Way a Woman Is" was as catchy as anything from the yet unformed genre called power pop. Songwriter/poet Jim Spencer and progressive rock acts as varied as Sigmund Snopek and Arousing Polaris stand alongside counterparts from around the world. In some cases, their efforts were documented by LPs released on the sort of small, independent labels that proved indispensable when the next wave hit: punk rock. It was at that point that my link to Milwaukee music was forged.

Punk rock sprang up in Milwaukee two years after it emerged in New York and London, but there was no shame. If 1976 was Year Zero for the movement, 1978 was the year it arrived in most cities around the world, from Durban, South Africa to Seattle, Washington. Ideas moved more slowly before the Internet, and that wasn't necessarily a bad thing. In places like Milwaukee, discovering punk could be a matter of fortunate encounters with the likeminded, followed by trips around town (and even out of town) to track down fanzines and vinyl. Punk wasn't a click away. It took work to find it and the effort translated into commitment.

For people of my sub-generation, the "Late Boomers" or tail-enders of the Baby Boom, punk rock and all that followed in the early 1980s represented an effort by those

---

1 For full citations see the Selective and Suggested Bibliography.

2 Mistakenly called the Shag(s), the group preferred "Shag" without the article (see Chapter 6).

too young to have participated in the 1960s to write our own music and form our own subculture. But only a slender minority of Late Boomers cared enough to make the effort. Ted Nugent ruled, along with anything else on album-oriented rock radio. The Ramones weren't just greeted with incomprehension; they were met with hostility. Launching a punk scene demanded devotion from tight circles of devotees. The scene that emerged in Milwaukee was like an unincorporated town—a Mayberry R.F.D. where everyone wore leather and knew everyone else. Soon enough the population grew to the extent that the character of the place changed and the boundaries with the mainstream became less clearly defined.

In the 1970s and 1980s Milwaukee was a city segregated by race and quartered into distinct neighborhoods. For punks, the East Side was the magnet, the center of gravity owing to a bohemian history dating from the Beat era (which arrived late in Milwaukee) and the 1960s counterculture (ditto). Punks may have claimed to hate hippies, but hippies defined the neighborhood where bands found cheap housing and places to play.

Coming from a city with a distinct history, Milwaukee bands had a different well to draw from than punks elsewhere. A lingering Germanic-Polish cultural heritage was still apparent, and the city's Socialist era had ended only in 1960. Little wonder the Haskels proclaimed themselves as "workers' rock and roll," the Blackholes explored the rhythm of "power polka" and Dark Façade sounded like a techno band from Weimar Berlin (see Chapter 9).

It was a wonderful place to be, especially in hindsight, and an exhilarating moment to come of age. Although I fantasized about becoming a musician and starting a band, my talents were decidedly elsewhere. I gained my ringside seat by writing about the bands. Along with Kevn Kinney, who did go on to be a musician and start bands (The Prosecutors, Drivin N Cryin), I launched one of Milwaukee's earliest punk fanzines. *The Sheet* (1978), a one-page photocopy job, rapidly morphed into a 12-page tabloid newspaper, *X-Press*, which by 1980 became *Express* and in 1987 merged with a rival to become the *Shepherd Express*, Milwaukee's alternative newspaper.

To a greater extent than any previous local music scene, punk rock fostered Milwaukee bands that took sway over imaginations around the world. Die Kreuzen influenced the spread of grunge; Plasticland was a leader in the psychedelic revival; the Stupid Frogs became the darlings of self-consciously hip musicians from across the U.S.; the BoDeans's music became the soundtrack of sitcoms; and the Violent Femmes' first album became the perennial touchstone for disaffected youth.

Like avant-garde art movements from the late nineteenth and early twentieth centuries, punk rock was initially unacceptable to mainstream culture and had to fight for attention and, eventually, a place in the culture. Punk rock's exponents could expect no easy handouts from the media or the entertainment industry. We had to do it ourselves. The Do-It-Yourself ethos remains one of punk's legacies and laid the foundation for the alternative rock that continues to be heard in the twenty-first century.

David Luhrssen
Managing Editor
Shepherd Express

by Phillip Naylor

The Haskels blasted through their set at Zak's. With the air still crackling from punk sonic waves, the Essentials took the stage. The timbre tempered; now it was soul, man, and it was very, very good. Their choreography and style reminded me of the O'Jays. But this wasn't the "Philadelphia Sound"; it was *a* "Milwaukee Sound" and I was proud of it.[3] Standing in that crowded bar situated at the social, racial, and musical interstice at North and Humboldt Avenues, my appreciation deepened for the city's diverse musical talent.

This book is *a* history rather than *the* history of Milwaukee rock and roll. It hardly claims to be comprehensive, nor is it meant to be (nor can it be), but it aspires to inspire other studies. The book, a collection of reflections, chronicles not only performers on stage—and there have been many important ones—but also those who played complementary roles such as promoters, photographers, artists, and DJs. It is also a history of the musical perspective of three people—Bruce, Dave, and me—three guys who have enjoyed Milwaukee music and appreciated its significance in our own way. In addition, we invited some of our good friends to contribute their perspectives and voices.

Milwaukee's accessibility to popular music has distinguished the city's history. Its intimate venues now gone (but replaced by others) included Teddy's (today's Shank Hall), the Scene, the Avant Garde, the Stone Toad, Zak's, the Landing/Tasting Room, the Palms, the Tamarack, and Century Hall allowed listeners to mingle with musicians in between sets. (Performers also made themselves available.) Being so close to Chicago facilitated transcultural musical transactions, especially regarding blues music. Many blues musicians came up to Milwaukee including Muddy Waters, Howlin' Wolf, Willie Dixon, John Lee Hooker, Koko Taylor, Albert King, and Jimmy Dawkins among others. One of the great ones stayed here—Hubert Sumlin (1931-2011)—and we can't forget blues piano man Aaron Moore (1918-2013) who moved to Milwaukee from Chicago. Local musicians, e.g., Jim Liban and Jeff Dagenhardt also inaugurated blues pilgrimages to Chicago's South Side. Furthermore, beginning in 1968, Summerfest offered Milwaukee musicians opportunities to interact as well as perform.

There are two people who particularly influenced my participation in this project. I met Jim Jablonowski (1944-89) at Marquette University when we were graduate students. He had an encyclopedic knowledge of rock and roll and blues. We attended clubs and concerts together. When I teach the rock and roll history course at Marquette University, I tell my students that this is Jim's course not mine.

The other great influence is my colleague and co-editor Bruce Cole, whose elephantine memory convinced me that Milwaukee rockers (like himself) needed and deserved deeper study. It is a pleasure working (and occasionally playing) with Bruce, "the real deal," according to the late Reverend "Chicago Steve" Wiest (1951-2003), the fine "harp" (harmonica) player of the Bullfrog Blues Band and the Western Civilization Blues Band. Bruce toured internationally with Charlie Musselwhite, the renowned blues harp

---

3   Blackwolf h'Allah Enubazz (Jesse Davis) of the Essentials (and later Kings Go Forth) recounted the group's association with the Haskels: "We opened for the Haskels. We had on tight, pinstriped, tan-belled pants on, with matching vests and pink satin shirts, with short tie-neck pink capes on, kickin' some Parliament songs. Hahaha! The audience went crazy" (Nodine, Beaumont, Carroll, and Luhrssen 2017, 157).

virtuoso, and backed scores of groups. He is now a librarian at Marquette University and the curator of the Jean Cujé Milwaukee Music Collection, which provided vital archival material for this book; he continues to "play out." Indeed, in multiple ways, he embodies the history of Milwaukee rock.

I have admired David Luhrssen as a cultural force in this city, given his editing and writing for the *Shepherd Express* and his cofounding of the Milwaukee Film Festival. He has also generously donated to Marquette's Cujé Collection. Dave is a scholar as well as a journalist and has published with university presses on an array of topics. By the way, Dave told me that he was at Zak's that aforementioned fateful night too, although we did not know each other at that time.

Dan Johnson, Marquette University's Chief Photographer, greatly assisted as "art editor" (and technical and photographic adviser) especially reproducing (digitizing) and preparing the Cujé Collection's artwork and that of other sources. We are particularly thankful for his enthusiastic participation.

Of course, the generosity of invited contributors to this book is especially appreciated as well as other friends' interests and inputs (see Acknowledgments). Thanks all.

Phillip Naylor
Professor
Department of History
Marquette University

Rockers at the Muskego Beach Ballroom (1962)

CHAPTER 1

Rock's Beginnings in Milwaukee

Bruce Cole's been there since the beginning. In this chapter, he describes Milwaukee's earliest bands and venues and how rock stirred the heart and soul of a teenager, notably when he was a member of the Savoys. Sam McCue is also featured. He remains a reverential figure in the history of Milwaukee rock. McCue inspired local (Shorewood) blues musicians Jon Paris (later a Johnny Winter sideman) and Steve Cohen, along with many others (see Chapter 7). He was Milwaukee's first rock star. McCue's career valorized and validated Milwaukee as a rock and roll wellspring. As Dave Tianen noted in the *Milwaukee Journal Sentinel* (12 March 1998), Sam remains "the legend to beat." Bob Berndt never had the success or celebrity of Sam McCue, as Stephen K. Hauser recounts, but he shared a love of rock and roll, particularly rockabilly. More than a "wannabe," Berndt courageously pursued his musical dreams like so many others. Les Paul's (1915-2009) influence is immense as a musician, inventor, and innovator. David Luhrssen and the late Martin Jack Rosenblum (1946-2014) provide a personal portrait. Although Les moved to New York, he still maintained a Milwaukee area connection jamming with Jon Paris on Monday nights at Manhattan's Iridium Jazz Club. Bruce Cole describes his widening appreciation of rock's rhythms given the Latin and Rhythm & Blues (R&B) beats and performances of "Little Artie" Herrera and the Pharaohs. The chapter concludes with Bruce's celebratory recognition of Larry Lynne's 60 years of rocking.

"Milwaukee, That's Near Chicago, Right?"

by Bruce Cole

> "Teen bands are flowering, rock shows are packing them in—1,500 at a time—in a cavernous dance hall and at least two Milwaukee rock bands are hitting the big time with fast selling records" (George Lockwood, "Teen Bands Booming as the 'Big Beat' Gets Bigger," *The Milwaukee Journal*, 21 October 1962).

It is, after all, only rock n' roll, so I don't have to be all that accurate. We can trace Milwaukee rock as far back as 1958.[1] Roland Stone, a working-class West Allis bass player and songwriter, had a 45 record out that year called "Moanin' Soul" (flipside was "Lost Love") on Chicago's U.S.A. label—probably the first rock record release in Milwaukee, maybe in Wisconsin. A North Side band called the Noblemen had a local hit record later that year, "Thunder Wagon." Sam McCue and Larry Foster started the Nomads around that time. The Bonnevilles revved up a little later. I heard about these bands and records from neighborhood kids, who had listened to the tunes played by their big brothers and sisters. Local newspapers, television, and radio didn't show much interest in rock.

So, the fourteen pages of information and full-page pictures of local bands in the 21 October 1962 *Milwaukee Journal* (right before the Cuban Missile Crisis) was a very big deal at the time. The *Milwaukee Journal* was *the* most important information source in town. (I'd been a paperboy the year before, and I knew that very few houses in West Allis didn't get a daily newspaper.) I was proud since I was in a band myself and I knew some of the musicians mentioned in that article. I was part of an elite club.

But as a 15-year-old wanting desperately to be a part of the Milwaukee rock world, joining the 18-year-old and older guys who had been at it for a couple years already left me feeling like I'd missed the best part of the story. I got serious in late 1961. I searched and studied the local popular music scene like someone possessed. I learned that Buddy Holly had played a Fender Stratocaster and that the cool bands had "Fender Showman" amps and Rogers drums. I hung around West Allis Music—*the* guitar store, and Faust Music—*the* drum shop on Kinnickinnic ("KK") Avenue. From the first time that I saw a kit (see also below), I knew that I wanted to be a drummer. I loved the sparkle with the skins. Meanwhile, I learned the names of all the nightspots, dance halls, roadhouses, ballrooms, and bars. I went and stared at the parking lot out on Bluemound Road where Les Paul once played his homemade electric guitar. I found out you could drink beer at 18 in these "teen bars" and roadhouses out on the "Ozaukee Beer Run" north of Milwaukee at Weilers and This Old House. Hundreds of teen bars around the state had live music

---

1   Of course, Milwaukeeans were exposed to rock via the media and by touring groups, e.g., Little Richard at the Colonial Theater in 1957. Rhythm and blues (R&B) groups played the Ron-De-Voo Ballroom at the Masonic Hall on 12th and North Avenue. Walnut Street's Bronzeville district from 3rd to 12th Streets featured rhythm and blues clubs before the construction of Interstate 43 severed the neighborhood succumbing its nightlife (see Widen 2014, 18-19).

six nights a week. (Milwaukee stayed "21" for hard liquor until the late 1960s.) Bands aspired to move from the teen bars to the nightclubs downtown. Traveling the state was tiresome and crazy. Spending five or six nights a week in your own backyard was a lot more profitable.

The venues included Marty Zivko's Ballroom in Hartford on Saturday nights and George Devine's Million Dollar Ballroom in Milwaukee on Sunday afternoons. (A gig at Devine's in late January 1959 began the fatal last tour claiming Buddy Holly, J.P. Richardson [The Big Bopper], and Ritchie Valens in early February.) Sock hops, roller rinks, and CYO (Catholic Youth Organization) dances invited bands. VFW and Knights of Columbus halls featured local DJs and "battle of the bands" contests. (Only the winner would be paid.) The Nightingale Ballroom and Bert Phillips Ballroom hosted Wednesday night dinner dances. Bands especially favored the Spa on 5th and Wisconsin Avenue. Marquette University and Carroll College frats hired bands for their parties. There were opportunities for bands everywhere during those years.

Among Milwaukee's earliest rockers were Sam McCue, arguably the "Father of Milwaukee Rock,"[2] Junior Brantley, a rhythm and blues (R&B) man (see Chapter 7), Larry Lynne (and his Skunks and Mad Lads) (see Myers 1994, 179-81 213-15; and below), and Little Artie and the Pharaohs, an R&B group. Artie was an amazing front man (see below and Myers 1994, 178-79). The Pharaohs held down the weekend gigs at the Wisconsin State Fair Grounds' Youth Building dances. The Youth Building was a big old brick warehouse-like building with little windows along the roof and a cold cement dance floor. Farm kids crashed there on their sleeping bags during State Fair week every August while their animals snoozed in the barns a few hundred feet away. Robert Beaudry, a West Allis lawyer, came up with a plan to promote dances there and it became a favorite destination for teenagers and, of course, bands. The other place to be in 1962 was the Muskego Beach Ballroom. About a thousand kids would pack the place every Friday, Saturday and Sunday night. Friday was the big night. During this time, the most esteemed group was the Legends, which included and increasingly featured Sam McCue. My rocker heroes were local.

The Legends had released their version of Gene Vincent's "Say Mama" that summer. They grabbed B-sides of hits and came up with slick rearrangements. Their harmonies were exceptional, backed by two guitars, electric bass, and drums. Like so many others, I realized that rock was here to stay in "Miltown" with its blue collar, industrial, gritty, fast, loud sound (a natural breeding ground later for garage and punk rock). As for me, it would be a never-ending learning situation.[3]

---

2   George Lockwood reported that "[Mickey] Sommers [of the Renegades]—and other Milwaukee rock musicians—attributes the music's high Milwaukee popularity to Buddy Holly, guitar player, arranger, singer and showman." Sommers added: "In the Milwaukee area, if you don't play Buddy Holly, you're out." According to Stuart Glassman, a record store manager at the time: "Holly was the Charlie Parker of rock n' roll" (*Milwaukee Journal*, 21 October 1962).

3   For a taped interview of Bruce Cole (2017) see http://mkemelodiesandmemories.weebly.com/storytime-with-bruce-cole.html.

Playin' with the Savoys
by Bruce Cole

I was 16 and I'd been playing drums about a year when I joined the Savoys, a Milwaukee cover band. They headed south four or five times a month to do gigs for Earl Glicken, a Chicago promoter, and manager of an ex-doo-wop group, the Ideals. My first job backing the Savoys was at Earl's North Suburban Synagogue Beth El in Highland Park, Illinois—a pretty high-end party. We opened for Jay and the Americans, and I ended up playing drums for them, too, because they traveled without a drummer or a bass player.

We did "Ideals" jobs at these old Chicago South Side ballrooms and night clubs and high school gyms. No African Americans in West Allis, my little blue-collar suburb. My high school, West Allis Central, had one slightly tan Hawaiian girl we thought might be black, and that was it. All of sudden I'm in this band car somewhere on the South Side of Chicago looking out the window at these endless rows of brownstone apartment buildings, and not a white person in sight. We'd unload at these terrific, colorful, but shabby old theaters. The guy at the door would stand guard while we brought in the gear. There would be a cardboard box also at the door for confiscated weapons. Everyone was dressed up. The ladies were beautiful, wonderful, and even exotic to me, a teenager. The men were all dressed sharp—and EVERYBODY wore cool hats.

The Savoys (from left to right: Mike Minikel, Bruce Cole, Ron Fait, Ron LaBode)

Courtesy of the Jean Cujé Collection

We would wait backstage while five or six soul acts—singles, duos, trios—would each get out there and sing along to their 45 while it played on this little turntable sitting on the end of the stage. Behind the curtains the singers would be passing paper-bagged bottles around, just like in a movie. It WAS a movie to me – and I felt like a star. All the acts did one or two songs and left. We would come out, and this totally black audience—maybe three or four hundred—would become quiet. But, as soon as we started playing "Go Gorilla" (the Ideals' hit from a year back), and the Ideals stepped out, the place would get loud and happy. We'd do the flip side of "Go Gorilla" and pack it all up and leave to do it again at another place. We'd do that about five times from about four in the afternoon until midnight on a Saturday. I never had the slightest idea where we were either. Usually we would have dinner at Leonard Mitchell's (I think it was Leonard's, but it might have been Reggie's or another guy's) mother's house—and it was the best fried chicken I ever had in my life.

We backed the Ideals at the Arie Crown theatre in McCormick Place opening for the Dave Clark Five, and a few weeks later at the same venue, Manfred Mann and Peter and Gordon (see Chapter 3). These concerts were promoted by Earl Glicken and Art Roberts (the popular Chicago DJ) and we played mostly for free, along with the Crestones, and a few other Chicago garage acts and even some Milwaukee bands (e.g., the Ricochettes). It was incredibly thrilling for me, and my only regret is that nobody filmed any of it.

When I returned to Chicago almost ten years later with blues bands, it was all different and sometimes scary. And, after around 40 years of going there now and again, I still don't know my way around Chicago. I never did the driving!

Sam McCue:
The Fountainhead
by Phillip Naylor

Born on 29 April 1941 to musical parents, Sam McCue was the essential figure in the development of Milwaukee rock. He grew up on Milwaukee's near South Side (see Roller 2013, 22-26).[4] Latin bands initially influenced McCue (namely the guitarist Ignacio Seragosa, who tragically perished in an automobile accident). Jukeboxes broadened his education introducing him to western swing, R&B, and rockabilly. These influences, including Slovenian polkas, contributed to his development as a great accompanying and lead guitarist (ibid., 7). Sam was a founder of the first great Milwaukee rock group, the Legends (originally the Nomads, named after a Chevrolet station wagon) and were signed by Capitol Records resulting in two albums (1963-64) (see Myers 1994, 171-77). McCue's playing has been compared to James Burton, the great guitarist who backed up Ricky Nelson and later Elvis Presley. The Everly Brothers, in turn, hired McCue as lead guitarist in their band. He toured the world with the Everlys from 1964 to 1973 and worked with them in the studio (including on the pioneering country rock album *Roots* [1968]). He also played in other groups including New Blues, A.B. Skhy, and Crowfoot. McCue met or played with some of the most renowned figures in early rock and roll including Carl Perkins, Chuck Berry, Johnny Cash, and Bo Diddley. While in Los Angeles, he played with session artists including Bob Glaub, the renowned bass player. He befriended younger rockers (e.g., Warren Zevon). He sat with Jimi Hendrix as the latter's masterpiece, *Electric Ladyland*, was being mixed.

An impressionable Bruce Cole was among the local musicians influenced by the Legends. He recounted how he "practically stalked" Jim Sessody, the Legends' drummer. In turn, Sessody helped Bruce become the drummer for the Grand Prix's (see Chapter 6).

---

4 For more biographical information see Piet Levy and Bruce Eder, respectively, http://archive.jsonline.com/entertainment/musicandnightlife/milwaukee-musician-sam-mccue-remembers-days-playing-with-phil-everly-b99177556z1-238779071.html; and http://www.allmusic.com/artist/sam-mccue-mn0001197298. In addition, see http://www.folklib.net/wami/wami_hof_bios.shtml#McCue,Sm. Bruce Cole provided additional information.

Bruce later joined McCue in the band Tempus Fugit in the late 1970s. He remains in contact with Sam. Bruce recalls: "He tried to bring out the musical best of band members. He was laid back and cordial—a pleasure to play with" (Conversation, December 2017).

Bob Berndt,
Elm Grove's Own Rockabilly Singer
by Stephen K. Hauser[5]

In the mid-1950s, American popular culture was changed forever by the unique voice and personality of a young man from Tupelo, Mississippi, Elvis Presley. By fusing the influences of black rhythm & blues and rural white country and gospel music, Presley popularized the rockabilly sound that captivated the nation, making him a teen idol and pop music sensation. Elvis's first commercial recording, "That's Alright, Mama," was released on Sam Phillips's legendary Sun Records label in Memphis on July 20, 1954. Heavy airplay on Tennessee radio stations WHBQ and WHEM made the record a big regional hit. Within two years, Elvis Presley had the number one song in the U.S. ("Heartbreak Hotel") and appeared on big national variety shows, such as the Milton Berle, Steve Allen and Ed Sullivan programs.

Robert P. Berndt celebrated his 22nd birthday on July 20, 1954. He didn't know it yet, but the release of Elvis Presley's first 45rpm recording on that same date down in Memphis would change his young life forever. Berndt had been born in Elm Grove where he attended St. Mary's gradeschool and went on to attend Pius XI high school in Milwaukee, but he left in 1950 when the Korean War broke out. He enlisted in the U.S. Army and was honorably discharged as a corporal when the conflict ended in 1953. He received a GED from Pius XI in 1954.

Berndt had always loved music and began to strum away on an acoustic guitar while in the service. He also enjoyed toying with his father Paul's radio set, pulling in faraway 50,000-watt AM radio stations, including WLAC and WSM from Nashville. It was there in his Elm Grove home on Wrayburn Road that he heard his first Elvis Presley songs, along with a potent mix of R&B and country tunes. Berndt was hooked and spent the next several years trying to break into the music business as a writer and a performer.

In 1961, Berndt traveled to Sauk City, near Madison, to cut a record of his own at Jim Kirchstein's legendary Cuca Records studios. (Kirchstein had recorded the original version of the Fendermen's #5 smash hit "Muleskinner Blues" the year before.) Berndt's 45rpm, "False Dreams/After Hours" (Cuca 1041), failed to chart, and today it is one of the more obscure (and hence more valuable) Cuca releases.

---

5   Adapted with permission from Stephen K. Hauser, the *Elm Grove NEWS-INDEPENDENT*, September 2012. Sources: Robert F. Berndt, the Berndt family, Gary E. Myers, Doug Tank, and Rocky Kruegel.

Undaunted, Bob journeyed to Nashville, Tennessee, to record for Nashville Records, a division of the powerful Starday Recording Company, which handled such big country stars as Johnny Bond and Red Sovine. Unfortunately, Berndt's release, "Just Step Back/Big Chi" (Nashville 5100), failed to make a dent. He did manage to record his 1962 sessions for posterity, however, by having a passerby snap photos of him outside the Grand Ole Opry and the WSM radio studios.

Bob Berndt in front of the Grand Ole Opry
(Ryman Auditorium in Nashville)

Courtesy of the Bob Berndt Family

Back in Elm Grove, Berndt approached Ralph Hanzel of West Allis Music Center on 89th and Greenfield to help him find a lead guitarist to play on a recording of four of his own compositions, "Down Home," "Walkin' Shoes," "Just Forget it," and "Whipperwill." Hanzel led him to Doug Tank of the Royal Lancers, one of Milwaukee's most popular bands. The Lancers had scored a big local hit the previous year with "I Fought the Law," a song penned by Sonny Curtis of the Crickets (and subsequently a #9 chart hit for the Bobby Fuller Four in 1966]).

A recording session was arranged at Dave Kennedy Studios on West Appleton Avenue in Milwaukee. Doug Tank worked out new arrangements for Bob's four songs, and brought in his friend Roy Malvitz, also of the Royal Lancers, to play bass. Berndt strummed away on rhythm guitar and sang.

An acetate was pressed of the sessions. If Kennedy had scheduled the tracks for release, they would have been manufactured at the RCA Victor pressing plant in Chicago. But it was not to be. Berndt's latest recording effort sank without a trace and would not be heard by anyone until Doug Tank, now living in rural Kansas, made a few remastered CDs available to friends in 2007.

Berndt went on to marry and raise three children in Elm Grove. He obtained a real estate license and founded his own realty company, served on the Elm Grove building commission, and dabbled in local politics. He ran unsuccessfully for state assemblyman in 1974 and for village trustee in 1976 and 1979.

Although he gave up his dream of musical success, he continued writing songs and recording them onto tape. He died February 17, 1983 at age 50 and is buried in St. Mary's parish cemetery.

"Les Paul: 'The Wizard of Waukesha'"
by David Luhrssen and Martin Jack Rosenblum[6]

In 1954 at a meeting of the Audio Engineering Society in New York, Les Paul proposed the ideal device for music listeners. He recalls his words as if the meeting had been held last week: "Ideally, it would be something you could carry in your pocket that had no moving parts and held every song you ever wanted to hear."

At the time it sounded as remote as interstellar travel. Fifty years later it was being marketed as the iPod. Although he foresaw a time when thousands of songs could be stored in a matchbox, Les Paul didn't actually invent the iPod. But even if he didn't invent several of the things careless writers have ascribed to him, the Wisconsin native known as the "Wizard of Waukesha" was, for several decades, at the leading end of audio technology while developing formidable skills as a guitarist. His name became etched in the history of rock music through the electric guitar he developed.

On June 21 [2008] Les Paul, who celebrated his 93rd birthday a week earlier, returns to Milwaukee for a performance at the Pabst Theater in conjunction with an exhibition at Discovery World, "Les Paul's House of Sound." Nobody knows who played the first electric guitar, but Paul was among the pioneers who tinkered with the potential of amplification. Paul's first stab at electrification involved jabbing the needle from a phonograph into the top of a Sears & Roebuck guitar and playing it through a radio receiver. By 1934 he built a solid body electric guitar, an early prototype of the famous Les Paul Gibson that went into production in the 1950s. And that wasn't Paul's only enduring accomplishment. Magnetic recording tape, developed in Nazi Germany, was first used in postwar America by Bing Crosby.

It was Paul, however, who glimpsed the new medium's full potential as he hammered out the basic tools of modern recording from the workbench of his garage. "How High the Moon," Paul's 1951 hit with his wife, singer Mary Ford, marked a breakthrough in multitrack recording, employing tape to overlap dozens of guitar and vocal performances.

Although reel-to-reel tape machines have been replaced by digital audio workstations, the method of assembling recordings like an aural mosaic from bits of separately recorded sound remains the way most contemporary music is produced.

It's been a long road from Paul's public debut, at age 13, at downtown Milwaukee's Schroeder Hotel (now the Hilton City Center) to the weekly residency he maintains nowadays at Midtown Manhattan's Iridium Jazz Club. As a teenager he performed a hillbilly vaudeville act on guitar and harmonica; soon enough his fleet fingers began wrapping themselves around the more challenging progressions of jazz. By the 1940s he became an ace sessions man, performing with Nat "King" Cole and other popular jazz artists.

But the insights from his early shows at Wisconsin Lions Clubs and band shells proved indelible. Performing at a Kenosha theater, he grabbed a banana from a backstage fruit bowl before strolling into the limelight. "The first thing I did was peel the banana,

---

6   Originally published by the *Shepherd Express*, 26 June 2008. Reprinted with permission.

toss out the banana and eat the peel. And then I started to play. I had the audience!" he says, still amused at his nerve as well as his digestive fortitude.

Even over a phone call from his home in Mahwah, N.J., Paul's personality shines. Like a favorite uncle who serves unconventional opinions at Thanksgiving dinner with a twinkle in his eye, he is a little zany at the edges. He is also earnest and unassuming.[7]

If the speaker at the other end of the line is an audience, he will be a trouper, an entertainer. He must have won over many peanut galleries as a teenager in Wisconsin. "The worst thing a musician can do is blame the audience," he remarks. "If you're not giving the audience what they want, it's your fault. As a guitarist I'm telling the audience with my hands what I'm feeling. [I should be able] to make them laugh, make them cry. One time there was a woman in the audience who wasn't responding. I stopped playing. I leaned over from the stage and said, 'Are you all right?'" He wasn't being sarcastic. Paul always wanted to tickle everyone's ear, whether in concert or on a recording. He wanted to please the public and be true to the sonic ideas carried in his head from a young age. It explains why the string of hit recordings made in the 1950s with Mary Ford were almost inevitably pitched in the key of relentless good cheer. By the time of those records, and the endearingly wacky network program he hosted with his wife, he had distilled elements of country and jazz into idiosyncratic, Sputnik-era pop sound of percolating melodies and caffeinated guitar riffs. It wasn't rock 'n' roll, but it pointed toward the technology that made rock, from the 1960s onward, possible.

Paul readily admits that he lost interest in the evolution of music even as he continued to develop new technology for creating music. The turning point for him was the bebop jazz of the late 1940s. Like the rock 'n' roll of the following decade, postwar bebop musicians "were no longer playing the melody." Whether or not he dug their melodies, Paul shaped the development of many rock musicians through multitrack recording and, perhaps more importantly, the line of Les Paul Gibson guitars. It has been the ax of choice for guitar heroes and has drawn musicians like Jimmy Page and Joe Perry to his gigs. Although Paul was not initially in the rock 'n' roll camp, he seems entirely pleased by the impact he made and welcomes the contributions of guitarists such as Jeff Beck and Keith Richards on his recent CDs.

Why has the Les Paul Gibson won so many devoted fans from the Rock and Roll Hall of Fame? For starters, it's as well-crafted as the handiwork of Old World luthiers. Because of its aesthetics, a guitarist can feel the resonance through the contoured top while hugging the instrument to his body. The guitar is beautifully shaped and proportioned with the neck set into the body, not bolted on as with other models. The humbucking pickups give the Les Paul Gibson a deeper, wider, warmer sound than the trebly, piercing Fender Stratocasters that are its major rival at instrument stores. Pop psychologists who deemed the electric guitar a phallic symbol might have gotten it wrong. For Paul, a guitar should be "your psychiatrist, mistress, housewife and bartender."

For him, the shapely Gibson is just like a woman. The solid body guitar bearing his signature represents the convergence of the two sides of Les Paul's coin, the knock-'em

---

7 Les Paul was best friends with Dr. George Miller, the father of Milwaukee native and Rock and Roll Hall of Fame inductee, Steve Miller (of the Steve Miller Band). Les was also Steve's godfather.

dead entertainer and the basement inventor. From an early age Paul was tinkering like a young Thomas Edison, eager to discover what new things the machinery of the modern age could accomplish. As a teenager he built his own crystal radio set, through which he discovered hillbilly music on the "Grand Ole Opry." He built his own PA system and electric guitars because "I had to be heard" in a world that was only getting noisier. He took apart his mother's piano in the parlor to figure out how it worked.

Among younger generations, the inventive impulse that moved Paul has shifted into computer software. He's not entirely happy with the influence this has had on music. "Digital technology bothers me," he says. "It is tinny. It has no warmth. Neither did the player piano. Remember, digital is either on or off like the player piano."

Paul has not retired from technology, however. Recently he was asked by the Gibson Company to design a new line of amplifiers. Paul was happy to sign on. "There is no speaker made today that can faithfully reproduce the sound of a solid body electric guitar," he explains. "You always lose the true sound value the guitar is capable of. It's easy for a bad guitarist to sound good given the amplifiers of today."

Any obstacle to reaching the sound he hears in his head has always frustrated and motivated the Wizard of Waukesha, whose goal has been to create a space where listener and musician can meet on common ground. "My whole life has been dedicated to chasing the sound," he says. "All of my inventions have been chasing the sound."

Becoming a Pharaohs Fan: Appreciating Artie Herrera
by Bruce Cole

I didn't know what to make of Little Artie and the Pharaohs that first time I heard them. I was a "top-forty" rock, pop music kind of "white-bread" kid. My "roots" (if I really had any) were in the Buddy Holly, Crickets, Chuck Berry, Jerry Lee Lewis, Bobby Vee school of rock. I liked most of what I heard when I turned on the local pop/rock radio stations we all listened to. I liked "Runaway" by Del Shannon, "Sea Cruise" by Frankie Ford, some Elvis, and some of that new surf music coming out of California.

The Pharaohs didn't play any of that stuff. They were a rhythm & blues (R&B), soul, funky kind of band that did things by people like Bobby "Blue" Bland, Bobby Marchan, Lee Dorsey, Rufus Thomas, and a lot of other artists I had never heard of. They did some New Orleans style blues/rock things, and some up-tempo blues shuffles and James Brown-kind-of-music. (I hardly knew who James Brown was.) The sax player often took solos instead of the guitar player, and the band did little steps together every now and then. They played "dynamics" and breaks throughout songs, and most of their tunes had that funky beat and not just a straight-ahead 4/4 groove garage rock bands lived on. At first, I wasn't sure what to think; I had this loyalty thing for "Joey Dee and the Starlighters," the "Ventures," and Duane Eddy-type grooves. The Pharaohs' rhythm and blues was foreign music to me, but it only took about five minutes to decide that I really liked it. There was plenty of room for this stuff in rock world's widening genre. Plus, I kind of knew inside that this band was a much, much better band than any of these primitive Buddy Holly-type combos I was used to hearing.

I went to those State Fair dances almost every weekend. I quickly became a devoted Pharaohs fan, and, mostly because of them, I started searching out the big names in black popular music of the time. I discovered entertainers like Major Lance, Alvin Cash, The Five Du-Tones, Chuck Jackson and Jerry Butler, as well as record labels like "Okeh" and "King" (James Brown's label) and "Atlantic." Luckily, I had some friends with older sisters and brothers who cruised record shops on the North Side and brought back "rhythm records" with that kind of energy and feeling you didn't hear on the top-forty, mainstream radio stations.

I learned a lesson early on: the great, important, interesting, lasting music, is often the music you *don't* hear on the radio every day. You have to search and find that special music. I learned that 50 years ago and it's as true now as it was then. Some things never change.

Larry Lynne's 60th[8]
by Bruce Cole

I have this memory of a sunny, spring, Saturday afternoon a long time ago. I was not yet a teenager and was sitting in the back seat of our 1956 (or 1957?) Nash Rambler waiting at a stop light. I glanced out the window and saw a live rock band, close-up, for the first time. These dudes all had high, Johnny Burnette-style oiled up hairdos, matching red jackets, thin black ties and slightly too short tight black pants. A Lucky Strike or a Camel dangling out of the corner of one guy's mouth, all five guys rolled out of a massive red 1957 Cadillac parked in the Rose Bowl (a West Allis bowling establishment near Highway 100 and Greenfield Avenue) parking lot and started unloading gear—little 30-watt amps, Fender guitar cases, mic stands—from the small U-Haul trailer hooked to the bottom of that big, Cadillac back bumper.

They were there to play an afternoon battle-of-the-bands show. And, of course, to complete the picture, out of yet another Caddy rolled those BABES—a couple really hot blondes with big bouffant 'do's' making particularly sure everyone noticed them.

Just before we turned right onto Greenfield I caught a glimpse of the red sparkle drums, and right there, on the spot, I decided. I was going to be a rock drummer as soon as I became a teenager. No doubt about it.

One of the band guys in that group was Larry Ostricki. At eighteen, he was already a well-known local rocker with a slightly crazy, definitely wild reputation. Originally from Stevens Point, the Ostricki family eventually headed for Milwaukee and ended out in the

---

8   Information for this essay was derived from an unpublished manuscript.

then rural community of Greenfield, Wisconsin, an oddly shaped area roughly ten miles south of downtown Milwaukee.

Twelve-year-old Larry worked that first summer at a truck farm off 27th Street loading freshly picked produce crates onto trailers; he spent the next couple summers working as a carpenter and eventually a roofer. Even as a kid he had that hustling, 1950s good-with-your-hands, ethic. It would stay with him for life.

A couple years later Larry was among the first enrolled at the brand new, ultra-modern Greenfield High School. He recalled: "There was a fence around the place, man, to keep the cows and horses out, I'm not kiddin'."

At sixteen, influenced by country music, rockabilly, boogie, and a desire for cool clothes, hot cars, and mellow chicks seen in those cheap, black and white triple-feature teenage exploitation drive-in flics, Larry changed his name to Larry Lynne, started teaching himself guitar ("first drums, then trumpet, then guitar"). He recalled: "My first guitar was a 1954 'Strat'[Fender Stratocaster]—paid fifty bucks for it." Larry figured it was just a matter of time before he would be the next wild rebel rocker like Gene Vincent.

It was a radical plan. There were no fulltime bands—rhythm combos, as they were known around Miltown in 1957—doing strictly rock music. Polka and country western trios featuring an accordion, a drummer and a horn were, primarily, the working live music of the time. Sometimes—rarely--an electric guitar would round out the group.

His first band (late 1957) was the Rock-a-tones: "We only did four gigs, though, and I don't really count that" says Lynne. It started for real, though, a year later with the Bonnevilles, probably Milwaukee's first rock band. Although another Milwaukee based group, the Noblemen, are usually credited with recording Milwaukee's first rock single, "Thunder Wagon," Larry and others contend that, technically, the Noblemen were not a true rock n' roll band. According to Larry: "The Noblemen were more of a '50/50' band— half polkas, half rock—but we were 100% rock n' roll, man."

Next to the Milwaukee Braves, the Bonnevilles were one of the hottest things in town for a couple years. There were tons of venues back then: night clubs, ballrooms on the outskirts of town, bowling alleys, theatres, supermarket parking lots, CYOs, proms, and high school and college weekend gigs. Larry hauled the trailer ("Bonnevilles," in red, painted on the side) with his white Cadillac convertible. He was often making around $100 a week. Not bad for a part-time job rockin' the weekends. It meant enough money for new cars, new toys and maybe even a house. At the time, blue collar, factory laboring guys like my Dad barely made that kind of money.

In 1960, the Bonnevilles landed a record deal with a major company—Coral Records (Buddy Holly's label). The "A" side of their first single was an impressive and moody instrumental arrangement of the old American Civil War ditty "When Johnny Comes Marching Home" called, simply, "Johnny." The record received decent distribution and sold (according to Larry) maybe a hundred thousand copies. It was, for sure, a "mid-western hit," with break out sales in a few other areas of the country. Two years out of the gate and Larry Lynne was almost there.

Close, but not to be; follow-up recordings went nowhere. Furthermore, the Bonnevilles were soon overshadowed locally by Milwaukee guitar icon Sam McCue and his group, the Legends. Lynne left the Bonnevilles and put together a solid, seasoned 4-piece

R&B-tinged group. Looking to abandon automobile names and phony titles, Larry jokingly called this new outfit the Skunks. With black and white furry striped suits, silver streaked hair and a powerful, highly professional approach to musical excellence coupled with a smooth, well-rehearsed show element, the Skunks raised the local musical ladder and quickly developed a huge regional following. Needing a 45 to peddle, and in keeping with their somewhat strange image and eclectic song list, the Skunks recorded a Dallas Frazier novelty number, "Elvira." Again, although a popular local and regional 45 like "Johnny," "Elvira" also failed to chart nationally. Oddly enough, around 13 years later, a strikingly similar arrangement of "Elvira," by the Oak Ridge Boys, became a platinum selling song and a signature number for that group.

The Skunks toured coast to coast for a couple years and Larry lived in California for a while. But the road got long and old and lonely, and eventually Lynne came home to his Midwestern roots and began again in Milwaukee where he had left off—working construction gigs by day and fronting popular, polished, excellent rock, soul, blues and country bands by night. We could do a page or two right here just naming the groups, but who cares? As they say in the music industry, "You're only as big as your last record." In the world of regional rockers with no hit records, it would be: "You're only as popular as your last band."

Larry Lynne, after 60 years in the band business, is indeed as big as his last band. In 2008, the Skunks re-grouped and re-energized, a show band in every sense of the word, and played festivals and corporate gigs throughout the year. Larry also maintains the Larry Lynne Group, Bootlegger, and the Rockin' Rebels. He was also out there playing guitar with the Doo Wop Daddies and a few other bands. And, of course, he still does his construction thing. Over six decades of roofs and rock.

It's 2018 as of this writing. Get out and see this well-preserved cat who works and plays with the energy and enthusiasm of a twenty-year old. A Wisconsin musical blue-collar icon; that's Larry Lynne and that's a fact. Happy 60th old friend.

MEET THE BONNEVILLES!

DBCD 1001

INSTRUMENTALS and VOCALS featuring

SENSATIONAL
BOBBIE MERKT

12-YEAR-OLD
WENDY COLBY

MEET THE ROCKIN' BEAT FOR YOUR DANCING FEET!

Courtesy of Dorothy Flanagan

The
Bonnevilles

Courtesy of Vince Megna (Galaxy Club, Cudahy [1962])

THE LEGENDS
Organized: April, 1959
Personnel: Jimmy Sessody (drums)
Jerry Schils (bass guitar)
Sammy McCue (guitar)
Larry Foster (guitar)
Favorite Songs: "Some Day" "Such a Night"
"Peggy Sue" "Think It Over"
Records: "Say Mama" "Lariat"
Engagement: Holiday House, parties,
Muskego Beach, rock shows

The Legends, kings of Milwaukee rock from the early to mid-1960s, on Bradford Beach (1962)

Courtesy of the Milwaukee Journal Sentinel

The Legends live at Marty Zivko's Ballroom

Courtesy of the Jean Cujé Collection

Les Paul

Photo by Erol Reyal

Larry Lynne

Courtesy of Larry Lynne

Little Artie and the Pharaohs added rhythm and blues to Milwaukee in the 1960s

Courtesy of Jim Lombard

Little Artie and the Pharaohs rocking

Courtesy of Jim Lombard

Nick Topping , Milwaukee's renowned impresario
of folk, rock, and world music, at the International House

CHAPTER 2

Milwaukee and the Folk Revival

The rediscovery of folk musicians (e.g., the Carter Family, Woody Guthrie, Pete Seeger, the Weavers, Jean Ritchie, Odetta, Lead Belly[1]) and their music in the 1950s and 1960s, along with contemporary renditions by appreciative, talented emerging musicians (e.g., The Kingston Trio, Dave Von Ronk, Peter, Paul, and Mary, Joan Baez, Bob Dylan, Tom Paxton, Phil Ochs, Ramblin' Jack Elliott), led to a folk revival. Blue grass music also gained popularity given the talents of musicians such as Bill Monroe, Earl Scruggs, Lester Flatt, Doc Watson, Earl Taylor, and the Stanley Brothers. Starting in April 1963, ABC televised Hootenanny on Saturday evenings celebrating a variety of folk music styles. As Stephen K. Hauser relates, the Coachmen (not to be confused with rock groups of the same name) from Waukesha were a particularly popular folk group. Although the Coachmen never cut a record, their numerous local television appearances besides live performances showcased the group's considerable talent.

Folk musicians' social and political activism especially interested Nicholas (Nick) Topping (1918-2007), a shopkeeper/impresario, who booked many international and national folk musicians for Milwaukee audiences. He is one of the great figures in the history of Milwaukee music,

---

1   Huddie William Ledbetter (also known as "Leadbelly") (1888-1949) epitomized a concurrent revival in traditional blues along with folk music. Other exponents included Son House, Brownie McGhee and Sonny Terry, and Lightnin' Hopkins, to name a few. Renowned for their electric blues, Muddy Waters, Howlin' Wolf, and John Lee Hooker played acoustically during the folk revival.

particularly remembered as the promoter who brought the Beatles (see Chapter 3) and Bob Dylan to Milwaukee in 1964 (see below). Nick's musical pursuits correlated with his commitment to social justice.

Milwaukee's folk tradition also featured the venerable Larry Penn, a truck driver and a union supporter. His social consciousness and civil rights engagement led to performances with Pete Seeger and Utah Phillips. Larry died in 2014 at the age of 87 and remains an inspiration.[2] Lil Rev (Marc Revenson), a steward of traditional folk, provides a heartfelt reflection. Like Larry Penn, David HB Drake performs in front of a variety of audiences from children to social activists. A native of Milwaukee, his wide repertoire features songs dealing with the Midwest. Bill Camplin began his folk career in the late 1960s (notably with his group, Woodbine) frequenting Milwaukee clubs and cafés; he continues to perform.[3] Other important singers with particular attachments to Milwaukee have included Claudia Schmidt, Loey Nelson, Barry Ollman, Jim Spencer, Jym Mooney, Willy Porter, and the folk/blues trio "Spider" John Koerner, Dave "Snaker" Ray, and Tony "Little Sun" Glover.

The Coachmen:
A Most Popular Folk Group of the Early 1960s
by Stephen K. Hauser[4]

By the start of the 1960s, America had been overwhelmed by the new folk music craze, with young musicians rediscovering many verses and melodies that were often long-forgotten echoes of the nation's past. The music proved a worthy soundtrack to the hopeful optimism generated in younger Americans by Senator John F. Kennedy's 1960 campaign for the presidency and the New Frontier policies of his administration. Milwaukee nurtured a folk revival during those years, but one of the finest local groups hailed from Waukesha County—The Coachmen.

In the fall of 1958, three young competitive swimmers caught the "folk bug" by the way of the constant airplay accorded to the new folk hits by Milwaukee's "Top 40" format stations: WOKY (920 AM) WFOX (860 AM), and WRIT (1340 AM). Leading the pack was the Kingston Trio's "Tom Dooley," which hit the number one spot on WOKY's "Hit Parade Survey" that November. Bruce Kerr, Walt Galloway, and Rich Reaves began singing along to the radio, clapping and playing bongos and strumming an occasional

---

2   At the unveiling of a portrait of Mayor Frank P. Zeidler at the Milwaukee Municipal Building, Penn performed "Spirit of Gene Debs" with music and lyrics by Mayor Zeidler (composed in the mid-1930s). Zeidler remarked: "Do I have any ambition at the age of 93? Yes, to play the guitar and sing like Larry Penn" (Wisconsin Labor Society Newsletter, 23, no, 2 (Winter 2005-06): 2-3 (http://wisconsinlaborhistory.org/WLHSproof1r.pdf).

3   Among the most prominent folk clubs were the Avant Garde (see Angeli and Goff 1975 [in Bibiliography], the Catacombs, and the Blue River Café (see http://www.milwaukeeindependent.com/profiles/gary-lukitsch-looking-back-at-the-blue-river-cafe/).

4   Adapted with permission from Steven K. Hauser and the *Elm Grove NEWS-INDEPENDENT*, August, September, and October 2016. Sources: Walt Galloway, Bruce Kerr, Rich Reaves, Steve Hoeft, Jim Duwel, and the *Waukesha Freeman*.

ukulele while riding to YMCA swim meets in the car piloted by their long-suffering coach Ray Hatch.

By 7th grade at Waukesha Junior High School, the three had begun to sing as a quartet with their friend Bill Illing in Mrs. Margaret Kamradt's music class. Walt Galloway and Steve Hoeft remembered Mrs. Kamradt as a tough taskmaster, quite adept at keeping the rambunctious junior high schoolers in line, but with a sincere love of kids and music. "She encouraged us," Hoeft recalled simply.

They adopted the name "The Coachmen," taking it from the Kingston Trio's song "Three Jolly Coachmen." So that each could sing a verse, an extra line was added, making it Four Coachmen. When Bill Illing decided not to continue, "He became the Pete Best of the Coachmen," Bruce Kerr quipped.

The remaining three were a trio only briefly. They were soon approached by fellow swimmer Steve Hoeft, a longtime friend. He informed Kerr that he had bought a guitar and was quickly learning to play it. "When you get good at it, come back and we'll talk," Kerr told him. "I returned the following week," Hoeft recalled. They became a quartet again.

After going on to Waukesha South High School in 1961, they were further encouraged in their musical pursuits by their swim coaches Rollie Bester and Phil Ciblik. Today, Coach Bester and Coach Ciblik are remembered as legendary Wisconsin coaches, as they led their swim teams to the championship level. "They motivated their swimmers, not just athletically, but to be successful in life," Galloway recalled. Kerr agreed, "They wanted you to do your best and instilled that in us. You can do anything if you believe in yourself."

The encouragement received at Waukesha South extended to the music department as well. Choral and *capella* director James Machan was appreciative of their singing talents. "He wasn't long on compliments," Kerr remembered. However, after the foursome sang the somber folk ballad "Seven Daffodils" at a high school concert, "Mr. Machan said to us as we left the stage, 'Don't ever forget how you boys sounded on that song.' I never forgot that."

The Coachmen began to widen their repertoire by learning a variety of album tracks and obscure "B" sides performed by national folk acts. "We tried to avoid some of the "obvious choices," Kerr remembered. "But the Kingston Trio's 'M.T.A.' became an audience favorite." Still, their sets even included some foreign language selections. "Since none of us spoke those languages," Galloway told me, "we had to write them out and learn them phonetically." As for the arrangements, "We all read music so Bruce would write it out for us by color coding the notes for each of our individual vocal parts to create the right harmony. My color was red."

The group also diversified their instrumentation. Hoeft added a banjo to the Coachmen's sound. "Musical instruments are fun because guys like gadgets," he told me. "There's nothing more fun than fiddling with a five-string banjo when you're first figuring it out." Meanwhile, Walt Galloway's parents bought him a used stand-up bass. "It was pretty beat up," he said. But it was functional. He learned to play it himself with the help of Kerr, adding the trademark thump-thump of the bass line heard on most folk recordings of the period.

They also developed a line of stage patter, marked by "self-depreciating humor," Kerr recalled. "We brought our friendship into the act with all four of us supporting each other no matter what happened on stage." Kerr even memorized some of the humorous introductions to songs used to great effect by Lou Gottlieb of the Limeliters at their concerts. Kerr still cites the Limeliters as his primary influence among the folk groups, while Galloway and Hoeft champion the Kingston Trio noting their commercial appeal. Reaves favors Canadian duo Ian & Sylvia Tyson of "Four Strong Winds" fame.

While the Coachmen remained popular playing at high school functions, they also began to perform at a wider variety of local events. "We played over thirty concerts a year for three years," Kerr remembered, including shows for the Waukesha Elks Club, the Woodside Women's Club, the Optimist Club, senior centers and nursing homes, the Wood Veterans' Administration Hospital in Milwaukee and even family parties for Kerr's parents.

Among their more unusual dates was a show at the Wales (Ethan Allen) School for Boys in 1965. Galloway and Kerr remembered it as their local version of Johnny Cash's famed gig at Folsom Prison, while Steve Hoeft recalled that the young men at Wales were disappointed to find that they hadn't brought "go-go girls" with them.

A few of the Coachmen jobs actually paid wages. One that did was a big fashion show for McCoy's Department Store in downtown Waukesha spotlighting Bobbie Brooks girls' sportswear in August of 1963. Another was an appearance at the *Music by Starlight* series at the Cutler Park bandshell the same month.

They also played local coffee houses, popular then with the college crowd usually without pay, but with all the coffee or tea they could drink. "We were just excited about playing," Kerr said. "But rock and roll bands were paid $50 a show at the local bars."

One job that Kerr, Galloway, and Reaves remembered with pride was a concert at Mukwonago Union High School auditorium to benefit the Waukesha County Peace Corps Service Organization in their efforts to raise funds for various Peace Corps-sponsored projects. To add an element of confusion to the event, another group on the bill that evening was another Coachmen, this one formed by three Marquette University students: Dan Schreiber of Elm Grove Joseph Kuemmel of Brookfield, and Peter Holzhauer of Wauwatosa. (The MU Coachmen later played a 1966 St. Patrick's Day luncheon at the Elm Grove Woman's Club, arranged by Schreiber's mother.)

Kerr was amused by the existence of the Marquette Coachmen, but when I informed him that the name had also been subsequently adopted in the late 1960s by a Milwaukee rock and roll combo who cut several records, he was surprised. He said he could understand another folk group choosing the name, but that it was an unlikely choice for a rock and roll outfit.

In their senior year of high school, choral director James Machan arranged for Kerr, Galloway, Reaves, and Hoeft to forgo study hall once a week for a special Coachmen rehearsal in the school's music room. "Sometimes, if we had a test coming up, we'd study anyway," Kerr recalled. Hoeft remembered that on one occasion, Mr. Machan brought in a new Ampex stereo reel-to-reel tape recorder and told the boys, "Just do your show." They played songs from their usual set list, including "Meeting here Tonight," "M.T.A.," "Risin' of the Moon," "Lonesome Traveler," "Blowin' in the Wind," and eleven more.

That old tape lay dormant and forgotten until 2004 when Mr. Machan, now retired but still a Waukesha resident, had it digitally re-mastered onto a compact disc. In 2005, he invited Walt Galloway to his home and played a few classical music CDs while they talked. Suddenly, he removed the classical CD, replacing it with a new one. "I heard Steve's banjo on the first track" Galloway told me, "and I immediately knew what it was. I hadn't known those recordings still existed." Galloway sent me a copy of the CD and I can testify that it sounds great, disclosing the real enthusiasm of four young men in love with their music being instantly contagious. "We love rehearsing and making music together," Rich Reaves told me. It is evident that he is right.

The Coachmen expanded their horizons by entering a local competition sponsored by WISN TV to appear as Milwaukee contestants on *Ted Mack's Original Amateur Hour*, then broadcast Sunday afternoons on the CBS television network. They did not make the cut to appear on the show but scored as runners-up.

During the 1964-65 television season, the Coachmen were booked to appear on Channel 12's "Singin' Here Tonight," a local half-hour "Hootenanny"-styled folk music show broadcast on Saturday evenings. Hosted by Milwaukee folkie James Murtaugh, a member of the Hitchhikers, a Marquette University folk group, the show received an award as the best produced local entertainment program in Milwaukee for 1965. Taped before a studio audience of local high school and college students, the programs spotlighted a different guest folk combo each week.

Rich Reaves doesn't remember it as a particularly enjoyable experience. "We couldn't really do our set," he explained. "We'd do one song, and then it was a break for a commercial. When we came back, the Hitchhikers would perform. Then we were back on for

The Coachmen

Courtesy of Bruce Kerr

another song. We couldn't really find our rhythm. The feel of the show was very choppy, and not very satisfying. It wasn't a great experience, although we were on TV. I'd prefer doing a live show. We were more in tune with our audience then."

The obvious next step was to make a record, but that was never done. Many local groups had trooped off to local recording studios to lay down a couple hundred bucks to press a few hundred 45rpm records that could be sold at shows. "Bruce Kerr may have thought of doing that, but I never did," Walt Galloway told me. "We never had a manager or a booking agent, so we sort of managed ourselves." Steve Hoeft agreed, "Bruce handled all the musical arrangements, but our bookings were taken care of by whoever was first contacted to set up a show." Kerr added, "We didn't know anyone we could have gone to, to do the job, so it never happened." Those who did hear them in concert, however, would concur that their harmonies would have sounded great in a recording studio.

Reaves does remember the closest they ever got to a proper recording. "Mig" Figi, the manager of WAUK radio (1510 AM) brought the Coachmen into the station's studios on West Main Street in downtown Waukesha. "He cut an acetate in the studio. We were jammed together, gathered around one mike, and sang as we watched the disc being cut. It was interesting to see the grooves created before our eyes. It was all done in one room, and I think the station did it as a 'dry run' to try out this new equipment. I'm not sure what we sang, and I don't know what happened to the disc."

Meanwhile, the group did score a local merchandising contract. Hoeft remembers that the Coachmen had to dress the part of 1960s era folk singers on stage. "Wool sweaters were $40 a pop, a lot of money back then, so we opted for $15 Gant and Van Heusen madras sports shirts instead. They had the first button-down collars I'd seen, along with longer short-sleeves that went to the elbow, and 'fruit loops', as they were called, at the back. The Kingston Trio wore 'em. Those shirts were still expensive to us."

Hoeft recalls that Jack Hunter, a salesman and manager at the Colonial Shoppe in downtown Waukesha, "offered us a merchandising deal. We'd wear clothing from the Colonial Shoppe, and we'd get to keep the shirts." Hoeft even made up a woodcut sign hawking "The Coachmen" with an old-style coach light beside the name. Beneath was lettered: "Sportswear by the Colonial Shoppe." "It was the first sign I ever made," Hoeft said. His brother later retrieved it and it was placed on stage at the group's 2005 and 2015 reunion shows. It is sad to note that the sign has survived the Colonial Shoppe by many years.

After their graduation from Waukesha South High School in June of 1965, The Coachmen prepared to go their separate ways. The *Waukesha Freeman* ran a front-page story about the group on June 24th, noting that Kerr was to attend the University of Michigan at Ann Arbor to study engineering, while Reaves would enroll at Beloit College as an economics major. Hoeft would study architecture at the University of Wisconsin-Milwaukee and Galloway would major in chemistry at Oberlin College in Ohio. All were planning career paths.

Still, the guys wanted to play a farewell performance at the Waukesha Civic Theatre at 506 N. Washington Avenue where they had given their first real concert three years earlier. The show was held on August 18th. It was the Coachmen's 100th show. (A surviving ticket from the concert notes admission was 50 cents.)

The Coachmen never played together again until 1988 when they reunited for a Waukesha South Alumni reunion, a performance they repeated in 1990. At their 40 reunion in 2005, Kerr, Galloway, Hoeft, and Reaves played for an alumni breakfast club at the Machine Shed restaurant in Pewaukee, at a class of 1965 reunion dinner and at a show open to the public at the Avalon Manor retirement home in downtown Waukesha. It was all so successful that the four repeated it all for their 50th class reunion in 2015. Present at both of the Avalon Square concerts was James Machan, their old high school choral instructor, who enjoyed their performance with the pride of a facilitator who had encouraged them along the way.

The four Coachmen have gone on to accomplish a number of things in their lives and careers and can look back with pride. The victories they achieved in athletic competition and the discipline they learned from musical performance and rehearsal stood them in good stead to compete for happiness in life.

Reaves surprisingly said, however, when he told me his fondest memory is of rehearsals with his friends. "I remember the process of working out the songs, bringing it all together and perfecting the harmonies. I liked working out our songs, seeing the music come to life. The process, that's what I liked best."

Folk Music and Nick Topping: Milwaukee's Inimitable and Irrepressible Impresario
by Phillip Naylor

Nicholas (Nick) Topping was a Greek American, a World War II veteran (Military Intelligence), but above all, a "cosmopolitan"—a citizen of the world. He proudly displayed the United Nations flag in his extraordinary sundries store, Topping & Company: The International House. Topping & Company was an entrepôt, a transcultural treasure house, which aimed to preserve and celebrate diverse ethnic traditions and identities through literature, food, and music that "language of the world," as Carlos Cortez proclaimed in his mural displayed in the store. (Nick also "exhibited" the paintings of Clarence Mente, a dedicated pacifist.) Nick was less a storeowner, but a host to all who entered Topping & Company. He would introduce customers to each other and converse (or sing!) in several languages, while offering services as a notary public, travel agent, income tax preparer, translator, and money order provider.

Politically, Nick was on the Left, existentially engaged in what he called "the good struggle" for social, economic, and political justice. On the other hand, Nick was neither dogmatic nor intolerant. He listened politely and patiently to customers and visitors with different opinions. For example, there was no pressure to sign a petition to oust controversial Police Chief Harold Breier. Nick and his young daughter Alexandra marched for

Civil Rights. Father James Groppi appreciated Nick's commitment.[5] Nick was a genial, modest person but also a shrewd businessman and promoter (the local musical representative of Triangle Productions).

Nick perceived music as a vehicle for social change. He pioneered "world music" in Milwaukee marked by an exceptional variety of albums (LPs) and 78s. An extraordinary impresario, he booked international activists Miriam Mekeba of South Africa and Mikis Theodorakis of Greece (scored *Zorba the Greek*, *Z*, and *Serpico*). Nick singlehandedly brought the national folk music revival to Milwaukee. He organized a folk music series and booked Pete Seeger, Sonny Terry,[6] Brownie McGhee, Josh White, Martha Schlamme, Jean Ritchie, and Theodore Bickel, among others in the late 1950s. In the 1960s, Nick booked the very popular Peter, Paul, and Mary to Milwaukee. Nick was described as a "music store man" (*Milwaukee Journal*, 6 October 1959) and appropriately "a music dealer"; he dealt music and musicians to Milwaukee to generate social consciousness and change.

In 1964, Bob Dylan was renowned for his "finger-pointing songs" and especially as "the voice of a generation."[7] His political and social messages mirrored Nick's; he naturally booked Dylan. The performance scheduled for the Oriental Theater on 21 November 1964 promised to be a particularly memorable one…and it was.

Apparently, "the regular sound system never arrived" and a "makeshift rig" was set up (see *Milwaukee Journal*, 22 November 1964). After singing "The Times They Are A-Changin' " and a chorus of "Talking John Birch Paranoid Blues," Dylan complained regarding the sound system. Nick quickly arranged with a local coffee house to have a new system installed. Yet Dylan and his road manager refused to cooperate. Nick had to announce to the audience: "We weren't able to install a substitute system and I couldn't persuade Mr. Dylan to perform."[8] Nick then offered refunds and exchanged tickets for upcoming concerts. Meanwhile Dylan provided his rationale for refusing to resume his performance: "I'm not going to make a fool out of myself. I've got a reputation to maintain, and I'm doing what my instincts tell me to do." Decades later Nick remained upset over the Dylan concert and disappointed by Dylan himself, a musician whom he had deeply admired.

On the other hand, by this time Nick had secured his place in local music history not only by introducing a wide variety of folk music but also by bringing the Beatles to

---

5   In a 23 May 1967 letter to Nick, Father Groppi wrote: "Thank you for your contribution to the work in which I am involved. The food you sent was quickly eaten as soon as I brought it to the Freedom House. The money will also be well used." On 7 July, Nick received another thank you note (Marquette University Archives).

6   Usually Brownie McGhee (guitar) and Sonny Terry (harmonica) played together. For Nick's folk series, Sonny played with Pete Seeger (see *Milwaukee Journal*, 20 October 1958) and Brownie played with Guy Carawan (*Milwaukee Journal*, 19 February 1959).

7   This title (or "the voice of his generation") burdened Dylan, especially at this restless time in his career. He was heading toward his own musical transformation (from acoustic to electric guitar and from topical to more personal compositions) as signaled by scenes in D.A. Pennebaker's *Don't Look Back*, a film that documented his 1965 England tour.

8   Marty Racine offered this account: "The major problem was the sound system, which was to be supplied by Milwaukee Sound Service. They never showed up and Topping feels they simply mis-logged the concert in their books. The concert proceeded anyway, with the Oriental's own system, which was inadequate. At the conclusion of the first song Dylan invited the audience to move closer to the stage, whereupon some climbed over the orchestra pit, on to the stage, and damaged the sound system…Topping quickly arranged for another sound system to be trucked in from a radio station. At this point, Dylan's road manager was pissed, Dylan was tired and pissed, and the concert was called off, even though the audience was willing to wait. Dylan and the crew split the Oriental immediately" (Racine 1975, 154).

Milwaukee in September 1964, rightly regarded by musicians and their audiences as a seminal, extraordinary event (see Chapter 3).

"Like a Lyric Low Down in the Prose:" The Life and Times of Larry Penn, Wisconsin's Legendary Folk Singer
by Lil Rev[9]

Driving along the bitter snow-covered North Country highways with Larry Penn is a lot like watching a gypsy traverse familiar terrain. His sense of direction is impeccable and nestled inside his GMC pick-up he surveys the road always ready to let some trucker know it's okay to switch lanes. He literally commands the road to carry him safely upon his journey.

And rightly so. Penn has earned many titles and paid a lot more than his fair share of union dues in his 70-some years of living. He is, for many of us here in Wisconsin, the Father of Midwestern Folk. This is his story told through the eyes of a young apprentice.

The world of Larry Penn is one of experience, and these are the visions that have painted his songs with the sweat and blood of the American working class. Penn echoes Woody Guthrie when he says, "I can never get it simple enough." In turn, Larry is extremely modest, and I have never known him to blow his own horn. So, I will.

In 1945, at 18 years old and fresh out of high school, Penn was drafted into the service. Though he didn't see any action driving a tank, it was to play an important role in helping him choose his career path. Returning home after World War II, he put his experience with heavy machinery to work driving trucks. He traversed the continent, hauling the industrial labor of the Midwest, writing down ideas, flirting with poetry and observing the world around him. By his mid-30s he was married and raising a family in Milwaukee. It was at this juncture that he began to teach himself guitar.

The Penn family would eventually include five children. One would think that the rigors of being a truck-driving man, father and budding guitarist might prove too heavy a load, but then again, the times-were-a changing. Milwaukee like so many other cities in the 1960s was roiled in the campaign for racial equality. Larry and his wife Pat marched for civil rights with Father Groppi. Throughout these defining years, Penn found himself writing, singing, marching and playing.

"Once you get applause, it's like a disease," Larry once told me. These years would also reinforce his sense of commitment to the working people of this nation as an active

---

9   This contribution derives from an unpublished manuscript dated 19 March 2004, and, in slightly different form, from "Like a Lyric Low Down, Larry Penn: Wisconsin's Legendary Folk Singer," *Shepherd Express*, 24 June 2004, 27-28). The author and the *Shepherd Express* provided permissions. See also https://www.larrypenn.com.

member of the Teamsters. Throughout his career, he would be called upon to sing for the people. Labor it seems, would not let him rest!

In an era of me first, one recognizes Penn as the embodiment of commitment and responsibility to family, community, and work. Men like Larry remind us that folk music comes from life and living; it is the voice of a hard day's work and the selfless act of giving your time to others. Penn in all of his humbleness, would never set himself apart.

Like his music, Penn is a man of many hats, father, husband, storyteller, photographer, musician, activist, and toymaker. His fascination with trains started when he was just a kid, when his dad brought him an electric train. Today, in addition to his well-crafted songs like "Run Kate Shelley Run," "No Self-Respecting Hobo," and "Julia Bullette." [10]he can be found working in his basement on quality wooden toys. You guessed it. Railroad whistles and toy trains—all hand cut, sanded, and polished. Larry says it's his wish that these toys not only spark the imagination of the kids who acquire them but that they could also be left out in the rain, pounced on, and played with, while still surviving the vagaries of a healthy childhood.

Larry first began to sell his toys at craft fairs and festivals. While he loved meeting people and seeing his hard work passed on to others, it was often at the expense of his not being able to perform as much as he wished. Today, Larry makes wooden trains to order, either by the piece or as a whole line. His wooden whistles are also a big hit at the schools and libraries where he sings, teaches railroad lore and shows kids how to build their own whistles with his kits.

Larry's fixation with trains is like a never-ending reservoir of material. From his songs and toys to his truly unique collection of photographs—which catalogue his interest in boxcar etchings (hobo graffiti). In his song, "The Tuscan Red Rose," Larry's strikes a poetic high in his search for the infamous female hobo, whose name he repeatedly finds scrawled on various boxcar walls: "A woman will do ya that way sometimes/Like a lyric low down in the prose/She won't let you be, you'll never be free/Can you tell me the name of that Tuscan Red Rose."

As the years flew by, Penn immersed himself in the music of Lead Belly, Josh White, Woody Guthrie, John Hurt, and Jimmie Rodgers, to name a few. His style evolved from jazzy chord strumming in a local duo with Bill Brown to a now well-honed finger-style approach that sends his right thumb barreling down on his Gibson six-string like the ringing of John Henry's hammer. His repertoire of original and traditional material comprises those themes that run closest to his heart: trucks, trains, tramps, hobos, labor, Great Lakes shipping, kids, and love.

We could write of the hundreds of rallies and protests where Larry's hand has held sway, or speak of the time he opened for Bob Gibson, Ramblin' Jack Elliott or Dave Van Ronk; the railroad museums, folk festivals, and greasy spoons have all left their own indelible mark on this man, but this is all given to us if we just listen for the sake of the song.

If it's true that elegant simplicity is equal to gold, then Penn's collection of originals represents the Fort Knox of American folk music. His songs have been covered from Pete

---

10 Penn's songs are included in the Smithsonian Folkways catalogue.

Seeger (singing "I'm a Little Cookie" at Carnegie Hall) to Claudia Schmidt, Lee Murdock, and Joe Glazer. Today approximately fifty performers have recorded his songs. "So Long Partner," an homage to the workers' constant struggle with free enterprise, is printed in the Wobblies' (International Workers of the World) *Little Red Song Book* alongside the poetry of Joe Hill and Woody Guthrie. *Carry It On!*—a history in song and picture of America's working men and women by Pete Seeger and Bob Reiser—included Larry's "How'd Ya Like to Give a Little Back," a poignant shot at the corruption of politics and business at the expense of the workers: "Politicians pander for a kickback or a dime/Business understands it takes a little grease sometimes/They must think that all of us are on the take like that/How'd ya like to give a little back?"

Larry Penn

Courtesy of the Larry Penn Archive (2018)

Like many of labor's finest poets, there is always a glimmer of hope amidst the biting commentary. Larry's "On My Grandma's Patchwork Quilt," an oft-requested original, reminds us of simpler times, long before the likes of NAFTA, Iraq, and the Patriot Act: "Around the world people wait/For a day when there's no hate/And we treat each one, like my grandma done/On her crazy patchwork quilt." On the other hand, "Bill's Riff" decries the chains of redundancy: "It's the same old Army/And the same old War/Same old Exxon spilling more and more/Same old corporations they don't ever get enough/And it don't look like my luck is gonna change."

Fellow folkie and retired California professor Fred Starner reiterated a statement made to him by Pete Seeger who said: "Larry's songs are as good as Woody's." For those new to folk music, this is the equivalent to a Gold Seal of Approval or for that matter, a Nobel Prize. Woody Guthrie, who wrote America's unofficial national anthem, "This Land Is Your Land," is said to have composed 1000 other songs and inspired countless generations the world over to pick up their guitars. I imagine Larry sitting next to Woody, soul brothers of sorts. I imagine them hanging out, sharing a drink, playing a rally or a house-rent party. I imagine these two men, cut from the same cloth, would have been blessed to know each other.

The dreams of a child have morphed into a life well spent. These days, Penn still resembles the gypsy trucker whom he sings about in his songs. Only now he is the wise ol'bard of the highway. His traveling companions are the ghosts who refuse to be buried; they tug at his sleeves requesting that they be immortalized in song. Yet, perhaps more than anyone, Penn has chronicled the corrosion of America—its vanishing folk-heroes, its villains, and its changing landscape. He shows us that the life and death of the railroad in America is inextricably intertwined to our health as an industrious nation. The consequences of job loss and off-shoring are found in his songs. He is forever trying to show us the ominous future to which we are headed, as in his autobiographical "No Self-Respecting Hobo." He laments: "The whistle on the midnight freight train/Don't sound the same/Now I still feel like rolling when I hear that mighty roar/But no self-respecting hobo rides the railroads anymore."

Sifting through old newspaper clippings about Larry, one read, "everything that's right with the American folk tradition." I pondered this while so many of his songs lingered in the air, ripe for the humming. I read on and happened upon adoring words others have used to describe this majestic poet, like "unassuming" and "a gentle giant." I wondered why trade magazines failed to include stories about one of America's greatest proletarian voices—how this giant in our midst has managed to avoid being spotted on the radar screen. But then it became clear. The life Larry has spent in pursuit of love (Larry and Pat have been together since time immemorial and she deserves a lot of credit too), family, and work doesn't really fit the model of those full-time musicians whom we've made our heroes. In doing so, we've lost sight of so many men and women like Larry who rarely, if ever, get the credit that they deserve. They are the FOLK in folk music.

For its devotees, folk music is a way of life.[11] Penn is as real as it gets for folk music. He is the mud on the boots and the calloused hands among working class heroes. True, you'll hardly see them, but, peer out your window on a cold winter's night. They are the ones behind the headlights, out there like Penn in the trenches of our cities and hamlets, working the schools, libraries, nursing homes, and pubs. Here there is no room for leaning, only lifting. With Larry, you'll never have to ask which side you're on.

---

11 Lil Rev reflects on his home page: "The way I see it, music isn't just about entertainment. It has the ability to uplift spirits and empower human beings, whether you're a kid, a senior someone with developmental disabilities, or just an average person just getting through your day" (see https://lilrev.com/about).

Nick Topping with Mo(ses) Asch,
the renowned folklorist and founder of Folkway Records (1956)

Nicholas Topping Presents

Folk Singers in Concert

Sunday
October 5

Sunday
October 19

Friday
October 24

JOSH WHITE

Ballads & Blues

all at 8:15p.m.

PETE SEEGER

with

SONNY TERRY

American

Troubadours

MARTHA

SCHLAMME

Songs of

Many Lands

Coming Soon

Sunday
November 30

JEAN RITCHIE,
"Kentucky's Ballad Girl"

Flowing Arrangements of English-American
Ballads accompanied on the guitar and
Mountain Dulcimer.

Saturday
December 27
and
Sunday
December 28*

The GATEWAY SINGERS and the
KAVKAZ DANCERS of Milw.

An exciting vocal quartet together with
Milwaukee's "Moiseyev" Dancers.

* Hall to be announced.

Sunday
February 15

Friday
February 20

SONNY TERRY and
BROWNIE MC GHEE

On tour after a successful 8 week
jazz tour in England.

THEODORE BIKEL
"Folk Songs in 15 Languages"

Like Martha Schlamme, a native of Vienna,
he later made Israel and London his home
and now the U.S. — a multiple artist and
musician, of Stage, TV and film.

Reproduction courtesy of the Nicholas Topping Family

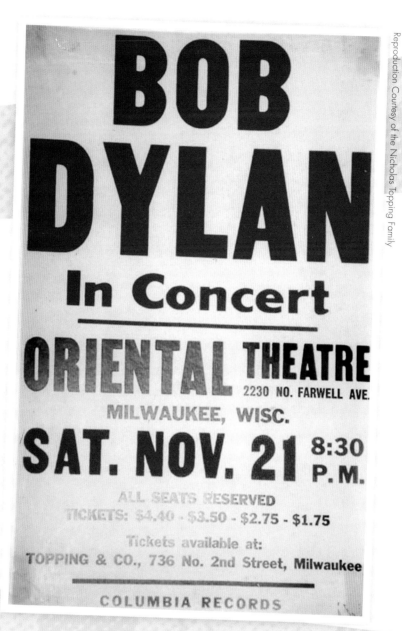

Jean Ritchie

SUNDAY, NOVEMBER 30, 1958

8:15 P.M.

NEW MEMORIAL CENTER

$2.00 — Tax 20c — Total $2.20

RIGHT ROW A

Courtesy of the Nicholas Topping Family

Courtesy of Nancy Penn

Courtesy of Lil Rev Archive

Lil Rev and Larry Penn at the Franklin (Wisconsin) Public Library for a program on hobo quilts and music (2013)

Lil Rev, a multi-instrumentalist, performing at the Northern Virginia Ukulele Society

Photo by Diane Poole

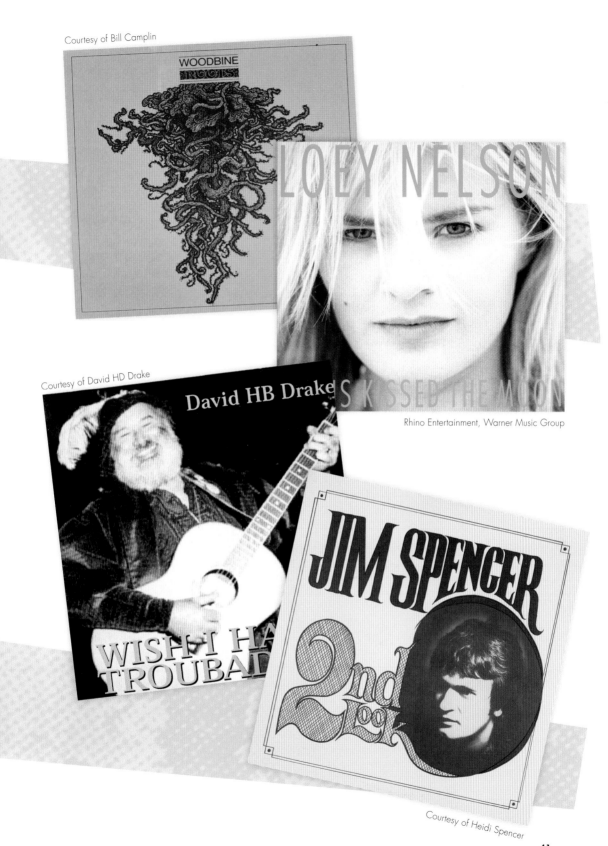

Courtesy of Bill Camplin

WOODBINE ROOTS

LOEY NELSON

S KISSED THE MOON

Rhino Entertainment, Warner Music Group

Courtesy of David HD Drake

David HB Drake

WISH I HA
TROUBA

JIM SPENCER

2nd

Courtesy of Heidi Spencer

Willy Porter performing at the Les Paul 100th Anniversary commemorative concert in Waukesha, WI

Barry Ollman, a featured performer at the Catacombs in the early 1970s

Photo by Rich Zimmermann

Bill Camplin performing with
his group, Woodbine, in 1971

The Beatles performing to a boisterous, enthralled audience in the Arena on 4 September 1964, an epic moment in the history of rock and roll in Milwaukee

CHAPTER 3

The British Invade Milwaukee

The British Invasion of Milwaukee is usually identified with the Beatles' legendary concert on 4 September 1964 (see below). Nevertheless, on 7 June 1964, the very popular Dave Clark Five (DC5) performed under tumultuous conditions at Milwaukee's Devine's Million Dollar Ballroom.[1] Future singer-songwriter Barry Ollman was there and describes the harrowing scene. By the time the Beatles performed on 4 September, one of the most important musical events in Milwaukee's history, the city was in the throes of Beatlemania and the British invasion.[2] The Rolling Stones (without Brian Jones who was ill) performed in November before many empty seats in the Auditorium[3] (and recently returned to open Summerfest in 2015). Consequently, Milwaukee bands opened for touring British groups (see Chapters 1 and 6).

---

1   When the Dave Clark Five returned to McCormick Place in December 1965, the Savoys with Bruce Cole on drums, played as an opening act and also backed up the Ideals, a Chicago group (see Chapter 1). Bruce recalled that Dave Clark pounded the drums so hard that the stage was littered by broken drumsticks.

2   DJ Bob Barry (see Chapter 4) quantified the group's popularity: "Listeners sent over 4,000 Beatle poems, voted Paul their favorite Beatle with 34,367 votes and entered a contest in which the winner wrote the word 'Beatles' 143,456 times, taking the girl a total of 6 days—8,607 minutes or 142 hours—and a total of seven pens" (Barry 1991, 420).

3   See Bobby Tanzilo's chronicle of Rolling Stones concerts in Milwaukee: https://onmilwaukee.com/music/articles/mke-historystones.html.

When the British Invasion
First Came to Milwaukee:
The Dave Clark Five at Devine's Ballroom
by Stephen K. Hauser[4]

The Beatles' inaugural appearance on the Ed Sullivan Show introduced them to the American public in February 1964. The group's performance on that program, watched by an estimated 73 million viewers, made them overnight celebrities in the U.S., and launched a phenomenon henceforth known as "Beatlemania."

Little attention has been given to what transpired the following month as Sullivan, recognizing immediately that he had tapped into something "Really Big," began following the entertainment news from Great Britain. Discovering that the Beatles' record "I Want to Hold Your Hand" had been knocked from the top of the U.K. music charts in January by a song called "Glad All Over" by the Dave Clark Five (DC5), he tracked them down in their hometown, the London Suburb of Tottenham, and booked them to appear on his show.

Ruggedly handsome, bandleader Clark had held day jobs as a motion picture stuntman, a boxing instructor, and a morning milkman. With a keen business sense, he had cashed in on the embryonic British beat boom in 1960 by teaching himself the drums and forming a rock 'n' roll band, hitting the English ballroom circuit. After some initial personnel changes, he settled on a lineup of Mike Smith on keys, Lenny Davidson on guitar, Denis Payton on sax, and Rick Huxley on bass, all pals with whom he had played amateur soccer.

With an organ and a sax, "The Dave Clark Five" produced a different, jazzier sound than the Beatles (something Clark was quick to point out), but it was still English-style rock 'n' roll, and their audiences seemed to love it. "We'd play whatever got them up and dancing," Smith recalled years later. Ballroom owners noticed too, and the Five were never at a loss for work. Recordings and television appearances soon followed.

When "Glad All Over" (actually their sixth release) shot to the top of the British charts, displacing the seemingly indomitable Beatles, they were signed by Epic Records, a subsidiary of Columbia, in the United States, and Sullivan inked them for his television show.

The Dave Clark Five landed at Kennedy International Airport in New York on March 1. They met with Epic Record executives to discuss "Glad All Over", already positioned at #23 on the U.S. charts, and lay plans for a follow-up hit and a publicity campaign for their first album release. On Sunday, March 8th, the Five made their inaugural U.S. appearance on Sullivan's variety show. Hedging his bets, the host had only scheduled them to perform one song, their current hit, but when he saw the reaction they created among audience members and the New York press (and noted solid television viewership

---

4   Adapted with permission from Stephen K. Hauser and the *Elm Grove NEWS-INDEPENDENT*, March 2014). Sources: Mike Smith, Bill Taylor, Artie Herrera, Barry Ollman, Mike Muskovitz, Gary Mason, the *Milwaukee Journal*, and Joel Whitburn's Record Research, Inc. See also Chris Foran, "Rock Arrives with a Riot," *Milwaukee Journal Sentinel*, 7 June 2017 and http://www.thedc5.com/Devinerevelations.html. By the time the DC5 played Milwaukee, the group's *Glad All Over* LP (album) had reached the 250,000 sales mark (*Billboard*, 23 May 1964).

according to the ratings), he asked them to return as headliners the following week on March 15th, performing three songs, including their new single release, "Bits and Pieces." (On a personal note, after viewing that show, I went to Hettiger's Hobby Shop in the Elm Grove Park & Shop and purchased "Glad All Over" for 99 cents, the first record I had ever bought.)

From that time on, the Five's success in America was assured. The press and the fan magazines dubbed them the DC5 and took delight in promoting a fictional "Beatles vs. Dave Clark Five" rivalry, which of course only served to garner more publicity and sell more records for both groups. An American tour was planned for the spring, and the DC5 kicked it off with a concert at New York's Carnegie Hall on 29 and 30 May and a return to Ed Sullivan's show the following night, playing their new hit, "Can't You See That She's Mine." The tour featured stops in 14 cities, including a show on Sunday, June 7, at Devine's Million Dollar Ballroom at the Milwaukee Eagle's Club on Wisconsin Avenue at 24th Street. The Dave Clark Five's appearance at Devine's was considered such a big event that WOKY radio dispatched two of their top disc jockeys, Bob Barry and Bill Taylor, to introduce the acts at the show. The venue held 7,000, but somehow 12,000 tickets had been sold. The size of the young crowd so overwhelmed the place that it violated local fire codes. Fans were crushed up against the stage, numerous teenaged girls fainted, and the *Milwaukee Journal* reported that ten were taken to the hospital by ambulance.

IN PERSON
THE DAVE CLARK FIVE
Coming to Milwaukee Sunday, June 7th
Appearing at Devine's Million Dollar Ballroom .... 2:00 PM

Courtesy of Stephen K. Hauser

Local performer Little Artie Herrera of the Pharaohs led one of the opening acts. Artie remembered the scene years later as "a madhouse. Kids were literally hanging from the balconies and the crowd on the main floor was standing room only. They're lucky something worse didn't happen."

Five songs into the DC5's set list, 35 Milwaukee policemen waded into the crowd and stopped the show.[5] The main attraction had played for only 15 minutes.[6]

5 The *Milwaukee Journal* had run a feature story the morning of the show headlined: "Dave Clark's Sprinters." The story noted that the group often could not finish their shows because of the pandemonium they generated. The article proved to be prophetic.

6 They managed to perform their three current chart hits: "Do You Love Me?", "Glad All Over," and "Bits and Pieces."

Chaos like this created publicity, which only increased attendance for the remaining tour dates.

It should be noted this was the first national U.S. tour by any British band of that era, preceding even the Beatles' first American tour by three months! The DC5 went on to appear on the Ed Sullivan show a record 18 times, more than any other rock or pop act. They placed 27 songs on the *Billboard* music charts between 1964 and 1968. (In May 1964, they could boast of four records on the Hot 100 the same week!) They made two motion pictures, sold in excess of 50 million records by the time they broke up in early 1971, and were inducted into the Rock 'n' Roll Hall of Fame in 2008.

In a broader sense, The Dave Clark Five redefined "Beatlemania" as the "British Invasion."[7] The Beatles created a phenomenon that revolved around one admittedly fresh and talented new band. The DC5 widened this to an American obsession with all things English and paved the way for dozens of young groups from the U.K. to place their own hits on the U.S. charts, appear on American television and tour the States. In their wake, the Rolling Stones, Hollies, Searchers and many more scored hit songs on the U.S. music charts. By the end of 1964, no less than 30 English artists had scored American hits. Some were "one hit wonders" to be sure, but dozens more would follow their lead in 1965 and 1966. The results of this half-century old cultural exchange still resonate.

"I Nearly Died"
by Barry Ollman

I nearly died at my first rock concert! It was a Sunday morning, June 7, 1964 and I was 11 years old. That morning a school friend called and asked if I wanted to go with him to see the Dave Clark Five, and he even had a ticket for me. Something happened to me in that moment and before I even thought of asking my parents, I said yes, absolutely, yes.

I had no clue how to go to a rock show and I actually remember putting on my only suit, a little shark skin number, and a tie. I don't remember if that was what I thought I was supposed to wear or if I actually thought I looked cool. That much is forever lost to History. I got a ride to his house and his dad drove us downtown early. We skipped to the front of the long line and as the doors opened, we ran right up to the stage.

Within minutes the crowd began to grow and before long I began to realize that I was in deep trouble. Suddenly I couldn't get a breath and the surge of screaming girls became a force that I had never experienced before or since. I have an old newspaper article that says that the promoter sold twice the number of allowable tickets that day. After what seemed like an hour, a team of police officers piled in and started lifting hundreds

---

7   The Dave Clark Five returned to Milwaukee on December 15, 1964. About 1,900 fans attended their performance at the Auditorium. According to *Milwaukee Journal*'s Michael R. Drew: "Milwaukee teenagers apparently don't love Britain's Dave Clark Five in December as they did in June." Nevertheless, he noted: "The teenagers who were on hand did their utmost to make up, in enthusiasm, for those who were absent" (Foran, *Milwaukee Journal Sentinel*, 7 June 2017).

of wilted and terrified kids on to the stage and many were put on stretchers and rushed to the hospital. I lay on a cot backstage until I felt a bit better and proceeded to watch my first real rock show, wandering in a daze around the back of the room. I remember the DC5 playing "Glad All Over" and "Bits and Pieces" and that's about it. One more thing—I remember a bunch of tough kids, "greasers" as we called them, kneeling in a circle toward the back of the hall, pounding out the drum part of "Bits and Pieces" on the dance floor of the giant oversold ballroom. The guys wore dark Ban-Lon shirts with cigarette packs tucked into the short sleeves. I felt like I was on a different planet and maybe I sort of was.

The whole experience was a total shock to me and all I could think about was going to another show!

That next show happened in September 1964 and I'm forever grateful to say that it was the Beatles. I think my ears still hurt from those screaming girls, and I could barely hear the Fabs, but it was a true life-changer for me.

The Beatles Invade and "Conquer"
by Phillip Naylor

The Beatles performed at the Milwaukee Arena on 4 September 1964. They arrived on stage at 9:10 PM and played for 30 minutes.[8] It was one of the most momentous musical events in the history of the city.[9] In its September 5th edition, the *Milwaukee Sentinel* proclaimed: "Beatles Conquer the City!" The approximate 30-minute concert, aptly called by the *Sentinel*, an "appearance," since their music could hardly be heard included the requisite "yelling and sobbing" that characterized Beatlemania. Gerald Kloss of the *Milwaukee Journal* reported that "George would swing a lissome hip or Paul would flash a sudden smile, and the roar from the crowd fractured the mortar between the bricks." He concluded that the Beatles were "less a musical attraction than a visual one" (*Milwaukee Journal*, 5 September 1964). The Beatles set featured music from their recently released successful film and album, *A Hard Day's Night*. Reporter Bernice Buresh reflected: "There is no experience like the Beatles" (*Milwaukee Sentinel*, 5 September 1964). Concurrently, at the neighboring Auditorium, Milwaukee bands also rocked featuring John Kondos and the Galaxies, the Seven Sounds, the Mojo Men, and Little Artie and the Pharaohs.

---

8 For details see the *Milwaukee Journal* and *Milwaukee Sentinel*, 4, 5 September 1964; Barry 1991. See also www.fab4milwaukee.com.

9 For example, anniversary articles of the concert appeared in the *Milwaukee Sentinel* on 2 September 1974, 3 September 1979; and the *Milwaukee Journal Sentinel* on 4 September 2009. A documentary film, "The Beatles Invade Milwaukee" appeared in 2014 and was produced by Milwaukee Public Television. Brief raw footage of the Beatles' concert is on https://www.youtube.com/watch?v=iyzxpvKIO48. An array of contemporary articles featured in Milwaukee's newspapers illustrated the extent of Beatlemania (notably Bernice Buresh's series "The Beatles Worshippers" beginning on 31 August in the *Sentinel*).

The Beatles stayed at the Coach House Inn,[10] practically besieged by "enrapt fans." The *Sentinel* reported that four girls managed to sneak in and "subsisted on one banana, Coke and cigarets [*sic*]," while hiding in a seventh-floor boiler room before being caught (5 September). Cindy Black, a sixteen-year old was given a byline and access to the Beatles (except John Lennon who had a sore throat). She asked if the fans annoyed them, which elicited a "definitely not" from Paul supported by George and Ringo. According to all news reports, the Beatles seemed to enjoy their short stay in Milwaukee. Tickets cost $3.50/$5.50 and could be bought at the International House owned by its "president" and "head clerk," the inimitable Nick Topping (see Chapter 2), the promoter of the concert.

When I asked Nick how he managed to bring the Beatles to Milwaukee, he replied: "Because I pay my bills." Yet he also believed that the Beatles could inspire positive, progressive change. He accurately, if not presciently, perceived something more in them besides the pop music of Beatlemania (see also Racine 1975, 154). Nick learned that the Beatles were reportedly bored in their Coach House Inn room. He sent over a record player and Bob Dylan albums, clearly intending to influence the Beatles' musical direction and potential. While the Beatles were undoubtedly aware of Dylan, Nick in his own indirect way may have contributed to their gradual musical and lyrical transition resulting in what are usually considered the group's best albums—the "Dylanesque" *Rubber Soul* (1965) and *Revolver* (1966). His store, Topping & Company: The International House" displayed an immense poster publicizing the Milwaukee concert (see chapter photo). He was obviously proud of his achievement.[11] Indeed, I invited Nick to my Rock and Roll History class at Marquette University to recount his booking and bringing of the Beatles to Milwaukee. He entered the lecture hall singing John Lennon's lyric: "All we are saying/ is give peace a chance."

---

10 The Coach House Inn (1926 W. Wisconsin Avenue) became a Holiday Inn. Today it is Marquette University's Mashuda (Residence) Hall. Nick also brought back the Dave Clark Five back to Milwaukee, who also stayed at the Coach House Inn (see *Milwaukee Sentinel*, 16 December 1964).

11 Grateful concert goers left thank you cards and even arts and crafts gifts in front of Nick's International House. The Topping family has saved some of these items.

The DAVE CLARK FIVE

—FIRST AMERICAN TOUR—

DIVINE'S

MILLION DOLLAR BALLROOM

2401 WEST WISCONSIN AVENUE

SUN., JUNE 7th - 196

—ALSO PLAYING—

★ THE CITATIONS ★ THE THUNDERBIRDS ★ THE
★ LITTLE ARTIE & THE PHARAOHS

$2.00 ADVANCE - $3.00 AT THE DO

—DOORS OPEN AT NOON—

Courtesy of the Jean Cujé Collection

Reproduction of original poster in which Devine's is misspelled.

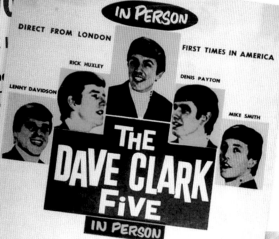

IN PERSON

DIRECT FROM LONDON

FIRST TIMES IN AMERICA

RICK HUXLEY

LENNY DAVIDSON

DENIS PAYTON

MIKE SMITH

THE DAVE CLARK FIVE

IN PERSON

BRUCE HALL

MILWAUKEE, WISCONSIN

TUESDAY DECEMBER 15

at 8:00 PM

Tickets: $4.75, 3.75, 2.75, 1.75 tax incl

On Sale: Topping & Co. 736 N. Second St. Milwaukee, Wisconsin

Reproduction courtesy of the Nicholas Topping Family

Poster displayed at Nick Topping's International House(s)

Courtesy of the Nicholas Topping Family

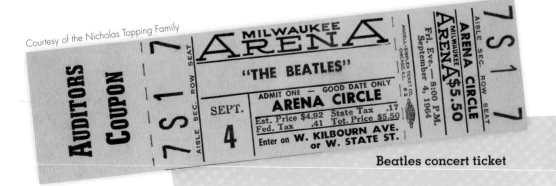

Beatles concert ticket

Photo courtesy of the *Milwaukee Journal Sentinel* and the Nicholas Topping Family

Beatles' interview at Coach House Inn, September 1964.
(John Lennon had a sore throat and did not attend.)

Photo by Benn Ollman; courtesy of Barry Ollman

Rolling Stones press
conference at Coach House Inn (November 1964)

Triangle
Theatrical
Productions

Franklin Fried
PRESENTS

THE BEATLES

Milwaukee Auditorium — Sept. 4 — Milwaukee

Beatles/
Beatlemania
program

October 2 • Orchestra Hall • $5—$4—$3—$2
PETE SEEGER

October 16 • Orchestra Hall • $5—$4—$3—$2
CLANCY BROS. & TOMMY MAKEM

October 30 • Orchestra Hall • $5—$4—$3—$2
EWAN MacCOLL & PEGGY SEEGER

November 20 • Orchestra Hall • $5—$4—$3—$2
BOB DYLAN

December 4 • Arie Crown Theatre • $5—$4—$3—$2
PETER, PAUL AND MARY

January 22 • Orchestra Hall • $5—$4—$3—$2
JUDY COLLINS

February 19 • Orchestra Hall • $5—$4—$3—$2
ODETTA

March 6 • Opera House • $5—$4—$3—$2
THEODORE BIKEL

March 19 • Orchestra Hall • $5—$4—$3—$2
CARLOS MONTOYA

March 26 • Arie Crown Theatre • $5—$4—$3—$2
THE MITCHELL TRIO
JOE FRAZIER, MIKE KOBLUK, CHAD MITCHELL

Triangle
Theatrical
Productions

FRANKLIN FRIED, EXECUTIVE DIRECTOR

4TH ANNUAL FOLK MUSIC SERIES 1964 1965

Mail orders for all concerts to: Triangle Theatrical Productions, Inc., Box B, 156 E. Superior St., Chicago, Illinois, 60611
Enclose self-addressed stamped envelope. Series tickets (all 10 concerts) Main floor and boxes $35.00, First Balcony
$28.00, Second Balcony $20.00. Gallery $14.00. Single admissions: Main floor and boxes $5.00, First Balcony
Balcony $3.00, Gallery $2.00.
Save as much as 39% by becoming a season subscriber. Single admission tickets will be mailed out three weeks before
each concert.

JOHN LENNON

PAUL McCARTNEY

GEORGE HARRISON

RINGO STARR

F
R
A
N
K
L
I
N

F
R
I
E
D

PRESENTS

THE

B
E
A
T
L
E
S

with

The Exciters
Jackie DeShannon
The Righteous Brothers
Bill Black Combo

congratulations

AND THE **ringo starr**

BEATLES

on your
TRIUMPHAL U.S. TOUR

Ludwig

EXPERIENCE / IMAGINATION / CRAFTSMANSHIP

WISCONSIN MUSIC CO.

960 No. 3rd Street — Phone 276-1878
Milwaukee, Wisconsin 53203

SAVE THIS PROGRAM FOR DISCOUNT
IMPORTED SOLID-BODY GUITARS

SAVE THIS PROGRAM

for

DISCOUNT

Available

EUROPEAN
TRAINED
REPAIRMEN

Contour Cut Solid Body. Pick-up especially made for Bass Guitar. Individual String Adjustment. Detachable warp-proof Neck—Steel reinforced. Size: 47" x 1½" — List $128.85

4 Pick-up Deluxe Guitar with Contour Cut Solid Body. 3 Piece detachable warp-proof neck—Steel reinforced. 8 Switches and Controls plus Tremolo Tail Piece for multiple effects. Adjustable Metal Bridge. Size: 40½ x 14½" — List $131.85

AMPLIFIERS, FOLK GUITARS

CLASSIC, FLAMENCO

BANJOS, UKES, MANDOLINS

INQUIRE ABOUT OUR

GROUP CONTEST

Your group may be
one of the winners

Solid Mahogany Body. Double Cutaway with 3 Piece Laminated Neck—Steel reinforced. Adjustable Metal Bridge. Volume and Tone Controls. In-put Jack. An outstanding value! Size 39½" x 12" — List $52.50

FABULOUS PRIZES

NOVEMBER 25

RETURNING TO MILWAUKEE

PETER, PAUL & MARY

WEDNESDAY 8:30

BRUCE HALL, MILWAUKEE

$4.75, $3.75, $2.75, $1.75

TICKETS BY MAIL ORDER C/O
TOPPING & CO.
736 N. 2nd ST., MILWAUKEE, WIS.

**Send Check or Money Order
Plus Self-Addressed Envelope**

NOVEMBER 21

BOB DYLAN

ORIENTAL THEATRE
SATURDAY — 8:30 P.M.

★ $4.40, $3.75, $2.75, $1.75

TICKETS BY MAIL ORDER C/O
TOPPING & CO.
736 N. 2nd ST., MILWAUKEE, WIS.

**Send Check or Money Order
Plus Self-Addressed Envelope**

*APPEARING IN THEIR FIRST
MILWAUKEE CONCERT*

THE DAVE CLARK FIVE

DECEMBER 15

TUESDAY 8:30 P.M.

MILWAUKEE AUDITORIUM

TICKETS: $4.75, $3.75, $2.75, $1.75

TICKETS BY MAIL C/O

TOPPING AND COMPANY, 736 N. 2nd, MILWAUKEE, WIS.

SEND CHECK OR MONEY ORDER PLUS SELF-ADDRESSED ENVELOPE

HEY GANG!

in MILWAUKEE it's

McDonald's

tasty food — thrifty prices

look for the golden arches

6 CONVENIENT LOCATIONS

• Appleton at Capitol Dr.   • Hwy. 100 at Burleigh
• Packard Plaza in Cudahy   • 76th St. at Oklahoma
• S. 27th St. at Morgan   • Hwy. 100 at National

MARCH 5

PETE SEEGER

BACK FROM
WIDELY ACCLAIMED WORLD TOUR

ORIENTAL THEATRE

FRIDAY — 8:30 P.M.

★ $4.40, $3.75, $2.75, $1.75

TICKETS BY MAIL ORDER C/O
TOPPING & CO
736 N. 2nd ST., MILWAUKEE, WIS.

**Send Check or Money Order
Plus Self-Addressed Envelope**

GET YOUR REAL-LIFE . . . FULL-COLOR
GIGANTIC **BEATLES** SHOW POSTER
WITH YOUR NAME PRINTED ON IT!

Your friends will be amazed to see YOU share the spotlight with world famous BEATLES at their LONDON PALLADIUM COMMAND PERFORMANCE. HUGE SHOW POSTER MEASURES 20" x 28". GREAT FOR WALL DISPLAY. Has PERSONAL AUTOGRAPHS of RINGO, PAUL, JOHN and GEORGE. A real COLLECTORS TREASURE! SEND FOR YOURS TODAY.

ONLY $2.50 with YOUR NAME
$1.50 without your name

MAIL TODAY TO: SHOWPOSTERS
P.O. BOX 245 • ELMHURST, ILL.
Please Rush Poster ☐ With My Name
☐ Without Name

MY NAME
ADDRESS
CITY   STATE

Enclosed is $ for   Posters
For more than 1 name poster be sure to enclose other names

BEATLES with JOHNNY JONES of the
LONDON PALLADIUM

The Legendary **WAWA** & DR. BOP

WAWA staff, including Dr. Bop, front left, and O.C. White, front right

CHAPTER 4

Milwaukee's Rockin' Radio

The role of radio, with its array of DJs and announcers, was crucially important in popularizing and amplifying rock. Milwaukee AM top 40 radio featured WOKY and WRIT. Bob Barry was especially popular on WOKY and interviewed the Beatles and emceed their performance in Milwaukee on 4 September 1964. Locally, he was referred to as the "Fifth Beatle" and "Beatle Bob," given his enthusiasm for the band.[1] Diana L. Belscamper recounts Barry's multiple significance regarding popularizing rock music in Milwaukee. With the rise of competitive freeform FM, AM stations (namely WRIT) occasionally offered "deep cuts" from albums and as Dewey Gill and David Luhrssen recount, played music by local groups. Stephen K. Hauser details the history of WAWA, an R&B and soul station broadcasting from suburban Elm Grove. Its on-air personalities and programs had consequential social besides musical significance. The chapter concludes with Bob Reitman, who remains the dean of Milwaukee freeform (see Spielmann 1975). Indeed, after retiring from WKTI, he resumed a freeform program at the site where he began, WUWM. Today, WMSE (transmitting since 1981 with a boosted signal) and WYMS (Radio Milwaukee since 2007) are also non-commercial stations featuring freeform rock programming.

---

1   See also http://catholicherald.org/special-sections/mature-lifestyles/catholic-upbringing-guided-bob-barry-s-star-filled-career/; http://archive.jsonline.com/entertainment/tvradio/bob-barrys-fifth-beatle-status-almost-didnt-happen-b99197212z1-243593801.html; and http://www.wisconsinbroadcastingmuseum.org/hall-of-fame/bob-barry/; Barry 1991.

Bob Barry: The Voice of Milwaukee

Diana L. Belscamper

Recognized locally and nationally for his broadcasting achievements, Bob Barry is the voice of Milwaukee (see Barry 1991, 2018). As one of the city's most popular DJs at WOKY in the 1960s and 1970s, Bob Barry became synonymous with Top 40 radio in Milwaukee, and he remains a local icon, decades later. Barry is best known to some for introducing the Beatles to Milwaukee—he was the first to play their music on the "Mighty 92," and he was the emcee at their Milwaukee Arena concert on 4 September 1964. However, Barry's roots and legacy extend much further. His ubiquitous voice has been heard on radio and television in Wisconsin for over 60 years, making him not just a household name, but a friend on the airwaves. At the peak of his career, his personal appearances at concerts, telethons, festivals, and community events often drew as many fans as the acts he introduced. Renowned celebrities sought him out to be interviewed, and his easy conversations with them brought them a little bit closer to his Midwestern listeners. Similar to Bob Uecker, another Milwaukee icon whose charm and enthusiasm are immediately identifiable as soon as he's heard, Bob Barry's voice is the sound of *home* for generations of Milwaukeeans.

Born and raised in Milwaukee, Barry knew from an early age that he wanted to be on the radio. He practiced baseball play-by-play and introducing records, emulating the voices he heard on local stations. By 1958, he was working his first professional radio shows—out of a farmhouse in Hartford, Wisconsin. Shortly thereafter, Barry was emceeing local dances and live performances, gaining a following of his own fans. Within a few years, Barry's career progressed to regular shifts on WEMP and WRIT, increasing his familiarity with his hometown audience. In December 1963, Barry signed his first contract with WOKY, the timing of which could not have been more opportune – for him or for Milwaukee listeners. Within months, The Beatles would make their first appearance on *The Ed Sullivan Show*, kicking off the British Invasion of Top 40 radio and the *Billboard* charts—with Bob Barry situated perfectly to be Milwaukee's envoy.

Given his smooth rapport with listeners and celebrities alike, Bob Barry was well-suited as a liaison between the two chaotic worlds of teen fandom and pop stardom. He was granted an exclusive audience with the Beatles when they visited Milwaukee in September 1964, and Barry was sure to deliver the exorbitant amount of fan mail and gifts that WOKY had received on their behalf. The kids knew that if anyone could get their letters, teddy bears, and jelly beans to their favorite Beatle, Bob Barry could—and he did. Securing his reputation as Milwaukee's "Fifth Beatle," Barry participated in the band's press conference at the Coach House Motor Inn, talked with them individually, and introduced them on stage at their Arena concert.

Though Barry etched his legacy in Milwaukee music history through his affiliation with the Beatles, his career and impact run so much deeper. He helped provide a sense of calm and continuity during times of crisis, such as the aftermath of the Kennedy assassination and the race riots of 1967. Barry transitioned to television in the mid-1960s, with appearances on local talk shows as a youth correspondent. He hosted the "Early Show" on WITI-TV, interviewing guests such as Chuck Berry, Bobby Sherman, and Brenda Lee. He spent nearly 20 years at WOKY and became one of the most recognizable names in Milwaukee media, his voice immediately recognized by generations of listeners. Known as "Milwaukee's Dick Clark," he introduced legions of pop stars to local audiences, emceeing concerts and interviewing acts such as the Rolling Stones, the Dave Clark Five, Herman's Hermits, the Monkees, Paul Revere and the Raiders, and countless others. His support of local bands gave them regional and national credibility, with the Legends, the Ricochettes, and the Robbs among those whose fame was boosted by Barry's play of their records.

Bob Barry garnered national media attention as well, featured in teen magazines during the 1960s as one of America's top DJs. He was recognized as the Billboard Top 40 Air Personality of the Year in 1975, drawing even more national attention to his successful broadcasting career. His "Bob Barry Calls the World" interview segment brought global celebrities from film, television, music, and politics to Milwaukee listeners, often with amusing anecdotes encouraged by Barry's smooth conversational rapport with them. Barry continued his radio career into the 1990s, with his last regular gig as a morning host on WRIT-FM, as he matured into the elder statesman of pop music in Milwaukee. Barry provided a glimpse of his history—and his archive—by outfitting the Solid Gold McDonald's on South 76th Street with personal photos and memorabilia collected through his decades in broadcasting. In 2001, Bob Barry was honored with induction into the Wisconsin Broadcasters Hall of Fame, confirming his iconic stature as the legendary voice who guided the soundtrack of Milwaukee for decades.

Dewey Gill Remembers When
AM Radio Played the Local Hits
by David Luhrssen

For many years Dewey Gill has hosted a pair of programs on WMSE, the alternative radio station licensed by the Milwaukee School of Engineering (see also Chapter 9). On his monthly Friday night show, Gill often explores the little remembered fluorescence of Wisconsin recordings acts during the early years of rock music. Gill grew up in Milwaukee during the 1960s and was an avid fan. He speaks of the era from memory as well as extensive research conducted in adulthood as a voracious and well-informed record collector.

During the early 1950s, Wisconsin was home to locally owned record labels that released polka, jazz and other genre recordings. After the emergence of rock and roll, regional independent labels also played an important role in circulating the new music; local music released by "indie" labels on 45rpm-singles often received airplay on commercial radio stations and were featured in Milwaukee Top-40 charts. By the early 1970s the influence of Wisconsin indies and the availability of airtime for area bands diminished as the result of corporate homogenization, especially the nationwide playlists the radio broadcasting industry imposed on disc jockeys.

Remarkably, some Badger State bands found themselves on a journey from the indies to major labels, usually resulting from the savvy of a regional network of music managers. While most of these men were not powerful in the coastal centers of the entertainment industry, some of them had enough clout to be heard. Their phone calls were sometimes returned.

Gill cites the example of the La Crosse band, the Unchained Mynds, responsible for "one of the biggest songs in Milwaukee." The Mynds originally cut "We Can't Go on This Way" for a small La Crosse label, Transaction. A Milwaukee-area company, Teen Town, run by entrepreneur Jon Hall, reissued the single. After becoming the Mynds' manager, Hall leased the master to a national label, Buddha, in 1969. Although "We Can't Go on This Way" never reached the Top-100, it was featured in Billboard's "Hot Happenings" chart. "It became one of the biggest selling records of the time from Wisconsin," Gill adds.

Indie label releases were usually issued in small batches and sold by bands at shows, albeit some local record stores such as Radio Doctors stocked them. Radio was the principal but not the only medium for exposing local music in the 1960s. DJs on AM stations such as WOKY and WRIT often managed the bands whose records they spun, a conflict of interest happily ignored by all parties. Some of the labels were operated by radio personalities, including DJs Lee Rothman's USA Records, which issued what was probably Milwaukee's first rock and roll disc, Roland Stone's "Lost Girl" (1958). After being sold to Chicago interests, USA achieved a level of national success with another Milwaukee band, the Messengers.

While "Lost Girl" is generally credited as leading Milwaukee into rock and roll, Gill acknowledges the difficulty in untangling the evolution of the music during the 1950s. "There was carry-over," he says. "There were a couple of good western swing records released here in the mid-'50s—almost a Bill Haley style crossover. Many of the early rock and roll era bands from Milwaukee had accordions—most of them never had a chance to record, and they dumped the accordions after a while."

WOKY and WRIT were the city's primary Top-40 rock and roll stations, but other broadcasters aired specialty rock shows, including WISN. Gill recalls "two or three local television programs that dealt with rock, including *Somethin' Else* on WISN." Allen Pozniak wrote a weekly column for the *Milwaukee Journal*'s popular Green Sheet section, "Badger Beat," that dealt with local and regional bands. The mid-1960s saw the emergence of *Action*, a Milwaukee music newspaper with band photos and notices of upcoming shows.

At that time, Gill recalls, anyone interested in local rock bands had no problem hearing their music or finding their shows. "Between 'Badger Beat,' what you saw on television and heard on the radio, the most popular bands became local heroes," Gill says. "Some of them had cult-like followings—a band like the Robbs stirred something like Beatlemania among the girls."

Some Milwaukee recording acts that never cracked the Billboard charts were able to receive airplay in other parts of the country. "There was a lot of communication between DJs in different cities—they often moved from town to town but kept in touch with each other," Gill says. "They could call in favors. That's how 'Thunderwagon' by the Noblemen on USA Records wound up on a San Francisco station."

At the same time that WOKY and WRIT promoted local rock bands, WAWA and WNOV were broadcasting Milwaukee acts from the parallel universe of rhythm and blues. "Milwaukee was segregated but there was some crossover," Gill says. "You had Little Artie and The Pharaohs, a Hispanic band with a reputation for playing for a tougher crowd, and the Legends out in Muskego Beach, with a more clean-cut crowd. Little Artie fans did not go to Muskego Beach to see the Legends."

As Gill recalls, "1971 was the last good year for local bands to get a break on AM radio. After that, it became increasingly tough," given the narrow-focused playlists imposed on DJs across the nation, not just in Milwaukee, as broadcasters began to follow marketing rulebooks rather than their own instincts. DJs no longer had the leeway they once enjoyed and were becoming little more than talking technicians, providing chatter in between dropping the needle on a prescribed roster of singles. By the end of the 1970s, some radio stations did away with DJs altogether and went with automated formats. The freeform FM stations that persisted through the mid-1970s, notably WZMF and WQFM, ignored local singles and gave only limited airtime at best for albums by Milwaukee artists such as Sigmund Snopek III (see Chapter 10).

Milwaukee on the Billboard Charts Hit Singles by Milwaukee Rock and Soul Acts, 1958-1971 (From Gary Myers 1994)	
The Robbs "Race with the Wind" (1966) Reached 103 on the Pop chart	**Harvey Scales &** **The Seven Sounds** "Get Down" (1967) Reached 79 on the Pop chart and 32 on the R&B chart
The Esquires "Get on Up" (1967) Reached 11 on the Pop chart and 3 on the R&B chart	**Thee Prophets** "Playgirl" (1969) Reached 49 on the Pop chart
The Esquires "And Get Away" (1967) Reached 22 on the Pop chart and 9 on the R&B chart	**The Messengers** "That's the Way a Woman Is" (1971) Reached 62 on the Pop chart

Elm Grove's Unlikely Radio Station: The History of WAWA

by Stephen K. Hauser[2]

In 1944, a promising career in local municipal politics came to an inauspicious end. Milwaukee attorney Herbert L. Mount, a Progressive stalwart, was defeated in the March mayoral primary by incumbent mayor John L. Bohn. He did run slightly ahead of Socialist candidate Frank P. Zeidler (who would be elected in 1948), but Mount retired from electioneering.

Instead he moved to Wauwatosa to concentrate on his law practice. A go-getter with an active mind, in 1959 he formed Suburbanaire Broadcasting, Inc., with plans to begin operating an AM radio station with programming designed to serve the needs of the growing suburban communities west of Milwaukee. Mount would serve as Suburbanaire's president. He promised that the new station would pay particular attention to the audience of young middle-class suburban housewives. Mount imagined these women as his loyal base.

A problem arose, however, when no one could quite figure out exactly what programming should be directed at female suburbanites. Other than a vague promise "mainly of news and music," Mount apparently didn't know either. A second difficulty was in finding a spot for the towers and radio transmitter site. A license was secured from the FCC and the call letters WAWA were approved. Mount had hoped to base the studios in Wauwatosa and the transmitter in West Allis, hence the moniker of WAWA for "Wauwatosa-West Allis." In the end, no suitable location was found in either community. A nearby alternate site had to be considered.

On 28 November 1960, Mount and newly-hired station manager Neil Searles appeared before the Elm Grove Village Plan commission to gain approval for the construction of a transmitter facility and four 200-foot towers at a seven-acre site located at 12800 W. Blue Mound Road. Mount gained easy approval for his new station, promising it would fill a gap in local programming, since current radio management in Milwaukee did not think about the suburbs in planning their broadcast day.

WAWA began broadcasting from its Elm Grove location in the spring of 1961 at a frequency of 1590 kilocycles. Its transmission power would be 1,000 watts, but the Federal Communications Commission (FCC) imposed a "sunset clause" on its broadcast day. The station could sign on following sunrise and had to sign off at sunset in the evenings. This, of course, necessitated a shorter on-air cycle in the winter months than in the summer.

WAWA leased studio space from the Polly Valley Motel immediately to the east at 12700 W. Blue Mound Road. The motel leased its units to long-term guests as residency suites with cooking privileges and efficiency accommodations. The unit at the far west of

---

2   Adopted from manuscripts and articles (appeared in the *Elm Grove NEWS-INDEPENDENT* [February-June 2013]) with permission of Stephen K. Hauser. Sources: Walter G. Beach, O.C. White, Earl Gissing, Phil Klingler, Ken Freck, Jim Cronin, Stu Glassman, "WAWA Soul Surveys," *Milwaukee Community Press*, the *Elm Leaves*, and the *Milwaukee Journal*.

the Polly Valley property adjoined the WAWA facilities and was perfect for rented studio space.

Station manager Searles hired Earl Gissing as the new station's program director and first air personality. Gissing would remain with WAWA for the next nine years. He recalled in 2014 that one early program was "Imaginary Ballroom." Big band favorites and crooner standards would be played, with hopes that housewives would dance with their mops and brooms, enchanted by a make-believe word of days gone by. Apparently, not many women chose to play along. The weekday show, along with many other supposed suburban-oriented broadcasts, fizzled. In response, Mount made a fateful financial decision that would earn him the reputation as a pioneering broadcaster, community patron, and civil rights activist.

Mount hit upon an interesting idea to gain income for the fledgling station while simultaneously repaying anxious investors. He began selling time to local ethnic and cultural societies and fraternal groups, allowing them to offer programs aimed at a narrow target audience. Those organizations and individuals buying the time could recoup their money by selling their own commercial time on their broadcasts to businesses that might wish to reach their specific listeners with a message or product particularly attuned to them.

Soon a deal was struck with one such early air personality entrepreneur. Austrian-born Louis Zimmermann, host of *Herr Louis's Café Vienna*, heard on WAWA Monday through Friday from 12:15 to 2:00 p.m. and Sunday afternoons from 4:00 to 6:00 p.m. Herr Louis played Continental music, ranging from Alpine folk songs to German polkas to Viennese waltzes. A sports fan, Louis also hosted the weekly soccer reports, sponsored by the *Deutsche Zeitung*, Milwaukee's German-language weekly newspaper. This programming naturally attracted German listeners and German advertisers as well. Restaurants serving up Germanic and Alpine fare, including the Golden Zither, Edelweiss Inn, Dietze's Bavarian Wurst Haus, John Ernst Café, Ritter's Inn, Alpine Village and the Schwabenhof were all aboard. German athletic clubs also ran ads, often read over the airwaves in German!

Another ethnic program, *The Voice of Sicily* soon joined the air-on schedule as well. Hosted by Phil Balistreri, the program featured traditional Sicilian folk music, along with news and sports from Italy. Mr. Balistreri was quite knowledgeable of Sicilian culture and history and prided himself in owning a fine record library of Sicilian music. His commentary on the various melodies that he played was very educational, even for the casual listener. Sponsors lined up for the show which aired from 1:00 to 2:00 p.m. on Sunday afternoons, including Milwaukee Italian restaurants such as Mister Marco's and Jack De Salvo's which featured Sicilian specialties on the menu.

The opportunities afforded by WAWA's new policy of selling air time to those who wished to reach a "niche" audience were not lost on an enterprising 29-year-old novice broadcaster named O.C. White. A graduate of Milwaukee's Lincoln High School, White had played semi-pro football for the Racine Raiders and had been employed as a foreman for Milwaukee General Construction Company in the late 1950s, he had also worked in local radio at WFOX and WMIL. As an African American, White longed to do a radio show that featured rhythm and blues (R&B) records and spotlighted merchants and businesses that served Milwaukee's black community. He believed that R&B music, which he loved, deserved to be heard in southeastern Wisconsin by both black and white listeners, and he felt that shops and stores in Milwaukee's central city would jump at the change to advertise their wares to a targeted audience of potential customers.

At the end of 1961, O.C. White signed a contract to host an R&B show on WAWA radio. Known as *Good Dr. White's Good Time Express*, it aired twice a day in a split-shift format Monday through Friday at 5:15 a.m. and 5:15 p.m., and again at 5:15 a.m. on Saturdays. The split-shift format had a purpose; during the middle of the day White was in Milwaukee visiting businesses to sell advertising to pay for his program! Soon, he was selling more ads on his show than he had ever believed possible. By 1962, O.C. White was hosting the highest rated program on WAWA. The station's owner, Herb Mount, was well aware of this, and he approached O.C. with a suggestion, a question and a colossal opportunity. WAWA was about to undergo a major format change.

Mount queried White with a proposition: would he agree to shepherd the station's transformation to an R&B music and news format aimed primarily at Milwaukee's black community? He also asked if White knew of other air personalities to fit the new format. It was a tremendous opportunity for White. It would make WAWA the first black format radio station in Wisconsin and would cast attorney Mount in the unlikely role of a civil rights pioneer. White's response? An enthusiastic "Yes!"

The R&B playlist took off like a rocket. New disc jockeys were hired, including young Larry Hayes and Pat Bell. By far the most dynamic new hire, however, was 33-year-old Hoyt Locke from Columbus Ohio, known on the air as "Dr. Bop." "I'm the cat with the fine brown frame," he would shout into the mike. "I'm 42 across the chest, a stone-cold lover and an ex-Golden Glover. Bop be my name and music is my game. Dr. Bop powers on from the Soul Empire!" His on-air braggadocio soon had him pegged as Milwaukee radio's answer to world heavyweight contender Cassius Clay. All in good fun, listeners enjoyed the bravado.

O.C. White, meanwhile, began publishing his own weekly soul music Top 40 survey in the spring of 1962, spotlighting such legendary African American artists as Ray Charles, James Brown, Sam Cooke, B.B. King and Chubby Checker. Coincidentally, these were performers that America at large was just beginning to gain awareness of, thanks to a new phenomenon—crossover hits—charting on soul format stations and White-oriented pop radio that also played the likes of Elvis Presley, Jerry Lee Lewis, Pat Boone, and Bobby Vee.

At the end of 1965, Herb Mount scored a coup in circumventing the FCC's "sunset clause." He secured a 102.1 FM frequency for WAWA, allowing it to simulcast with the AM outlet during the day and continue to spin soul music through the nighttime hours after the AM signal had been put to bed.

The 24-hour format required hiring of additional on-air staff. An integrated roster of air talent was brought aboard, including local jazz and blues musicologist Manny Mauldin, All Ballard, Jim Frazier, Chuck Smith, Bob Wilder and Phil Klinger. Phil Klinger, who had adopted the on-air persona of Nassau Daddy, eventually became the chief engineer for Milwaukee stations WOKY, WMIL, WRIT and WISN.

The air staff was not the only integrated aspect of WAWA's programming. Listeners not only heard soul hits by Aretha Franklin, Sam & Dave, Stevie Wonder, Marvin Gaye and Milwaukee's own Esquires, but were also treated to tracks by British Invasion rockers like the Beatles, Hollies and Yardbirds, as well as American pop by the Byrds, Young Rascals, and the Buckinghams. Even local garage bands like the Mustard Men got a spin or two of their late 1965 release, "Another Day."

O.C. White's fledgling soul survey had evolved into "Milwaukee's Weekly Bag of 50 Gems," available to customers at record outlets throughout Milwaukee, including Radio Doctors on 3rd and Wells Street downtown, the largest record store in Wisconsin. Dr. Bop, meanwhile, saw his celebrity grow to such an extent that he was asked to host his own weekly television program on Sunday nights on Milwaukee's independent UHF station, Channel 18. The show featured local bands, and was sponsored by Milwaukee's hip clothier, Johnny Walker's (whose salesmen sang their own commercial spot on-air). The Doctor was also busy hosting CYO dances, even at Our Lady Queen of Peace parish on Euclid Avenue at S. 27th Street on the predominantly white south side of Milwaukee.

WAWA had become a successful radio station, reaching an audience far beyond what its originators would ever have imagined. As the turbulent decade of the 1960s wore on, however, big changes were in the wind, including the introduction of public affairs and talk format programming, civil rights controversies, and even a presidential campaign, along with the arrival on the scene of a former Green Bay Packer with an offer to purchase the station.

The station began 24 hour-a-day FM broadcasting in January 1966 and in June a new 350-foot FM tower was constructed at the transmitter site on Blue Mound Road. On 20 July 1966, station founder and owner Herbert L. Mount died of a sudden heart attack at age 62. In his

Milwaukee's original R-B hit list

This Weeks Bag Of 50 Gems

EFFECTIVE MARCH 27, 1967

LAST WEEK	THIS WEEK		
2	1	I NEVER LOVED A MAN	ARETHA FRANKLIN
1	2	THE WHOLE WORLD IS A STAGE	THE FANTASTIC 4
7	3	SWEET SOUL MUSIC	ARTHUR CONLEY
4	4	I LOVE YOU MORE	LEE WILLIAMS
5	5	THE HUNTER GETS CAUGHT BY THE GAME	
			THE MARVELETTES
8	6	JIMMY MACK	MARTHA & VANDELLAS
12	7	I DON'T WANT TO LOSE YOU	JACKIE WILSON
13	8	EVERYBODY NEEDS HELP	JIMMY HOLIDAY
17	9	HIP HUG HER	BOOKER "T" & THE MG'S
9	10	NOTHING TAKES THE PLACE OF YOU	
			TOUSSANT MC CALL
15	11	YOU ALWAYS HURT ME	THE IMPRESSIONS
22	12	TELL DADDY	CLARENCE CARTER
3	13	LOVE IS HERE AND NOW YOUR GONE	THE SUPREMES
20	14	THE JUNGLE	B. B. KING
21	15	LET THE DOOR HIT YOU	JIMMY MCCRACKLIN
6	16	MERCY, MERCY, MERCY	CANNONBALL ADDERLEY
14	17	OOH BABY	BO DIDLEY
11	18	BELLY RUB	DAVE CORTEZ
	19	THE LOVE I SAW YOU IN	THE MIRACLES
33	20	GIRL DON'T CARE	GENE CHANDLER
38	21	YOU'RE ALL I NEED	BOBBY BLAND
10	22	KANSAS CITY	JAMES BROWN
19	23	SKATE NOW	LOU COURTNEY
25	24	RAISE YOUR HAND	EDDIE FLOYD
32	25	BERNADETTE	THE FOUR TOPS
16	26	WHY NOT TONIGHT	JIMMY HUGHES
27	27	TRY A LITTLE TENDERNESS	OTIS REDDING
41	28	LATER FOR TOMORROW	ERNIE K. DOE
	29	EIGHT MEN, FOUR WOMEN	O. V. WRIGHT
18	30	LOOK AT GRANNY RUN RUN	HOWARD TATE
46	31	SOMEONE	FENTON ROBINSON
49	32	EVERY BODY LOVES A WINNER	WILLIAM BELL
31	33	SHOW ME	JOE TEX
39	34	GIRL I NEED YOU	ARTISTICS
44	35	ALL SOLD OUT	THE APOLLAS
45	36	A WOMAN WILL DO WRONG	HELENE SMITH
	37	I FOUND A LOVE	WILSON PICKETT
40	38	DRY YOUR EYES	BRENDA & TABULATIONS
	39	FEEL KING OF BAD	THE RADIANTS
34	40	A KNIFE AND A FORK	KIP ANDERSON
	41	GET YOURSELF TOGETHER	THE CAESARS
	42	HIJACK	JACKIE HAIRSTON
48	43	WITH THIS RING	THE PLATTERS
36	44	OUTSIDE LOVE	JOHNNY TAYLOR
50	45	HERE COME THE TEARS	DARRELL BANKS
	46	LOSING BOY	EDDIE GILES
	47	CLOSE YOUR EYES	PEACHES & HERB
	48	PRECIOUS MEMORIES	THE ROMEOS
	49	YOU'RE MY BABY	NAOMI & HARRIS
	50	MAKE LOVE TO ME	WINTERS-THUNDER

"Mellow Ain't They?"

Courtesy of Stephen K. Hauser

obituary, the *Milwaukee Journal* noted his graduation from Marquette University, his successful law practice, his past presidency of the Milwaukee Bar Association, his unsuccessful race for mayor of Milwaukee in 1944 and his longtime association with Wisconsin's Progressive Era governor, Philip Fox La Follette. His ownership of WAWA radio was not mentioned.

WAWA led its newscasts the following day with the story of Herb Mount's death. He was recalled there as one who gave a voice to Milwaukee's black community and offered African American broadcasters a chance to work in their chosen profession. After his death, station ownership passed through his estate to his widow, Isabel Mount (who held 32% of company stock), along with chief engineer Jack C. Krause, attorney James A. McKenna and co-founder Neil K. Searles.

Initially, not much changed at WAWA. Program director O.C. White continued to preside over the playing of the top R&B and soul hits of the day. Often airtime was given to records not heard elsewhere in the Milwaukee radio market. A prime example was the national hit "When A Man Loves a Woman" by Percy Sledge. Now considered a soul classic, this million-selling record placed at #1 on the *Billboard* Hot 100 for two weeks in May 1966 but did not even chart on Milwaukee's two Top 40 stations, WOKY and WRIT. It only received local airplay on WAWA and climbed to #3 on the WAWA weekly soul music survey.

By 1966, the WAWA chart listings were accurately compiled from area record sales with the help of Stuart Glassman, president of Radio Doctors. With two locations, at 3rd and Wells Street and 3rd and North Avenue, Glassman's shops sold more R&B records than any other music stores in Wisconsin.

During this time, WAWA began experimenting with new forms of programming. The Milwaukee Braves left for Atlanta after the 1965 season. During the absence of major league baseball in Milwaukee, a contract was signed with the Minnesota Twins allowing for broadcast of Twins games over WAWA from 1967 through 1969. (Other Milwaukee radio stations picked up Chicago Cubs and White Sox games at this time.)

O.C. White hired Rev. John E. Jackson, a central city pastor, as WAWA religion director in 1968. With the assistance of his daughter, Brenda Wallace, Rev. Jackson developed a playlist of spirituals and gospel recordings to be played in a regular rotation on Sundays, as the station devoted much of the day to religious programs. Live broadcasts were relayed from several city church services as well.

Meanwhile, Dr. Bop continued his daily broadcasts on the AM band, and had become perhaps the most entertaining of all Milwaukee air personalities. In October of 1967, the good Doctor announced a faux campaign for the U.S. presidency in 1968. His running mate for vice president was Arkansas "red neck" stand-up comic Dick Davy, who had two best-selling comedy albums on Columbia Records. Their satirical campaign lampooned the prevailing racial stereotypes of the day in ways that would no doubt be deemed politically incorrect by some today. When asked by *Milwaukee Journal* columnist Michael Drew whether their candidacy was merely a publicity stunt for WAWA, comedian Davy responded, "Hell, Dr. Bop has already spent $14 on bumper stickers and buttons, so you know he's serious!" On Election Day, Dr. Bop did receive some write-in votes in Milwaukee, but lost to Richard Nixon.

Public affairs involvement of a less tongue-in-cheek sort came when WAWA management hired Dr. Walter G. Beach II as news director. Beach began a nightly topical call-in program airing from 11 PM to midnight. Promising listeners that there would be "no sacred cows," Beach pledged to be "unbossed and unbought." He regularly angered both the white establishment and the black community, prompting some to call him "an equal opportunity offender." On more than one occasion, he called the Elm Grove Police Department for an escort to his car after receiving anonymous threats while on the air. He later would recall that he found the Elm Grove police to be cooperative and helpful. Beach left WAWA after five years and later ran twice as a Republican for Milwaukee's 5th district U.S. congressional seat, in 1980 and 1982. He remained active in local community affairs for many years.

Walter Beach's late-night call-in show was among the earliest of its type in the Milwaukee radio market. With expansion into sports programming and a round-the-clock FM listenership, WAWA had become a force to be reckoned with in local broadcasting.

Throughout the 1970s, WAWA continued to offer Milwaukee area listeners the best in soul and R&B hits, adding new popular styles like funk and instrumental jazz as times and tastes changed. Contemporary artists such as Isaac Hayes, Bill Withers and Barry White joined old favorites like James Brown, Wilson Pickett and Aretha Franklin to create a new, hip, youth-oriented format that attracted a widening pool of diverse listeners.

On 25 February 1976, the *Milwaukee Journal* stunned readers by informing them of the sudden death of Dr. Bop from a heart attack the previous day. Since arriving in town in 1963 from a stint hosting an R&B show in his hometown of Columbus, Ohio, Hoyt Locke (his real name) had come to define personality radio in Milwaukee. His Sunday evening TV program on Channel 18 and his frequent appearances at clubs, CYO dances, and record hops had made him recognizable on sight to

WAWA FIRST 45 SOUL SURVEY

O. C. White
6:00 - 9:00 A.M.

Phil Klingler
9:00 - 12:00 A.M.

Jim Frazier
12:00 - 4:00 P.M.

Dr. Bop
4:00 - Sign off
(FM till 9:00 P.M.)

on
1590 AM   102.1 FM

Week Sept. 14-19 *1970*   Milwaukee, Wisc.

1. War - Edwin Starr
2. Don't Play That Song - Aretha Franklin
3. Still Water - 4 Tops
4. Down By The River - Buddy Miles
5. Ain't No Mountain - Diana Ross
6. Express Yourself - Watts 103rd St. Band
7. I Understand - Freddie Hughes
8. Love Uprising - Otis Leavill
9. It's a Shame - Spinners
10. Patches - Clarence Carter
11. Signed, Sealed & Delivered-Stevie Wonder
12. Somebody's Sleeping - 100 Proof
13. Dear Ike - Sister & Brothers
14. Yours - Joe Simon
15. Seems Like I Gotta Do Wrong - Whispers
16. Stay Away From Me - Major Lance
17. Mail Call - Mel & Tim
18. Nobody Wants to Get Married-Jesse James
19. Get Up--Sex Machine - James Brown
20. I Need Help - Bobby Byrd
21. Baby Turn On To Me - Impressions
22. Something Strange - Ted Taylor
23. I'll Be There - Jackson Five
24. Part Time Love - Ann Peebles
25. Stand By Your Man - Candi Staton
26. I Gotta Get Away - Ray Godfrey
27. You're Gonna Make It - Festivals
28. I Stand Accused - Isaac Hayes
29. Ain't No Reason - Esquires
30. Hey Romeo - Sequins
31. Groovy Situation - Gene Chandler
32. If I Didn't Care - Moments
33. Heart Association - Emotions
34. I've Learned - Mavis Staples
35. She Said Yes/Engine No. 9 - Wilson Pickett
36. Cross My Heart - Billy Keene
37. When Love Calls - Darrow Fletcher
38. Need Your Love So Bad - Brenton Wood
39. Gimme Some - General Crook
40. I, You, We - Brothers of Love
41. Pure Love - Betty Wright
42. If This Is Your Last Song - DeeDee Warwick
43. We Can, Pt I - Lee Dorsey
44. Mellow Dreaming - Young Holt Unlimited
45. Push & Pull - The UDWI Peoples

SURE SHOT - Let Me Back In - Tyrone Davis
BEAST AROO - Lead Me On - Given McCrae
WAWA MONSTER - Baby, I've Got It - Popular Fiv
SLEEPER - Get Into Something - Isley Bros.

Courtesy of Stephen K. Hauser

many, an unusual feat for a radio personality. The *Journal* would note in his obituary that he was only 48 years old, but subsequent coverage by newspapers back in Ohio indicated that he was in his mid-60s! It didn't really matter to fans, as many had considered him timeless, and as current as the music he played.

The man who had once intoned, "I'm so tough I should have been triplets" was gone. It was a real blow to the identity of WAWA. For listeners, Dr. Bop had been the heart of the station. As its format and playlist continued to evolve toward a "maximum music mix" that allowed for less patter and braggadocio from disc jockeys, the good Doctor's passing seemed to mark the end of an era. Milwaukee radio fans would not see or hear his like again.

In a 1974 newspaper interview, WAWA program director O.C. White had predicted that African American ownership of the station was not far away. His prediction came true five years later when, in 1979, the station was purchased by All-Pro Broadcasting group, headed by retired Green Bay Packers legend Willie Davis. All-Pro Broadcasting also owned FM stations in Los Angeles and Houston, Texas. Davis and his associates believed that the future of music radio was on the FM band. This hunch proved prophetic and has been borne out since. By 2015, only two Milwaukee area AM stations still featured a music format.

All-Pro ceased the simulcasting of WAWA's FM signal, rechristening the 102.1 FM frequency as WLUM, with a high energy "contemporary urban" approach of "more music/less talk." On weekends, however, WLUM also began to appropriate much of the discussion and public affairs programming that had previously been heard on AM at WAWA. Willie Davis was committed to providing programs that not only entertained but also served community needs for information and education. I was a guest on Arnie Wheeler's Sunday morning interview program on WLUM in 1989, and found it to be a well-produced, professional show. That is what the station strove for in community programming.

The fate of WAWA, meanwhile, was in doubt by the end of the 1980s. Its low fidelity AM sound and limited 1,000 watts of transmission power coupled with the dawn-to-dusk broadcast day restrictions placed upon it by the FCC made the station something of an anachronism. In late 1988, unable to sell the 1590 frequency to a new owner, All-Pro pulled the plug on WAWA and its signal went dark.

O.C. White was named corporate vice-president of All-Pro Broadcasting and moved his on-air responsibilities to newly-acquired WMVP at 1290 AM where he hosted a talk show and an R&B oldies program. He founded O.C. White's Soul Club, an agency in the central city that trained at-risk youth in skilled construction trades. He served on the Milwaukee Metropolitan Sewage District board and the Milwaukee County Parks Commission, operated his own Bar-B-Que restaurant on Capitol Drive and received an honorary doctorate in communications. He died on October 19, 1992, at Milwaukee County Hospital while awaiting a heart transplant at age 60. White had shaped the future of WAWA back in 1961 when he began playing rhythm and blues records and selling advertising to merchants in Milwaukee's black community. He had changed local history and Wisconsin radio in the process.

WLUM-FM continued to broadcast from its 12800 W. Blue Mound Road location until new studios were ready at 2979 N. Mayfair Road in Wauwatosa, just north of Mayfair Mall. The United Parcel Service purchased the old WAWA property and razed the studios. The defunct FM tower on site was used to transmit coordinating instructions to UPS trucks on their rounds, but in October 1999, the tower was taken down, cut into sections and hauled away. The last vestige of WAWA's decades long tenure on the property, an old bridge that crossed the Underwood Creek and led to the station's parking lot, was removed in 2006.

Back in 1959 attorney Herbert Mount envisaged a suburban radio station. His dream came true with the founding of WAWA AM in Elm Grove in 1960. He could never have imagined all of the future musical and social ramifications of that dream. It truly changed Wisconsin broadcast history.

Bob Reitman and Freeform FM Radio[3]
by Phillip Naylor

It's a Sunday evening about 9:00 PM in 1972, almost time for *The Dylan Hour* hosted by Bob Reitman transmitting from WZMF in Menomonee Falls. I have my Magnavox radio strategically perched on the windowsill of my studio apartment to best capture WZMF's relatively weak signal. Reitman introduces *Highway 61 Revisited* and my friend Jim Jablonowski and I settle back to listen to the entire album. It's freeform FM exercised by a master host who was with it and who still has it—Reitman.[4]

Born in Oklahoma and raised in Whitefish Bay, Reitman received an English bachelor's degree from Marquette University and a master's urban education degree from the University of Wisconsin-Milwaukee (UWM). Essentially, however, Reitman is a poet. (He was also the poetry editor for the underground newspaper *Kaleidoscope*.) Reitman participated in readings at Milwaukee coffeehouses and other venues, e.g., the Avant Garde on Prospect Avenue just south of North Avenue (see Angeli and Goff 1975). His poetry would be accompanied by jazz and rock music. His style evoked the Beats and predated Patti Smith (whom he admires) as can be heard on his spoken word album, *The Eleventh House* (1972). In 1966, he recited on *Sense Waves*, a poetry program on WUWM-FM and later hosted the show. (His first radio director was Ron Cuzner, the inimitable host of an all-night jazz program *The Dark Side*.) Meanwhile albums arrived at the

---

3   See https://en.wikipedia.org/wiki/Bob_Reitman; https://onmilwaukee.com/buzz/articles/reitman.html; https://www.youtube.com/watch?v=Vd6vTjAb5aE; http://wuwm.com/programs/its-alright-ma-its-only-music; https://www.youtube.com/watch?v=e3nongY6JZM; and Spielmann 1975. Conversations with Reitman over the years also contributed to this essay. Reitman has generously shared his professional and personal history with Marquette University students.

4   Reitman seemed omnipresent during these years emceeing concerts, e.g., at State Fair Park, County Stadium, and the Alternate Site (see Chapter 6).

station. Reitman requested and received more air time where he presented a rock music program in 1967, *It's Alright Ma, It's Only Music*. WUWM "got ratings."

Reitman chose what he wanted to play. Given his poetic proclivities music of Bob Dylan, Lou Reed (and the Velvet Underground), and Leonard Cohen were among his favorites, which he shared with his growing audience and later included Bruce Springsteen and Patti Smith.[5] The freeform format allowed Reitman to be, as he has often called

THE LIFT PRESENTS

THE ELEVENTH HOUSE

with bob reitman

it, a "benevolent dictator." Reitman also educated not only about music, but also life. His "Dear Doctor" segment featured a physician addressing the drug scene in Milwaukee (and its risks). Later, Reitman appealed to men to have their prostate tested, given his own experience as a cancer survivor. Indeed, Reitman was, and still is, an educator.

Moving to WZMF, Reitman continued his freeform performance with his program the *Eleventh Hour* until "ZMF" began changing its format to attract a wider audience. He left the station. (Reitman also had stints with WAWA and WTOS, the latter turning into an easy-listening station in 1971.) Reit-

man joined WQFM, where he enjoyed a freer format. (In 1976, he set the Guinness world record for the "Longest Continuous Broadcast on the Air by a Disc Jockey [222 hours and 22 minutes.]") Nevertheless, with freeform fading (and uneconomic) and finally with "nowhere to go," WKTI hired Bob in 1980 and teamed with Gene Mueller in a highly successful morning program. "Reitman and Mueller" broadcast from six Olympic Games and, notably, the liberalizing Soviet Union in 1985 as Mikhail Gorbachev promoted *glasnost* (opening, greater freedom) and *perestroika* (restructuring) as the Cold War thawed. Bob retired in 2006. In the following year, Reitman returned to where it all started—WUWM—and revived the freeform *It's Alright, Ma, It's Only Music* program in 2007 (now accompanied by his son, Bobby).

Why do I still tune in Reitman on WUWM? Because, even before I knew him, he was a guy I felt you could trust. Musically and aesthetically, he had your best interests in mind and heart, and still does. Just listen.

5 See https://onmilwaukee.com/music/articles/patti-smith-milwaukee-bob-reitman.html.

Courtesy of Bob Reitman

Courtesy of Stephen K. Hauser

now it's Pepsi
for those who think young

PEPSI·COLA

W-RIT SPOTLIGHT LP's

	Title	Artist	Album
X	Meet The Beatles	The Beatles	Capital
	You Make Me Feel So Young	Ray Conniff	Columbia

HOT PROSPECTS

X	DAWN	Four Seasons
X	GOOD NEWS	Sam Cooke
X	ABIGAIL BEECHER	Freddie Cannon
	SHIMMEY SHIMMEY	Orlons
	BLANG DONG	Doctor Feelgood & Interns

Courtesy of Stephen K. Hauser

The New **W-RIT**
RIGHT MUSIC SURVEY
1340 in Milwaukee

BILL MC COLLOUGH 6-10:00 am — BILL ERICKSEN 10 am-1 pm — LEE ROTHMAN 3-6:00 pm — GEORGE MICHAEL 6-10:00 pm — EDDIE DOUCETTE 10-12:00 m — BUDDY CARR 12 m-6 am

NEW W-RIT SONG SURVEY

Last Week	This Week	EFFECTIVE JANUARY 19, 1964
7	1	I WANT TO HOLD YOUR HAND-Beattles-FDC
1	2	THERE I'VE SAID IT AGAIN—Bobby Vinton
6	3	DUMBHEAD—Ginny Arnell
10	4	FOR YOU—Ricky Nelson
14	5	YOU DON'T OWN ME—Leslie Gore
8	6	OUT OF LIMITS—Marketts
5	7	MIDNIGHT MARY—Joey Powers
3	8	DRAG CITY—Jan & Dean
2	9	AS USUAL/LONELY, LONELY ME — Brenda Lee—FDC
4	10	LOUIE, LOUIE—Kingsmen
11	11	DAISY PETAL PICKIN'—Jimmy Gilmer—FDC
15	12	ANYONE WHO HAD A HEART— Dionne Warwick
21	13	IN THE STILL OF THE NIGHT—Santo & Johnny
12	14	POPSICLES & ICICLES—Mermaids
19	15	THE SHELTER OF YOUR ARMS— Sammy Davis Jr.
22	16	A FOOL NEVER LEARNS—Andy Williams
23	17	UM UM UM UM UM UM UM—Major Lance
9	18	SURFIN BIRD—Trashmen
13	19	WHISPERING—April Stevens & Nino Tempo
16	20	NEED TO BELONG—Jerry Butler—FDC
29	21	HEY LITTLE COBRA—Rip Chords
35	22	CALIFORNIA SUN—Rivieras
Debut	23	SHE LOVES YOU—Beatles—FDC
32	24	THAT GIRL BELONGS TO YESTERDAY— Gene Pitney—FDC
40	25	TALKIN ABOUT MY BABY— Impressions—FDC
37	26	SLIPPIN & SLIDIN—Jim & Monica
36	27	WHAT KIND OF FOOL DO YOU THINK I AM—The Tams
17	28	HEY LONELY ONE—Paul Steffen & Appollo's
18	29	LODDY LO HOOKA TOOKA—Chubby Checker
Debut	30	JAVA—Al Hirt
Debut	31	BLUE SKIES—Jack Scott
20	32	NITTY GRITTY—Shirley Ellis
30	33	BABY I LOVE YOU—Ronettes
24	34	FORGET HIM—Bobby Rydell
Debut	35	GONNA SEND YOU BACK TO GEORGIA — Timmy Shaw
Debut	36	COME ON—Tommy Roe
Debut	37	STOP & THINK IT OVER—Dale & Grace—FDC
Debut	38	TONIGHT YOU'RE GONNA FALL IN LOVE WITH ME—Shirelles
Debut	39	SOUTHTOWN USA—Dixiebelles
Debut	40	WOW WOW WEE—The Angels—FDC

FDC: A FORMER DISC COVERY ON THE NEW W-RIT

Courtesy of Stephen K. Hauser

Courtesy of Stephen K. Hauser

Courtesy of Stephen K. Hauser

WAWA'S FAMOUS 1590 AM
DR. BOP
WAWA'S FAMOUS 102.1 FM
72 *for* **PRESIDENT** 72

Courtesy of Stephen K. Hauser

Dr. Bop
enterprises

Courtesy of Stephen K. Hauser

WAWA

DR. BOP

WAWA
1590 K.C.   102.1 M.C.

MON. thru FRI. 6:00 AM to 9:00 AM
SAT. 6:00 AM to 9:00 AM & 10 to Noon

DR. BOP ENTERPRISES
3379 North 20th Street
Milwaukee, Wisconsin 53206

ATTN: UNIVERSITY FRATS. & SORORITIES
HIGH SCHOOL & ALL SOCIAL CLUBS

DR. BOP ENTERPRISES
871-6919
FOR PERSONAL APPEARANCES

CALL OR WRITE SOON FOR ADVERTISING
ON **WAWA** OR **DR .BOP** PERSONAL
APPEARANCES

ADVERTISING & MUSIC
IS MY GAME

DR. BOP'S
SOULFUL **45**
The Music That Moves
DO IT TO IT
MON-SAT WAWA 1590KC 6:45-9:00 A. M.
SUNDAY   WUHF TV 5:30-6:30

DR. BOP
WAWA'S FAMOUS 102.1 FM
for **PRESIDENT** 72

Paul Cebar
(see Chapter 10)
promoting
freeform WMSE

Photo by Erol Reyal

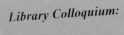

Library Colloquium:

ROCK n' ROLL n' RADIO ... THE LAST 50 YEARS

Featuring:

Bob Reitman,
Marquette Alum,
Pioneering 1960s DJ,
WKTI Personality,
Rock 'n Roll Historian,
Raconteur,
Poet

Wednesday, November 2, 2005
2:00 P.M.
Raynor Library Conference Center
Beaumier Suites B & C (Lower Level)

Jointly sponsored by the Marquette University Librarians' Assembly and the
Association. The event is free and open to all. A Marquette I.D. card is requi
Library; members of the general public are required to register (at least 10 m
program) at the library entrance with a photo I.D.

For more information please contact
Alberto Herrera at 288-2140 or alberto.herrera@marquette.edu

Courtesy of the Jean Cujé Collection

Bob Reitman, DJ, poet and educator, the dean of freeform Milwaukee FM radio, at the Reitman Gala Farewell Party at the Riverside Theatre (2006)

Photo by Erol Reyal

Courtesy of the Jean Cujé Collection

Harvey Scales, Milwaukee's "Godfather of Soul,"
a celebrated composer, producer, and performer

CHAPTER 5

Milwaukee's Rhythm and Blues (R&B), Soul, and Hip-hop Heritage

Jamie Lee Rake provides a detailed survey of Milwaukee's rich R&B and soul heritage and includes hip-hop. Stars like Harvey Scales, Al Jarreau, Eric Benét and Speech are among the constellation of musicians identified with Milwaukee and these genres. Jarreau and Penny Goodwin especially bridged soul and jazz.[1] Currently, Milwaukee hip-hop community is particularly vibrant and features WebsterX, IshDARR, Tyrone "DJ Bizzon" Miller, Damon "Jank" Joy, BoodahDarr, D.J. the Jenius, and Kane.[2] These artists are attracting greater national besides local attention.

---

1 Regarding Milwaukee jazz musicians, see Pinkham 2010.

2 See https://noisey.vice.com/da/article/6e4m7p/milwaukee-rap-scene-report-2015; and https://www.jsonline.com/story/entertainment/music/2017/08/31/five-milwaukee-rappers-rise-selected-ishdarr-websterx-and-others/600572001/.

Milwaukee Rhythm and Blues (R&B) and Soul to Hip-hop

Jamie Lee Rake[3]

The rise of R&B in Milwaukee coincides with the decline of the city's African American Bronzeville neighborhood, an epicenter of activity in the 1940s for the blues, swing, and jazz—the musical vernacular among blacks locally and nationwide.

Though never having developed a trademark "Milwaukee sound," as in other cities with significant African American populations, Milwaukee R&B acts produced singles, LPs, cassettes, mix-tapes, and CDs, displaying unique artistic invention and interpretation admired by local and occasionally national and international audiences. Milwaukee R&B acts continue to produce a steady stream of recorded music. During the past quarter-century dominated by hip-hop, Milwaukee's most renowned export in that genre, Speech, would take a roundabout way to greater attention by moving to Atlanta before achieving worldwide acclaim.

Like rock and roll, R&B took time to catch hold in Milwaukee. Though strains of it could be heard in Bronzeville venues, it was not until 1958 that local rhythm and blues surfaced on record with Big Mack & His Shufflers' "Someday You're Gonna Sing the Blues"/ "Out of My Mind." Just as Big Mack was laying down his 45, the first act that would give Milwaukee R&B/soul notoriety had formed. The Esquires got together in 1957 in high school with siblings Gilbert, Alvis and Betty Moorer as the group's nucleus. A decade later, after many personnel changes, they were an all-male vocal group about to explode with the most nationally successful record to come from Milwaukee in the 1960s.

Chicago label owner Bill "Bunky" Shepherd brought the Esquires' "Get on Up" to Top 5 soul/Top 15 pop success in 1967, and he was not the group's only Windy City connection. Chicago's male vocal trio, the Impressions, served as an exemplar for the Esquires' quartet-to-quintet use of high tenor lead singing atop lower backing vocals and bass fills at the bottom. The Esquires actually attempted to interest Curtis Mayfield, the Impressions' own high tenor co-lead, in signing them to the companies in which he had a hand at the time. Mayfield's disinterest made for Shepherd's good fortune.

The follow-up to "Get on Up" led to soul Top 10/pop Top 25 sequel "And Get Away." The two hits combined as the name of the only Esquires' album, *Get on Up and Get Away*. They would continue to record until the early 1980s, occasionally charting. The Esquires' limited degree of success, however, did not inhibit their hometown's flourishing R&B/soul scene.

Betty, the sister to the group's Moorer brothers, issued 45s both before and after her siblings' hit streak. She recorded for the same label to which her brothers were under contract at the time, Specter Records' subsidiary Wand Records, and marks one of the few times a Milwaukeean made an "answer record" to a national smash. Copying the arrangement of the Isley Brothers's hit, "It's My Thing," Betty replied: "It's Your Thing,"

---

3   Interviews conducted by the author in 2013-14.

belting like Etta James in one of her feistier moments. Another singer emerged with an Esquires stint in his résumé and an early 1960s affiliation with Sauk City's prolific Cuca Records. He went on to significantly greater heights as a songwriter.

Harvey Scales, who was to become "Milwaukee's Godfather of Soul," was born in Osceola, Alabama, and moved to Milwaukee from South Bend, Indiana, as a child. He graduated from North Division High School.[4] Not long after his work with an early iteration of the Esquires, he issued his first record as Twistin' Harvey, a nickname earned by his out-dancing at a local concert Chubby Checker, the popularizer of early 1960s dance craze, "The Twist."

With his band, the Seven Sounds, Scales adopted a smooth delivery akin to Sam Cooke's satiny croon. Taking in a James Brown concert at the armory on South 16th Street and Mitchell Avenue drew him into a different direction. "James Brown blew my band's mind," said Scales in a 2014 interview. Upon seeing the Godfather of Soul's incendiary showmanship and his band's tight interplay of brass, he thought to himself: "That's what I want to do." And so he did with his own spin on a run of singles for Chicago's Magic Touch Records, peaking with 1967's "Get Down." The single cracked the soul top 40 and the lower 70s pop chart. Its B-side, "Love-itis," would bring Scales royalties from covers by other R&B acts plus Boston rockers the J. Geils Band.

Other dance craze numbers, such as "Broadway Freeze," "The Funky Yolk," "Electric Robot" and "Funky Football" would follow for numerous labels throughout the rest of the 1960s and into the 1970s. Scales channeled the same sort of social consciousness amplified in the early 1970s by Motown artists like Marvin Gaye, Stevie Wonder, and the Temptations on "Trying to Survive," among other releases.

If his and the Seven Sounds singles weren't doing bustling business, Scales composed LP tracks and singles for other soul acts including the O'Jays, the Dramatics, and the Facts of Life. It would be a veteran Stax Records hit maker who had recently signed with Columbia who gave Scales his most indelible mark on his resume.

Not a disco record as such, but a funk song about disco is how Scales describes "Disco Lady." That stylistic disparity didn't prevent it from becoming Johnny Taylor's biggest single (1976), topping both pop and urban sales and air play charts and becoming a favorite on Don Cornelius' African American *American Bandstand* complement, *Soul Train*, for the song's mention of the show.

"Disco Lady's" blockbuster status coincided with the establishment of a sales certification award higher than gold by the record business trade group the Recording Industry Association of America (RIAA). Scales' best-known co-writing credit earned all parties concerned a platinum award for U.S. sales exceeding 2 million copies. Though he insists that he hasn't yet received his rightful share of income from it, he doesn't sound embittered by the corruption endemic in the music business. "Disco Lady" afforded Scales other career options, including taking his own recording career to a higher level. Neither of his LPs for Casablanca Records, the label best known for signing Kiss and an un-

---

4 Scales (1941-2019) died as this manuscript was being prepared. See Piet Levy's obituary/article in the *Milwaukee Journal Sentinel*: https://www.jsonline.com/story/entertainment/music/2019/02/12/harvey-scales-milwaukee-godfather-soul-disco-lady-writer-dies/2847266002/.

leashing deluge of disco, came anywhere near "Disco Lady" numbers. With the second of those efforts, *Hot Foot (A Funque Dizco Opera)*, Scales followed the lead of Casablanca label mate Alec R. Costadinos and reigning disco queen Donna Summer by making a thematically ambitious disco concept album. It also contained "Dancing Room Only," Scales' most-sampled composition, used by rappers the Beastie Boys and Kriss Kross, among others.

Post-Casablanca, Scales continued to write and record, including his first compact disc release, *All in a Night's Work,* for a Canadian concern in the early 1990s. Now residing in Atlanta, he remains active finding new challenges, among them singing the theme song for 2011 campy monster movie *Super Shark* with un-ironic retro-relish and dabbling in gospel and Southern soul. He also fits in concert dates throughout the U.S. and Europe.

Scales' lengthy array of credits is an extreme exception given the considerably less prolific recording tenures of his contemporary Milwaukee R&B artists. For one singer born in the city, a brief stint in soul music was a fluke on his way to recognition as a successful jazz singer whose career would encompass cross-genre appeal. "No regrets… but we've gone somewhere else," Al Jarreau said in a 2014 interview to summarize his duo of mid-1960s 45s for Milwaukee studio owner/producer Ray Kennedy's Raynard Records. In the years immediately following the attainment of his degree in social work from Ripon College, the Major Lance-gone-Motown strains of a brassy dance tune like "Shake Up" from one of those singles would not have meshed with the more genteel crooning Jarreau plied at local venues including the Pfister Hotel and the clubs further west where he would connect with Warner Brothers, his main label for the first 20 years of his national career.

Jarreau recalled that Kennedy's connections netted those Raynard releases a few spins on Milwaukee radio; he never really performed them live. Dynamic performances those surely would have been, their memories live on as their status as collectibles from one of the most internationally successful acts from Milwaukee in any genre. They also wound up as turntable staples among some DJs in the 1970s England's Northern soul subculture, an outgrowth of the earlier mod movement where U.S. obscurities with up-tempo danceability fueled all-night dances among mostly white youths (and continues to be foundational in the country's idea of pop music). Jarreau and Scales are only the best known among Milwaukee acts to have received the approval in Northern soul and other R&B-enthused subcultures elsewhere throughout the world.

Jarreau's 1980s crossover hit "We're in This Love Together," the theme song to the Bruce Willis/Cybil Shepherd TV show *Moonlighting,* would net him R&B and pop viability for a while, but he was by that time not strictly known as a Milwaukee personality. Though the interview for this essay was the first time Jarreau was reminded of his Raynard recordings in years, he recalled them pleasantly as he has moved on to more eclectic territory. "It's great that it didn't happen for me," he reflected. R&B may have impeded his idiosyncratic career.

In the 1960s and 1970s most Milwaukee R&B acts would neither release full-length albums nor benefit from their singles receiving support from national radio and record retailers that could have widened their popularity beyond local dates or regional touring. Exceptions of one stripe or another abound, however, through the period. After one late-1960s 45 on the local Odessa label, A.C. Poston saw fit to start his own venture, Sympathy Records, for his next two offerings. His mid-to down tempo tunes drew from the secularized gospel testifying of deeply Southern artists like Percy Sledge and James Carr. Arguably more inventive may have been his entrepreneurial determination. In the early 1970s bar climate where jukeboxes often provided musical entertainment, Poston was one R&B promoter so sold on the influence of the money-taking machines that he courted the companies that catered to their trade. He was referenced in a September 1971 issue of *Billboard* in the context of jukeboxes disseminating what he hoped would develop as a "Milwaukee sound."

Neither would Jarreau be the only Milwaukee act to go from recording straight R&B to variants of jazz. Teenage 11-piece Aalon Butler & The New Breed Band started in 1967 proffering rugged, horn-infused party soul made for dancing. Ten years on, Butler had left for Los Angeles, made a connection with Animals singer and War collaborator Eric Burdon and led a band named Aalon for one album, blending poppy rock and fusion jazz with a side potion of disco. Butler manifested Milwaukee pride by naming that lone collection for the color of the bricks for which his former home was known, *Cream City*.

Around the time the New Breed Band changed their name to the hipper A Different Bag (releasing a single by the even hipper title of "Mother-Fudge Cicle") and moved to Memphis, joining them for a time was a singing keyboardist who went by the name Bobby Mack. He would later revert to his real name, Bobby McFerrin, and launch a career of innovative jazz vocalizing that commercially peaked in the reggae-hued 1988 #1 pop hit, "Don't Worry, Be Happy." Later joining the act would be James Ingram, best known for his collaborative pop, R&B, club and country hits with Quincy Jones, Patti Austin, Linda Ronstadt, and Michael McDonald, among others.

During a decade when the Supremes scored heavily among pop and R&B listeners alike, Milwaukee produced only one female vocal group with similar potential as Diana Ross, the Mar-J's. Their lone 7-inch, the deceptively joyous "Got to Find a Way Out," (1967), was likely backed instrumentally by Harvey Scales' Seven Sounds band and was released on the source for so much of Scales' work, Magic Touch Records.

More lyrically substantive and sonically diverse fare from a feminine perspective arrived seven years later via Penny Goodwin. Her 1974 *Portrait of a Gemini* could have caught the attention of adventurous fans of prominent female singers such as Roberta Flack, but in terms of Goodwin's spacious acoustic arrangements, she sounds like a precursor to turn-of-the-twenty-first-century neo-soul females Jill Scott and Angie Stone. A Japanese 2004 CD reissue of *Gemini* coincided with the issuing of a concert album by Goodwin the same year in that country.

The band backing the late Marvelle Love (sometimes spelled Marvell Love), the Blue Mats (later the Blue Match), did the Seven Sounds and the New Breed Band one better, emulating James Brown's ensemble by including dual drummers. That doubling of percussive power was put into the service of one of the most literally titled (hoped-for) dance craze records ever, "The Dance Called the Motion."

Love, apparently, wasn't satisfied with only making music; his New World Records turned out an intermittent flow of 45s from urban Milwaukee acts. Production was uniformly captivating in one way or another, but sometimes a bit rustic compared to contemporaneous, nationally charting hits. If this counts as a manifestation of Poston's hoped-for Milwaukee sound, mission accomplished. Many record collectors would concur, considering the prices some of Love's productions command today.

A handbill advertising the Essentials, a Milwaukee soul group which also shared the stage with the punk band, the Haskels (see Introductions)

Courtesy of the Jean Cujé Collection

Other record companies native to the city, mostly specializing in singles, aimed to accommodate local talent and hoped for hits as the 1960s turned into the 1970s. Brewtown Records' foaming stein logo assured quality throughout the Nixon-Ford-Carter years. One highlight of its catalog? Eddie Jackson's frantic "Memories of a Dream," combining funky horn charts with co-ed background vocals. Alternately, Vic Pitts Cheaters' "Loose Boodie," distinguishes itself not only by mining a deeply rubbery funkiness, but also cribbing *two* contemporaneous Alka-Seltzer ad slogans: "Try it, you'll like it" and, more mystifying, "I can't believe I ate the whole thing."

Cal Monegar's Calgar Records was about as prolific as any other Milwaukee R&B specialist label of the time. That is to say, not very. Some recordings received local soul radio airplay, including Brothers by Choice's 1973 slow jam, "You Think That I'm a Fool." They also released a 1979 slice of disco, "Get Up and Dance," on New World Records.

Calgar's only act with multiple releases, Black Earth Plus, was an ensemble led by the late singer/guitarist Duchie Rogers. Not only did those 45s showcase a stunning use of wah-wah pedal ("How Can You Say You Love Me") and a lyrically minimalist celebration of the city reminiscent of Donny Hathaway or Gil Scott Heron ("Milwaukee"), but they were also the introduction of a musician with a historical pedigree whose travels would make him an ambassador of his city's musical good will to the world.

Rogers' maintained Black Earth Plus as a working unit long after their 1970s Calgar work, playing for U.S. troops in Hawaii, Germany, Korea and Japan. A solo trip to England led him to opening for and playing with soul music queen Aretha Franklin. At least once he played in Milwaukee with his more famous cousin, blues great B.B. King, though Rogers and Black Earth Plus were booked regularly at local venues and events like Potawatomi Casino, Summerfest, African World Fest, Pewaukee's late Piano Blu and elsewhere. All of this would occur when Rogers wasn't working his day job of assisting disabled people.

Rogers' seeming ubiquity in live settings was belied by a slim discography. Over 20 years after the aforementioned Black Earth Plus singles, a partnership with Jonnie Lee Mills Junior birthed one seven-song EP of modern adult R&B with smooth jazz touches, *I Kissed You in the Right Place*, as Du/Jon. Highlights include the danceable mid-tempo titular track and "Don't Turn Your Back on Love," as well as the statelier lament over inner city youth violence, "Another Life Lost."

Fourteen years later, and only a couple years before his passing, local producer Godxilla, best known for his work in hip-hop, oversaw Rogers' crowning achievement, *Heat*, an album that did justice to the eclectic reach of Rogers' sensibilities while infusing it with more modern elements that never seem gimmicky. For a devoted churchman and son of a Church of God in Christ pastor, the album's flirtations with pimp culture—and its concomitant misogyny—brought an unsettling edge to Rogers' usually creamy bass/baritone singing. *Heat*, nonetheless served as a late-career triumph and received considerable play in some of Milwaukee's inner city "grown folks" night clubs, according to the eulogizing given Rogers by veteran radio personality Ernest "Ernie G" Mitchell on his Saturday afternoon show on WMCS AM 1290 at the time of his 2011 death.

Rogers' Black Earth Plus shouldn't be confused with the similarly monikered, also Milwaukeean and roughly contemporaneous Black Society. Their Stax single from 1972, "Look Around You," was followed the next year on MCA with a remake of the Four Seasons' "Sherry." From there, the group disappeared.

A confluence of black rock music's evolution in the wake of Jimi Hendrix's death, the rise of the Latin rock interpretations of Santana, and a cerebrally heavy take on funk brought about another of Milwaukee's major label graduates, Cane and Able. Listening to their two 1972 Epic Records long-players, one might assume the octet would have found an audience among fans of Sly & the Family Stone, Funkadelic, Buddy Miles and the guitar-heavy direction the Isley Brothers were taking at the time. Their albums have yet to see reissue.

Popular media conceptions of disco peg the dance music's peak in the post-*Saturday Night Fever* 1970s. Though that may have been the period of saturation, the term had already gained currency as far back as the summer of 1974 when the fledgling genre garnered its first two back-to-back #1 pop hits (The Hues Corporation's "Rock the Boat" and George McRae's "Rock You Baby"). Milwaukee musicians contributed to the sounds early on.

Male vocal group the Quadraphonics became the first Milwaukee entity to adapt a disco sound with "Betcha if You Check It Out," which climbed to the middle of *Billboard*'s soul survey in 1974. Already, disco's trademarks were in place: the 4/4 interlocking of hi-hat cymbals and snare and bass drums, and the integration of horns and strings cultivated by Kenny Gamble and Leon Huff's Philadelphia International Records productions earlier in the decade. Milwaukee's Calgar and New World operations saw fit to issue disco, too. Regarding the Quadrophonics' Warner Brothers-distributed hit, local operators paired dance rhythms with slower-paced romance. Calgar's the Perfections waxed tender for the A side of their only 45, "Till I get Home"; its flip, "Can This Be Real," paired their silky harmonizing to a beat scape keeping up with the disco times, with electronic fills accenting the arrangement's brass and thump. It is a few steps up in sophistication from the Esquires' 1976 revamp of "Get on Up," where a more insistent back beat undergirded a close approximation of the original version from nine years before.

New World gave the city its loosest as well as its tightest disco sides in 1979. Claps redolent of Rose Royce's "Car Wash," keening trumpet stabs and relatively informal vocal interplay make Brothers by Choice's "Get Up and Dance" culminate in a booty-loosening party vibe. The more complex and beat-dropping structure of Lo-End's sophomore single for the label, "Le-Beat," uses the balance of lushness and austerity distinguishing New York disco specialists such as Chic and GQ to commanding effect. Clocking in over 4:30 and ending starkly on the beat, it may be New World's slickest offering and worthy as any Milwaukee offering of national dissemination.

Were the "Le-Beat" to have received wider promotional attention, Lo-End still may not have been competitive in the bustling club music market at the end of the 1970s. Twelve-inch singles 12 were *de rigueur* in discos' DJ booths by this time. It would take a white interloper to club sound-tracking to produce the city's first 12-incher—Jim Spencer, who was better known for folk rock and poetry.

His initial disco seven-incher was a 1979 collaboration with local band Son Rize on his own Armada imprint. "The Blues Are Out to Get Me" matched a depressive lyric to a bed of flute, saxophone, and galloping bass situated between a lush Italian approach to the music *à la* Cerrone and the Doobie Brothers' yacht rock take on it. Manic mixed gender background singing of the title, add to the uncharacteristically paranoid entry into a genre more commonly associated with celebration, or at least catharsis.

The tempo dropped considerably on Spencer's 1979 12-inch single (also savvily issued as an edited seven-inch), "Wrap Myself Up in Your Love." Spencer presciently anticipated the rise of lower beats-per-minute dance music popularized in clubs, especially African American ones, after the disco backlash that climaxed with Chicago rock radio DJ Steve Dahl's disco record explosion at Comiskey Park (12 July 1979). Spencer's seductive couplets, far less troubled than those of its predecessor, played in the song's favor, too. Sticking more highly energized remakes of Cole Porter's "Begin the Beguine" and Glenn Miller's "Moonlight Serenade" add another layer of eclectic mystery to Spencer's disco intrigue.

The enigma continued two years after Spencer's death in 1983 with a seven-inch released on New World Records, for which he enlisted Milwaukee blues harmonica player Jim Liban and drummer Kenny Baldwin, African American owner of punk/new wave nightclub The Starship and member of nationally signed electro-pop band Colour Radio. One track from it, "Take Her by the Hand" fomented a lean funk/rock hybrid that may have been a stretch for buyers of other New World releases, but not entirely out of their frame of reference, either.

Spencer probably would not have been anyone's idea of a harbinger of change in R&B, but the 1980s marked shifts in urban music that reverberate to the present day. Though rap and hip-hop culture generally would take a while to influence Milwaukee artists after its late 1970s rise from East Coast cult phenomenon to national spotlight, other bustle was afoot.

One of those bustling hustlers beat the trend of male R&B singers going by one name (i.e., Usher, Lloyd) by about a decade. Harold (last name Stewart) managed the fairly unheard of feat of landing a self-released indie single into the lower reaches of *Billboard*'s soul singles chart in 1982. Released on his own Je-Har label, "In the Cool of the Night" used Harold's friendly tenor to pleasing quiet storm effect. Thirty years on, its more frenetic B side, "Shortage of Love," is preferred by collectors bidding on rare black dance music; its opening *faux* news report concerning the song's titular scarcity makes for a cute touch on a gracious tune.

Three years later, Stewart released a six-track cassette to local retailers, promoting *Night Time Fun* with a vinyl single of its title cut. He resumed recording only in the 2010s, with two independently issued albums worth of romantic, political, and spiritual ruminations in what he calls a "crossover balladeer" style synthesizing elements of R&B, jazz, folk and country.

A more concentrated burst of creativity arrived mid-decade from a promising teenager whose musical aspirations seemed to have burned briefly and brightly, only to be extinguished as quickly. Timothy Marrow involved himself in two records that received significant local R&B airplay within a year of his 1985 high school graduation. The 12-inch EP he produced by a group named the Kee is the sort of lite jazz-skirting electronic R&B with which English keyboardist Paul Hardcastle ingratiated himself among urban radio listeners and break dancers with 1984's "Rain Forest." The Kee added vocals on "Traffic Violator" and "You Turn Me Out," the latter packing slightly more "oomph," the former enlivened by the odd burst of what sound like video game effects. It's the record's last selection, absent from a simultaneous 7-inch pressing, that's the real revelation. "The Game Is Over" could be the only piece of Latin freestyle, or inadvertent approximation of it, to come from Milwaukee, with staccato drums machine work and high-pitched synthesizer programming in a minor key, vaguely Hispanic melody would work comfortably in a club set of songs by TKA, the Cover Girls, Exposé, and other vocal trios and soloists who wouldn't be recording for another year or two.

The apex of Marrow's short foray into music, however, was "Killer Moon." Either in its 7-inch version or extended 12-inch with slightly different keyboard tones and other touches, the melodic debt to Michael Jackson's "Billie Jean" is easy to hear; yet Marrow's use of the sinister motif is more genuinely unsettling. As with Marrow's freestyle turn on the Kee's record, "Moon" anticipated popular taste by at least several months. It's not difficult to hear it as a counterpoint to Timex Social Club's cautionary, paranoid "Rumors," which slowly climbed into the pop, R&B, and club play top 10s by the end of 1986.

Hip-hop, the greatest stylistic innovation in African American music of the century's last quarter, was introduced in the city in an almost haphazard way. As with disco,

Marvelle Love had an ear for what might have seemed like a fad at the time, releasing in 1982 the city's first rap side, "Class A," as the B-side of 7-inch single by local male harmony group the Majestics. Compared to the nearly quarter-hour-plus duration of early genre hits such as the Sugarhill Gang's "Rapper's Delight," the Majestics' foray into hip-hop's rhythmic speech was relatively brief, being under four minutes. Though their music possessed the same kind of loose studio funk as Kurtis Blow's contemporaneous work, the rhyming was significantly more casual than what was being produced on the east and west coasts. Curiously, the party-hearty lyrics referenced more than once the group's possession of a "double Dutch bus," an obvious reference to Frankie Smith's 1981 #1 R&B/top 30 pop rap about African American Philadelphia's pidgin English and jump rope games, "Double Dutch Bus."

It would be at least a couple of years before a steady stream of 12-inch singles and EPs by local hip-hop crews could be found regularly on the shelves of record shores on the city's Northwest side, notably Audie's on West Capitol Drive. Commercial airplay of such releases in the city was next to (or entirely) non-existent, but that didn't impede the nurturing of the innovative style. One white Milwaukee comedian saw rap's potential to gently lampoon economic recession and race relations and had a local radio hit in 1983.

Layoffs in Milwaukee's manufacturing sector and Grandmaster Flash and The Furious Five's groundbreaking "The Message" inspired Rip Tenor (a.k.a. Art Kumbalek) and His Cavalcade of Top Bananas' "White Men Out of Work." Of "The Message," Tenor says, "It was the first/rap hip-hop record to really knock my socks off." He and the track's co-rapper, Dave Maleckar, eschewed that piece's harrowing ghetto scenarios for pointed laughter, with the eventual punch line, "There goes the neighborhood!" The record's spoof of newly unsuspecting welfare recipients garnered spins on several Milwaukee stations. For Tenor, it was "thrilling to hear it on WNOV. It meant our satire was getting through."

Records from the city's actual hip-hop community followed soon enough, a good many of them on the format of choice for street DJs disseminating the genre, the 12-inch single. Perhaps most significant among the stream of local vinyl in the second half of the '80s were a pair of EPs of the same size.

The historical significance of Royal Dynasty's 1986 *Strictly on the Record*, with four vocal tracks on its A-side and the instrumental versions on the reverse, lies not only in its recorded introduction to Dr. B. As arguably the city's most ubiquitous hip-hop ambassador, he has, according to the website of his B-Boy Productions company, won turntable scratching and mixing battles in several states and has held residency and made guest appearances on several of city's commercial and non-commercial radio stations.

Contrasting with the hard boasting and pounding lyrical approach of Royal Dynasty were A-Tack. Their 1986 debut 12-incher emphasized turntable dexterity. They refined their persona later the same year with the *My Car* EP on one of the city's few labels to release multiple hip-hop releases, VU Records. The group's leader, M.C. Todd Thomas, rapped of his beater automobile and spoke with caution of imbibing alcohol; the effect was like a less upscale iteration of novelty leaning Philadelphia rhymer Will "Fresh

Prince" Smith's early shtick, though it may have been at odds with Thomas's status as the son of the publisher of one of the city's weekly newspapers servicing its black community, the *Milwaukee Times*.

Thomas's matriculation from Rufus King High School to the Art Institute of Atlanta would bring significant change to his musical outlook. Likely influenced by the varying strains of "alternative hip-hop" that came to the fore after De La Soul's sample-heavy, hippie-minded 1989 debut album, *3 Feet High and Rising*, he took a more idiosyncratic route. Instead of the militant Black Panther and Nation of Islam templates for African American authenticity abundant in post-Public Enemy hip-hop, Thomas adopted the griot-like stage name of Speech, grew dreadlocks and gave his new ensemble, Arrested Development, a pastoral vibe indebted to his childhood visits to extended relations in rural South.

Speech's/Thomas's kind of machismo-lite Christianity-imbued alternative rap would recede from the commercial limelight by the end of the 1990s as permutations of gangsta nihilism and affluence-flaunting commercial rap took over. But 1992 found Arrested Development accruing three top 10 pop and R&B singles from their first long-player, *3 Years, 5 Months and 2 Days in the Life Of ...*; its platinum-certified sales success bred enough good will for an album of the group's *MTV Unplugged* session to go gold. Their reception in the U.K. was nearly as warm.

By the time their second studio album, *Zingalmanduni*, dropped a couple years later, the formula had played out in terms of receptivity by commercial radio listeners. Between the two studio sets, Speech had enough pull with his label to get hometown Milwaukee friends Gumbo, a deal that lasted for one alt-hip-hop album, *Dropping Soulful H20 on the Fiber*; a couple of singles, a *Soul Train* appearance and some MTV rotation ensued to little fanfare. Speech nurtured a solo career for much of the rest of the 1990s, finding a substantial audience in Japan, before reforming Arrested Development in the early 2000s while continuing to record on his own.

Hip-hoppers from the city not fortunate enough to reap international chart acclaim still found local and regional followings. A-G-2-A-Ke (say "a g to a key," as in parlaying $1000 to a kilogram of street pharmaceuticals, presumably) proffered gangster hardness with occasional mellow choruses. They shared a label, Houston's Rap-A-Lot, with shock gangsta group the Geto Boys. Coo Coo Cal would start with local genre indie Infinite Recordings before a brief fling with legendary New York City rap and EDM imprint Tommy Boy Records, scraping *Billboard*'s R&B top 20 with "My Projects" at the turn of the century, abetted by a video filmed in inner city Milwaukee. The enterprising artist calling himself Reality based his confrontationally profane artistry in both Atlanta and Milwaukee, maintaining a North 27th Street record shop in the latter for a while. Kali Tribe reportedly moved over 30,000 copies of its 12-inch EP of Afrocentric, positively vibed rhymes akin to the Jungle Brothers; the trio's main M.C. has toured with NYC electro hip-hop innovator and Zulu Nation patriarch Afrika Bambaataa.

As the 1990s progressed, indigenous vinyl releases would share shelf space with compact discs and cassettes at inner city music retailers specializing in urban sounds. Newer Downtown and East Side shops such as the Scratch Pad mingled hip-hop with an inventory of the techno, trance and less radio-friendly house styles heard at the raves that filled Milwaukee warehouses with young, multi-racial audiences.

Vocal R&B would be a less dominant phenomenon in Milwaukee in the 1990s, but at least one star emerged with more than his music to interest the public. Mobile-born, Milwaukee-raised Eric Benét's name entered then consciousness of celebrity gossip journalists for his marriage of several years to actress Halle Berry. By the time of their 1997 nuptials, he was a burgeoning name of note, having issued his first Warner Brothers solo outing, *True to Myself*, the year prior. The effort resonated with a 1970s retro-soul flavor similar to contemporaries such as Maxwell and D'Angelo.

Benét emerged from his late-1980s tenure with Milwaukee-based, regionally popular dance-pop band Gerard (which also launched the career of poppy dance singer Keedy who made the top 20 in 1991 with "Save Some Love") and a duo with his sister Lisa. The duo's lone album for EMI Records explores romantic yearning in the "new jack swing" style made pervasive in late 1980s-early 1990s urban music thanks in large part to the productions of Teddy Riley on acts like Guy and Johnny Kemp; the siblings added touches of smooth jazz. Eric Benét's recording career continues in the twenty-first century.

Courtesy of Gusto Records, Inc.

Harvey Scales performing at the Rhythm N Brews in Saukville, WI (2010)

Photo by Erol Reyal

Courtesy of the Jean Cujé Collection

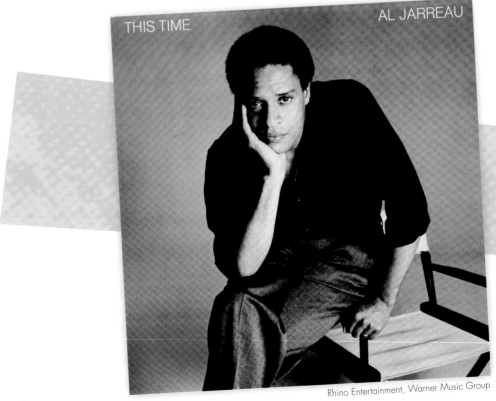

Rhino Entertainment, Warner Music Group

Rhino Entertainment, Warner Music Group

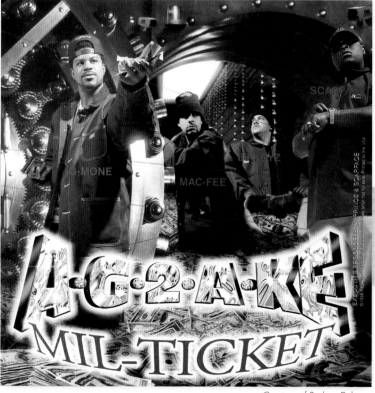

Courtesy of Rodney Deberry

91

A promotional photograph of the Ricochettes,
known as "Milwaukee's Beatle Band"

CHAPTER 6

Rockin' in the 1960s and into the 1970s

Bruce Cole contends that there were three periods regarding Milwaukee rock in the 1960s—before, during, and after the Beatles. The Beatles exemplified a rock and roll band which Milwaukee groups, like those in other American cities, emulated (see Barry 1991). The 1960s marked a golden age of rock in Milwaukee as local/garage bands often charted with national and international groups (see Roller 2013; Barry 1991). Indeed, several Milwaukee bands gained national notoriety, e.g., Shag and the Corporation. An overview begins the chapter providing context. Bruce Cole follows with recollections of bands he belonged to during this period. Milwaukee hosted a "Midwest Rock Festival" in July 1969 where some of the greatest rock talent of the time performed—an extraordinary event, which in some ways prefigured Woodstock. Outdoor performances began along the lakefront at the "Alternate Site," featuring Milwaukee musicians and occasionally mayhem. Proliferating clubs and bars not only showcased local talent but also national and British bands.[1] One of the most important venues, as Rob Lewis recounts, was the Scene. In the 1970s, rock "fused" with jazz and a new genre emerged. Kevin Lynch provides a particularly personal account of Milwaukee's fusion era.

---

1 Gary Myers, who notably drummed for the Cashmeres and the Mojo Men, also provided a photographic chronicle of the clubs where he played from 1962 to 1966, which he has shared digitally: https://onmilwaukee.com/music/articles/1960srockclubs.html; see also Bobby Tanzilo's article at https://onmilwaukee.com/music/articles/deadandgoneclubs.html; Bruckner 1975; and Racine 1975.

"A Golden Age"
by Phillip Naylor and Bruce Cole

According to Paul Greenwald, co-founder of Shag: "The Beatles came along and we bought instruments—we had the hair already—and we just started teaching ourselves how to play. We started doing Stones-like stuff." Playing at O'Brad's on East Locust Avenue as well as Le Bistro and the Scene, "We became such a sensation, and it was mainly because we had costumes and lights and explosions and smoke bombs and everything you could think of" (Myers 1994, 209.) The band moved to the San Francisco area and also gigged in Los Angeles (including at the Whisky a Go Go). Shag returned to Milwaukee for the Midwest Rock Festival in July 1969 (see below).

Another important group at this time was the Skunks, formed by Larry Lynne (see Chapter 1). The band members distinguished themselves by dying their hair black and then adding white stripes. According to Gary Myers: "If the Legends were Milwaukee 60's band Most-Expected-To-Make-It-But-Didn't, the Skunks may be runners-up" (Myers 1994, 214). Lynne left the band and formed the Larry Lynne Group. Other important groups included Tony's (Dancy) Tygers; Little Artie and the Pharaohs (see Chapters 1, 3); the Esquires (see Chapter 5); John Kondos and the Galaxies; the Mustard Men (two-time winner of the WRIT "battle of the bands"); Freddy and the Freeloaders and the Hound Dog Band, featuring Fred Bliffert's vocals (from the local lumber and hardware family); and the Palmettos, among scores of others (see Roller 2013). Shag, the Corporation (emerging in the late 1960s [included John Kondos of the Galaxies and his brother, Nicholas]), and the Invasion particularly performed psychedelic rock. [2]

Bruce Cole exemplified the 1960s Milwaukee rock musician. He drummed for an array of bands notably including—the Grand Prix's (1962-64; thanks to the Legends' drummer Jim Sessody's recommendation [see Chapter 1 and below]). The Grand Prix's were among a select group of bands to share the stage with the Legends at Muskego Beach. Then there was the aforementioned Savoys (1964-65), who backed up the Ideals at a variety of Chicago venues including the 1964 McCormick Place gig headlined by the Dave Clark Five (see Chapters 1 and 3). Bruce also filled in a couple of jobs with Jay and the Americans (see Chapter 1). It was not unusual belonging concurrently to several groups. For example, in 1964, Bruce also played with the Triumphs with whom he recorded the garage rock classic, "Surfside Date" (which featured his furious drumming). He also opened for Memphis guitarist Travis Wammack and England's Peter and Gordon and Manfred Mann. While with the Ricochettes (1966-67), he opened for numerous groups (see below) including the American Breed, B.J. Thomas, Wayne Fontana and the Mindbenders, and the Flock. As covered below, he played with the Van-tels intermittently for over two decades. He joined Poor Richard's Almanac and the Invasion in 1968. While with the latter, he opened for a variety of groups at the Scene (see below) including

---

2 See Wikipedia articles on Shag and the Corporation (https://en.wikipedia.org/wiki/The_Shag and https://en.wikipedia.org/wiki/The_Corporation_(American_band).

Frank Zappa and the Mothers of Invention and Cream. Before the latter's performance (see below), Bruce recounted:

> I watched [Cream drummer Ginger Baker] 'prepare' the beater side of his bass drums with glued on circles he cut from a stack of bass drum heads. After he left (I was warned by the two Cream roadies not to get near his drums.) I got behind his drums and hit the pedals and it was like hitting a hard wall, but the sound that came out the other side was like a bomb going off…You had to be there I guess (email to Phillip Naylor, 4 January 2018).

These were glorious years to be a musician in Milwaukee (see also Shurilla 1991).

A Drummer's Odyssey:
Memories of Bands along the Way
by Bruce Cole

The Van-tels began in the early 1960s and continued into the late 1970s. I played in this band three different times. I can remember at least 20 musicians who played for the group over the years, and many more passed through, I'm sure, before leader and founder Joe Piccolo shut it down for good. This was a fine rhythm & blues/soul show band that often worked six nights a week, 50 weeks a year—sometimes for a couple years straight at the same place.

I was seventeen the second time I played with this group, and we used to play Marty Zivko's ballroom in Hartford every weekend. Saturday nights drew at least 800 teenagers (supposedly all eighteen or older). The drink of choice was a "shorty Pabst," a little eight ounce bottle. The end of the night left the wooden dancefloor a slippery expanse of broken glass.

After one summer of living in a bus and playing nearly every night in northern Wisconsin teen bars, I bought a new Pontiac Catalina with the money I'd saved. Pretty cool for a high school junior without a job!

Joe Piccolo was big on promotion. He also kept excellent financial records and took care of the band's transportation. Joe was a good bandleader and business man. He was a friend, but he could be pretty stern about the way things were in his band. Discipline, practice, hard work. We practiced at least three nights a week in Joe's basement unless we were playing out of town. Then we would practice in the afternoon in the bar we were at. We had lots of band clothes, paid union dues on time, and filed self-employment tax returns every three months. We kept receipts for dry cleaning, gas, food, motels, and band instruments. We traveled together to jobs so everyone would be on time and share the setup toil equally. We had our price and never took less. Every year the band improved musically and earned more cash. Its eventual and final incarnation was as a tight seven-piece "horn" band working six nights a week in the better Milwaukee nightclubs.

Sixteen-year old North side guitar player and singer Ar Stevens (Kriegel) and bass/organist Herb Honke put together the Ricochettes in 1964.[3] They practiced hard, concentrating on British invasion tunes with three and four-part harmony, and within a year were one of the most popular bands in the Milwaukee area. They not only developed a strong, loyal, local fan base, but they also began drawing pretty well around the state and into Illinois. They were known as "Milwaukee's Beatle Band." They even recorded and released a Lennon-McCartney tune, "I'll be Back."

They had a terrific manager who got them great gigs opening for visiting English rock stars like the Hollies, the Animals, and the Rolling Stones as well as Chicago area hit groups like the Cryin' Shames, the Shadows of Knight, and the Ides of March. And, they had a regional hit record, "Come in My Love," in 1966.

They should have had at least a taste of national success. Their original recordings were catchy and commercial. Their musicianship was way above the average garage bands of the day, and their vocals were excellent. But, for whatever reasons, their singles never cracked the national charts, and their brand of bright, clean, harmony pop rock faded fast. Their last effort, "Find Another Boy," an original, catchy, three-part harmony lead vocal number with some nice echo and 12-string effects, was maybe six months too late. The garage rock movement would be morphing into darker, moodier genres by the end of 1967.

I joined the group in 1967 and it was probably the most fun I ever had in a band. Although we never did any national touring, and we were generally broke because most of the money we made went back into the group (paying for matching outfits, equipment, promotional material, etc.), we always projected that rock star image on stage and expected stardom to "happen" any minute--or, in the very near future anyway. We wore makeup on stage and custom-tailored (well, somebody made them for us) British-look suits. (You tried to have a London Carnaby Street look, whatever that was.) We had a couple of roadies, two fan clubs, and we were usually busy doing radio spots and DJ record hop personal appearances every weekend. Or, we were trucking down to affluent Chicago suburbs to do big proms, Bar Mitzvahs, and battle-of-the-bands competitions.

Even though I was still a teenager, by the time I joined the band, I considered myself a seasoned pro with four years, already, of roadhouse, nightclub, and bar experience behind me. I was surprised when I found out the Ricochettes almost never did bar gigs. It was usually a venue that included at least a couple hundred yelling teenagers. Stranger still was the fact that none of the band members had cars or apartments of their own. They were lucky if they had two or three dollars in their pockets. One of the hottest up-and-coming bands in town and they were practically homeless! In fact, without their

---

3   See also https://onmilwaukee.com/music/articles/ricochettes.html.

parents' help, they would have been. They couldn't believe I actually had a new car (a Mercury Comet Cyclone) and a little cash.

I'd seen both sides now: quick cash playing for little crowds of crazy beer drinking wild ones in the backwoods, and the do-or-die, all-or-nothing attempt to make records and be famous that left you happy, but hungry. The focused, hard practicing happy-but-hungry band was more fun. Of course, in the end I went for the steady money in the joints.

While with Poor Richard's Almanac, we gigged with Sam the Sham and the Pharaohs, that is Mr. "Wooly-Bully" himself, Domingo "Sam" Samudio. I got his picture and autograph when we opened for him at a night club in Madison, Wisconsin. Must have been 1967 or early 1968.

I liked "Wooly-Bully" when it first came out—but we played it to death. Plus, it got way too much radio play too. Local bands played it too fast, too slow, too wrong. No bands I worked with could seem to find that Tex-Mex groove it needed. (Nobody I played with knew what Tex-Mex music was anyway.) And no one could sing it like Sam, of course.

"Wooly-Bully," "Louie, Louie," "Mustang Sally," "Gloria"—the sweaty teen bar kids wanted to hear those tunes over and over again. With Sam Samudio, to make it even worse, he followed up "Wooly" with "Little Red Riding Hood," and all the bands had to do THAT one to death. Singers were supposed to howl like wolves, but they all just kind of yelped like little dogs.

The Sam and the Pharaohs band we played with included a six-piece R&B horn section from Texas. I thought they were great. They played my two favorite Chuck Jackson songs, "I Don't Wanna Cry" and "Any Day Now." Another attractive thing about this two-week gig was the "Shamettes"—Sam's three back-up girl singers. Everybody in our band wanted to get close to the "Shamettes." Sam, though, kept an eye on them. They stayed backstage all the time and seldom talked to anybody. After the gigs Sam took them back to the motel and locked them up.

One of the "Shamettes" came up and complimented me after our

Courtesy of Bruce Cole

first set. I sang a Bob Dylan song, "Stuck Inside of Mobile with the Memphis Blues Again" from the *Blonde on Blonde* album. I was convinced I did a great Dylan impersonation. She also thought I did a good job on the song and told me so.

I told the guys in the band that I had to do more Dylan stuff. Obviously, if this back-up singer with this "famous" band thought I sang Dylan songs well, we ought to put a few more into the set to show off my gift to greater advantage. They didn't agree. In fact, they finally confessed that they were a little embarrassed by my "Dylan voice" impression, and maybe it was time to just, well, drop the song, period.

Okay. Fine. And all along I had thought these guys were "professionals." Obviously, it was time for a new band.

This last version of the Invasion looked and acted like the acid rock, underground, heavy psychedelic outfit it thought it was. Loud was all we were. It was 1968, and we threw the band together to keep a four-night a week gig going at a dying downtown Milwaukee nightclub called Gallagher's. Nobody was going downtown anymore, but there was still a last gasp of pre-classic rock craziness in the late 1960s at a few spots in the city that still fit the description of "nightclub."

Benedetta Balistrieri sort of managed the Invasion for a few months in 1968. And, around that same time she got into booking rock acts into the Scene, a nightclub on 2nd Street just south of Wisconsin Avenue (see below). Just like that she booked Frank Zappa and the Mothers of Invention, Cream, Jimi Hendrix, Rod Stewart and the Faces, the Allman Brothers, and a bunch of other brand-new happening groups into that venue. We were the opening act for both Zappa and the Mothers and Cream. The Cream show was in May 1968.

The Scene was a plush, red-carpeted converted old theatre then featuring guys like Sid Caesar and Jerry Vale. I think it probably sat about 500 to 800 or so. Zappa and the Mothers played two nights, I think. Probably about three bucks to get in. Sadly, not many people showed up.

Unless you listened to "underground"/freeform radio, you probably didn't know who Frank Zappa was or what that whole new underground thing was all about. The Mothers practiced every afternoon, and, according to the band guys, Zappa was a hard boss. No drugs, no goofin' around, be on time to rehearsal, and learn your parts perfectly. They were proud of their group, but one of the drummers (the band had two) told me the tour was not going well—thin, puzzled crowds. If things didn't start looking up, the band would fold. I was shocked. They were the most amazing thing I'd ever heard.

We played the Cream show, the first of their two-night stand at the Scene (see above). Our song list was mostly our lame renditions of Hendrix, Grateful Dead, Allman Brothers, and Doors material. Of course, we did every "Cream" song on the albums. Whatever was on the hip stations, we tried to learn. The "promotion" for the show was a couple of small ads in the paper. Like with the "Mothers," the price to see this first, great, legendary rock monster trio that Cream was would be about three or four bucks. I was really excited about opening this show, but, unfortunately, that was greatly tempered by the fact that we were pretty bad, and I knew I would feel embarrassed and small. On the other hand, I think the audience really didn't care. Loud, stupid – so what?

The Cream show crowd was probably around 600 or 700 that first night. People came to see Eric Clapton, who had turned guitar god a couple years previous. Later, we all trooped over to the Midway Motor Inn. I think that's where they stayed on State and Prospect on the East Side and hung out with Eric, Ginger, and Jack (Bruce).

Memories of Shag
by Gordon Elliott

I grew up musically in Milwaukee. I had a total love for most everything I heard on the radio as a kid. My first musical aspiration was to be a "Jordanaire" and back up the likes of Elvis and Ricky![4] (This was about 1960.) By early high school, I had had a few guitar lessons and "knowing it all," I began playing with friends in school. We started a group called the Outlaws and played CYOs, sock hops and the like. Eventually, that led to playing numerous gigs at the many "teen bars" across the state. I formed and played with a number of Milwaukee bands, including 4MOR, the Notations," and the "Saints Five." Milwaukee had a big club scene offering numerous venues and steady work.

I went to the downtown junior college (MIT; Milwaukee Institute of Technology, as it was called then [today's Milwaukee Area Technological College; MATC]), where I met Bruce Cole. Together, Bruce and I went through three versions of a group called Poor Richard's Almanac (PRA). Sometime later, I met another person at MIT. His brother played in a popular local band called Shag. Meanwhile, I continued to play regularly with PRA throughout the Midwest. At some point, I ended up jamming with Shag and found much common ground. I ended up leaving PRA and within two weeks, I joined Shag and we composed two sets worth of original music and totally decorated a local club called O'Brads. This included a new light show, a dance floor painted to honor M. C. Escher (the Dutch graphic artist), and a strobe light causing dancers to doubt their balance as the band played songs in assorted time signatures. We often tried varying themes of music, lights, costumes and any sort of craziness that Milwaukee might inspire.

Nevertheless, for me, Milwaukee at that time was a bleak, stifling, and oppressive town, especially if one had the urge and passion to further art and ideas. The powers that be noted that we were guilty of destroying the fabric of the youth culture. It led to several forms of harassment, leading one to dream of a more open, progressive, and enlightened culture.

During a musical intermission at O'Brad's (our "headquarters), we were offered a management deal which would offer Shag new horizons. Within weeks, we headed to San Francisco and eventually settled down in an unbelievable and refreshing area across the Golden Gate Bridge in Marin County. We found an old ranch near a very small town

---

4   Ricky Nelson was featured in the television series featuring his parents, *The Adventures of Ozzie and Harriet*. Ricky occasionally performed at the end of the show with guitar great James Burton.

called Nicasio. It was situated in a magnificent redwood forest. It was certainly a far cry from Milwaukee's East Side. There we entered into a whole new culture and lifestyle. We built a studio ten feet from the house. The equipment was always set up and ready to go. In that studio, we would often gather all sorts of visiting players. Many were local players and many Wisconsin players made it to the San Francisco Bay Area in the late 1960s as well, like Jim Peterman and Tim Davis of the Steve Miller Band and A. B. Skhy (see Chapter 7). Rick Jaeger brought Sam McCue (a guitar hero of mine [see Chapter 1]) out one afternoon, to my delight, for a musical romp in the redwoods.

Parties, gatherings, new influences, great new people, new attitudes, new energy, new vibes, etc., were all part of the new era for Shag. We had found a magical place. The group started writing all new material in the studio. The three art school graduates in the band began making sculptures and stage props for our assault on unsuspecting audiences and the the record industry. Everything got painted including numerous stage props, such as Hollywood smoke delivery "statues," along with two sets of drums and congas as well. Everything!

We finally felt ready to rock and roll and were booked to play two weeks in Aspen, Colorado, at Galena Street East. It was a hippie, biker, ski bum, drinking and "all that kinda crowd" establishment. Those two weeks helped us put our act together in front of an audience. It was a fun but exhausting two weeks. The Aspen crowd was wild and welcoming. They all thought those Wisconsin boys could sure drink. That reputation followed the band.

In that era, San Francisco had several fabulously great FM stations. While listening (and to our complete surprise), we heard an unbelievable advertisement touting a concert in Golden Gate Park that weekend featuring Jefferson Airplane with Shag as the opening act! We brought out all the stops for that gig and experienced a dream of playing in the park to many (10,000 to 20,000) "beautiful people." I thought we had arrived!

We started to play the many venues and events in the area and built up a bit of a following. We shared the stage with some fine talent. We did our best to give the crowd a show of lights, smoke, costumes, loud original music, and a headful of what we worked so hard to offer. We also ended up commuting to LA often, where the audience was, surprisingly, a little more open to the complete show. Playing the Whisky a Go Go several times, we finally had a showcase there seeking to impress the record folks. We went all out and found ourselves bathing in the LA rock and roll scene and the craziness it had to offer. LA can be fun if you are happening.

While back in Marin, I recall a bright, sunny Nicasio afternoon. I wandered down our dirt driveway that led out to the road. Another dirt driveway opposed ours and two strangers were also walking toward the road. "Howdy!" They yelled. "We're the Grateful Dead." In the middle of nowhere, a premier San Francisco band had taken up residence across the road. Bob Weir, roadies, and company had moved into an old horse farm. They named it "Rucka Rucka." We became good neighbors. Our landlord was from India and our place soon became "San Geet Kuteer" or "House of Song."

Around this time, the Dead were at Pacific High Recording in San Francisco, doing their *Workingman's Dead* album. We were able to get in the studio on a few off days and were able to record some songs. The songs sat around for years until I eventually re-mastered and digitized the tapes later released as a CD on Gear Fab Records called *Shag 1969*. An LP was also released in Europe.

We returned to Milwaukee to play at the Midwest Rock Festival in State Fair Park (25 to 27 July 1969 (see below). It included major acts of the day. This gave us the chance to display a new Shag experience to the hometown crowd, with new sets and songs. We played sets on all three days sharing a stage with the likes of Blind Faith, Led Zeppelin, and Pacific Gas & Electric. It rained really hard one of the days. Everyone hoped for the best. The show went on for those hearty, devoted music fans. I thought it was great that the Midwest got a taste of what some fine groups of the day had to offer.

We had a good time at the festival, a good visit, rubbed some elbows and then headed back to California. We continued to play around Northern and Southern California in some great and not so great venues. We met and shared experiences with other groups looking for their break. The band entertained some serious recording offers, but terribly poor management as well as changing times and fashions made closing a deal tedious and eventually fruitless.

After years of effort, magnificent dreams, and attempts to move the band forward, the writing was on the wall. Sadly, after several years of "all in," I eventually left Shag. I went off to play with remnants of a Chicago band called H. P. Lovecraft. Shag's Don Luther was eventually called upon to play bass. We called the group Elixir and had some open doors, and sometimes great offers and gigs like opening at Winterland for Ten Years After. Eventually Elixir dissolved; that's another story.

Rah Kahn!

The Midwest Rock Festival (State Fair Park, 25 to 27 July 1969)
by Phillip Naylor

"I could have gone to Woodstock in 1969, but I didn't because right around the same time Jeff Beck, Blind Faith, and a bunch of other great bands were playing a weekend festival at Wisconsin State Fair Park" (Rick Nielsen of Cheap Trip) (Widen 2014, 6).

"Well, it looks like Milwaukee is finally getting what everyone has been begging for: a live honest-to-God rock festival" (John Kois, *Kaleidoscope*, 4-17 July 1969, 8).

The comingling and musical cross-fertilization of British and American bands, included those in Milwaukee, as particularly performed by the Ricochettes and even the Invasion. While covering songs, local bands often charted with English groups and even feigned

English accents! One of the greatest examples of British and American groups sharing a common stage in Milwaukee occurred in July 1969.[5]

A few weeks before Woodstock (15-18 August in upstate New York), Milwaukee had its own three-day rock festival.[6] The array of musical talent was phenomenal. Singer-songwriter Barry Ollman, an attendee, remembered a "fantastic lineup" that was "world class and everyone knew it. We were ecstatic."[7] Consider the scheduled musicians (not in order of performance):

> Friday, 25 July: Buffy Sainte-Marie, The First Edition, Pacific Gas & Electric, The SRC, Shag, Sweet Water, Led Zeppelin.

> Saturday, 26 July: Blind Faith, Delaney and Bonnie, Taste, The SRC, The MC5, Shag, John Mayall.

> Sunday, 27 July: Jeff Beck, Shag, Jethro Tull, The MC5, Johnny Winter, The Bob Seger System, Jim Schwall Blues Period, Joe Cocker and the Grease Band, Zephyr.

According to the *Milwaukee Sentinel* (26 July): "Subterraneans arose from the underground" to attend the "first annual Midwest Rock Festival at State Fair Park." With an initial approximated grandstand crowd of 10,000 (many entered via counterfeited tickets), an estimated 41,000 attended the three-day festival. Dean Jensen reported: "The crowd seemed incredulous that Milwaukee was hosting a major rock festival." He added: "After all, it was only a week ago that the National Polka festival was held here." The stage was a flat-bed truck trailer parked before grandstand seats. The Fillmore East's Pablo Light Show was projected behind the performers. Pierre-Rene Noth reflected that performers like Blind Faith, Jeff Beck, and Johnny Winter, "to the young, [were] equivalent to that of Stan Kenton, Frank Sinatra, and Charlie Parker were to another day and time." He referred to the event's historical significance: "Never have so many here had a chance to hear so much live rock for so long." He referred to the crowd as "affluent bohemians" (*Milwaukee Journal*, 26, 28 July). The Festival competed with "Summerfest," then in its second year with music venues dispersed throughout Milwaukee, e.g., a concurrent "Afro-American" concert in Lincoln Park.

On Sunday, a "driving rain," lasting four hours, failed to disperse the crowd, although the weather forced the cancellation of some of the acts (Jeff Beck, Jethro Tull, Jim Schwall Blues Period, the MC5, and the SRC). Nevertheless, the situation foreshadowed

---

5   I would like to acknowledge Tad Meeham, a former student. I referred to a copy of a paper that I assigned to him and supervised regarding the July festival.

6   The *Milwaukee Sentinel* and the *Milwaukee Journal* provided limited coverage of the Festival in their 26, 28 July issues. WOKY organized a "M'WOKY Pops Festival" at County Stadium in June 1969 featuring the Monkees, Gary Lewis and the Playboys, Andy Kim, Stevie Wonder, and the Guess Who. About 29,000 attended. The station organized two more festivals (1970 and 1971) (see http://archive.jsonline.com/greensheet/rival-rock-festivals-gave-fledgling-summerfest-a-run-for-its-music-money-b99749631z1-384766691.html).

7   Conversation with Barry Ollman, 8 September 2018. *Kaleidoscope* featured a photographic spread of some of the artists who planned to perform (7-18 July 1969, vol. 2, no. 17 [42], 6-7). The festival also featured local and regional groups, e.g., Bloomsbury People, Soup (from Appleton), Omaha, and, Woodbine.

Woodstock: "They danced and they clapped, they huddled under blankets together, they ran barefoot with their hands high in the air… The harder the rain fell, though, the closer Milwaukee's hip community moved toward its ideal—brotherhood and peace" (*Milwaukee Sentinel*, 28 July). Pierre Rene Noth observed: "For many, the festival must have been a revelation. Never had there been so large a gathering of the clan" (*Milwaukee Journal*, 28 July).

Regarding the performances, Cree Indian folk singer, Buffy Sainte-Marie, who opened the festival, Joe Cocker and the Grease Band, and Johnny Winter were particularly acclaimed.[8] Milwaukee's Shag "received a hearty welcome home" (*Milwaukee Sentinel*, 26 July). On the other hand, the First Edition "plugged their records and upcoming TV appearance between every number and to the flower power generation, that smelled of money hunger and sellout" (*Milwaukee Journal*, 26 July; see also recollections below.)

Although there were some drug arrests, charges were dropped. A State Fair policeman remarked: "I'd rather have these people than a fair crowd any day. They are really very polite" (*Sentinel*, 28 July). Assemblyman Robert T. Huber (D-West Allis) "compared state fair park…with Haight-Ashbury, [the] area of the San Francisco hippie community, and accused Vernon G. Wendland, state fair administrator of allowing the park to become a pigsty…Wendland labeled Huber's charges ridiculous" (*Milwaukee Journal*, 28 July; see also *Kaleidoscope* 8-21 August 1969, 2-6).

Consider these accounts by concertgoers:

Courtesy of the Jean Cujé Collection

> Three days, and I was there every day. I had what you might call 'backstage access'—which meant, in this case, walking around the infield of the racetrack; a lot of small trucks and roadies, amps and stands, stage lights and black drum cases everywhere. I kind of remember there being three or four small mobile homes the bands used. The stage was a flatbed truck. I was walking around this area early the first day, talking

---

8 While in Milwaukee, Buffy Sainte-Marie announced her intention to endow an Indian language program at the planned Indian Community Center (*Milwaukee Sentinel*, 26 July 1969).

to friends. I can't remember why, but I just climbed the two or three steps, opened the door, and walked right into one of the trailers. It was very small, and when I walked in, I nearly ran into a huge head of long, curly black hair. It was Jimmy Page of Led Zeppelin. He was bent over his guitar and perched on a little table with his feet on a chair. He looked up and said something like 'just tunin' up' and got back at it. I stood there for a minute or so, said something like 'okay man!', turned around, and walked out (Bruce Cole email to Phillip Naylor, 5 January 2018).

A Led Zeppelin URL (http://www.ledzeppelin.com/show/july-25-1969) offered these recollections:

I attended all 3 days. Tickets were $15.00 for the 3 days. I still have a playbill/poster of the event in pretty good shape. It rained Sunday afternoon so Jeff Beck and Jethro Tull did not play. Joe Cocker did, John Mayall did and the headliner was Johnny Winter…Zeppelin was great Friday night…Blind Faith was equally fantastic on Saturday. Taste, with Rory Gallagher, made their United States debut. This was…BEFORE Woodstock and I'm sure most people have never heard of it. (Roger S.)

One of the best times of my life…Even with rain and no music everybody gathered into the covered grandstand and had fun and shared whatever any of us had. It was really one of the only times I felt I belong[ed] to a community of like[-]minded people and was very comfortable…They tried to cover the stage with clear plastic sheeting to protect the performers. It did to a point, Joe Cocker came on and was outstanding until the water build up burst right over his head[.] He continued to complete his set…$15.00 in today's money would convert to $1500.00 easy. ([M.] Mueller)

A letter to *Kaleidoscope* assessed:

I think that it is fair to say that the effort spent by everyone involved was worthwhile. Then, I think it's also fair to assume that we can expect a 2nd annual Midwest Rock Festival.

In planning for next year, there are quite a few things that should be carefully considered, and problems corrected. First there was the continual delays between the groups. 10 or 15 minutes is OK, but an hour is absurd…

The major [problem], though, was the omission of a covering over the stage. Was everyone so hyped up that they thought it can't rain on OUR rock festival? Now, that nice big truck was fine, but it took a lot away from the groups, by cramming them in with their mounds of equipment. But, the real issue here is the fact that due to poor planning, six national groups, including Jeff Beck and Jethro Tull, had to be cancelled. There were a lot of people who traveled a long way to see that show, and particularly those groups…

Another thing which bugged most of the people (at least me) was the price…They could probably have cut the price of the tickets, gotten twice as many people, and still made out all right.

Well, there's almost a year to plan for the second annual MRF. If the time is used carefully, there is no reason why we can't have a fest that will outdo Atlanta, Atlantic City, Woodstock, and even Monterey (D. Tupper, *Kaleidoscope*, 8-21 August 1969, 4).

"Phase II" of the Midwest Rock Festival occurred on 30 August 1969 at County Stadium. Turnout was approximated 4000. Headliner Chuck Berry was late and wanted his payment up front, according to the *Milwaukee Journal*'s Dominique Paul Noth (31 August). WTOS-FM's Bob Reitman (see chapter 4), serving as the emcee "countersigned an IOU from the festival" and Berry performed. Phase II featured Cat Mother and the All Night Newsboys, Taj Mahal, the great bluesman Howlin' Wolf (Chester Burnett) (Noth reported regarding the latter: "He was an 'in' figure with many in the crowd and he certainly is an 'old daddy with a lot of class,' as one person yelled to him, but about half of what he did was of interest mostly to historians and extreme devotees" (see Chapter 7). Bethlehem Boogie Band, Bloomsbury People (a Milwaukee a proto-prog rock group [see Chapter 10]), and the Soup (from Appleton) also performed as well as Elyse Weinberg, the Illinois Speed Press, Mother Earth, and Clayton Fletcher. There were some drug arrests. Phase II ended up being the concluding event of the summer's Midwest Rock Festival phenomenon. Nevertheless, a new outdoor musical venue became popular attracting audiences and fomenting altercations.

The Alternate Site[9]
by Phillip Naylor

In the late 1960s, Milwaukee youth often congregated at the end of East North Avenue at Water Tower Park above Lincoln Memorial Drive and adjacent to St. Mary's Hospital to play or hear rock music. In 1970, clashes with police led to the County Park Commission (as suggested by Alderperson [and Civil Rights pioneer] Vel Phillips and Mayor Henry Maier) to consider allocating public space for concerts. The County approved a location west of Lincoln Memorial Drive across from McKinley Beach in 1971. Naming the space provoked considerable controversy, e.g., "Woodstock Park," and "People's Park. Milwaukee members of the Youth International Party—"Yippies"—favored "Czolgosz Park

---

9 See Chris Foran's article: https://www.jsonline.com/story/life/green-sheet/2017/08/29/when-music-found-alternate-home-milwaukees-lakefront-1971/606587001/.

after Leon Czolgosz, an anarchist who assassinated President William McKinley. As the *Milwaukee Journal Sentinel*'s Chris Foran noted: "What became known by default as the Alternate Site proved a popular weekend destination." Sam Friedman of the Hound Dog Band stated at the time: "It's a gas to play to these people. Furthermore, the publicity helped the bands: "It's good exposure, we've got nothing else to do on Sunday afternoons anyway. You get a wider group of people here, not like playing at a club."

Sunday concerts drew on an average about 5,000 people during the early 1970s. Crowd behavior and police confrontations eventually forced organizers to move to an alternate, Alternate Site along the lakefront north of the Milwaukee Gun Club and south of the Milwaukee Water Purification Plant. The first concert at the new concert grounds occurred in July 1974. Unfortunately, chronic confrontations with the police occurred later in the season, including arrests and the use of tear gas. Altercations continued in 1975. Consequently, concerts became infrequent although still mounted into the 1990s.

The Scene Ballroom:
A Balistrieri Legacy
by Rob Lewis

Advertised as the place "Where The Action Is!" and where you could "Make the Scene," (*Milwaukee Journal*, 1 October 1965), the Scene was the closest Milwaukee ever came to Bill Graham's Fillmore West Theater in San Francisco. Located at 624 North 2nd Street, the 1924 ballroom evolved into a musical entertainment center in the 1960s. From 1965 to 1971, the Scene was hipper than the usual music venue. The influential and controversial Balistrieri family made it all possible.

The long-forgotten ballroom in the now razed Hotel Antlers had an evolutionary history. Morphing from a Broadway theater to an intimate music venue, the Scene's ballroom had a capacity for 2,000 spectators and was acoustically perfect. The venue benefited greatly from the remnants of its predecessor, the Swan Theatre, which was ambitiously remodeled by Ray Boyle. The updated ballroom featured moveable stages, stage lights, and an accommodating backstage area. Inside the Scene's marquee entrance, a red and gold staircase led to the hotel's second floor restaurant and bars, where music was the main attraction. A lounge room, and bar room, complemented "the big room" which was a 100 x 100-foot ballroom, allowing the Scene to accommodate a myriad of musical settings with plenty of panache.

Overshadowed by his reputation as Milwaukee's crime boss, Frank Balistrieri was a local club owner who had a passion for managing bar-side entertainment in many of his Theatre District establishments. To his credit, Frank took over the lease on the hotel theater and established a music venue like no other in Milwaukee. (Frank's brother, Peter Balistrieri, was especially instrumental securing ownership of the theater.) Frank used out-of-town connections, and his experience in booking talent, to promote the Scene.

Eventually, the established Balistrieri family enterprise, Bals Inc., enabled certain family members to participate in the business of running the Scene.

Beginning in 1965, local bands like Dee Robb and the Robbins (the Robbs) and Junior (Brantley) and the Classics, entertained in the lounge featuring go-go dancers. Concerts in the ballroom occasionally used emcees, or comedians like Dick Gregory, to open for main acts. Popular Hit Parade groups like the Turtles and Tommy James and the Shondells headlined. House bands like Shag, the Messengers, and the Destinations showcased some of the best local musicians in town. Eventually, Little Richard, and the Sam and Dave Revue rock and rolled the ballroom.

Chuck Berry played the grand opening at the Scene, with a five-day run in September 1965. Among the local bands playing at the lounge, Little Artie and the Pharaohs were a favorite. According to Little Artie's saxophonist, Phil Zinos: "In 1963 we played at a Milwaukee nightclub called Gallagher's, which was Balistrieri-owned. The family subsequently opened the Scene and booked us into the lounge, where we played for a couple of years. Benny [Benedetta Balistrieri] was a young woman at this time and had nothing to do with the club, as I remember. She came on the scene in the late sixties."[10] In 1966, Frank began delegating the Scene's concert promotion and management to Benedetta, his oldest daughter. Under her father's advisement, she became Milwaukee's leading concert promoter of the late-1960s era, booking a plethora of local, national, and international bands.

Motown, soul, and R&B genre acts were most popular the first couple years at the Scene and included Smokey Robinson, Stevie Wonder, the Four Tops, Gladys Knight, and the Impressions. As the first of Benny's concerts, Ray Charles played five days straight in September 1966. She remembered: "At the Ray Charles concert I sat in the balcony, overlooking the stage, and it was the most enjoyable time I ever experienced at the Scene... before I became totally responsible for running the place. [11]

The Scene, Milwaukee's premier rock, rhythm & blues, and jazz venue—at 624 N. 2nd Street

Photo courtesy of Michael and Edward Muellenbach

---

10 Email to Rob Lewis via http://www.milwaukeerockscene.com, 21 May 2013.

11 Interviews of Benedetta Balistrieri by Rob Lewis (6-7 April, 6 May, and 3 June 2003).

Benny managed the Scene's club business, with subsequent family involvement. Jack Gesell, a young patron of the club, said: "I was aware of the Balistrieris because my dad was in the restaurant business. I remember seeing Frank occasionally at shows, but only a quick pop in and out. It obviously was not his thing. It was Benny's baby. You saw her walking around at every show. Benedetta had long black straight hair. She was beautiful. The bartenders had that 'Sopranos' look about them. These guys were not hippies tending bar, and we all thought they were mob guys."[12]

The Avant Garde Coffeehouse was a place where Benny liked to go with friends to watch underground art films and listen to folk music, and blues.[13] One night, she was greatly impressed with Jim Liban's harmonica playing ability, and booked his band, Knu Bluze, to play at the Scene for a two-week engagement in early 1968 (see Chapter 7). Rich Mangelsdorff reported: "The management of the Scene is to be congratulated for showcasing the state's best rock band... Liban is forging one of the most powerful and original harp styles in the U.S. ... I sincerely hope that everyone encountering the Knu Bluze at the Scene can enjoy them and have their minds blown" (*Kaleidoscope*, 2-15 February 1968, 8).

Liban's connections with fellow local musicians became intricately woven into happenings at the Scene. Of importance was Junior Brantley, whose band, Junior and the Classics, was a house band at the Scene. The other big influence was Sam McCue, Liban's music mentor and bandmate in Knu Bluze. Interestingly, McCue played at the Scene in three different bands, including the Legends, Crowfoot, and New Blues, a group whose name was recorded under several spellings, among them the aforementioned Knu Bluze.

Knu Bluze was known as a local band of all-stars when they played the Scene in 1968. Soon after, they reinvented themselves without McCue and left Milwaukee. In San Francisco, the band re-formed again and changed their name to A.B. Skhy. Before releasing an album, the band experienced playing at Bill Graham's Fillmore West and The Family Dog's Avalon ballroom.

The year 1968 was particularly memorable for the Scene's entertainment agenda. In February, the Jimi Hendrix Experience played for two nights, and it was, symbolically, the biggest event since the Beatles played the Arena in 1964. Concertgoer Jack Gesell recalled:

> Every musician in town had to see what this cat was all about, and he just blew the doors off the joint! Jimi Hendrix was just one of those points where everything seemed to change. It proved that acts of his size could come to Milwaukee and that we could support these acts... It justified the Balistrieris act of bringing other people into town... really the first step in Milwaukee having a regular concert scene. From 1968 it just kept building.[14]

---

12 Jack Gesell interview by Rob Lewis, 26 February 2002.

13 For more on the Avant Garde see Angeli and Goff 1975.

14 Gesell interview.

To improve all-age shows, the management restricted liquor during concerts and permanently removed the old theater seats. The in-house Uni-Verse Light Show Company accentuated psychedelic music with colored light projections from the balcony, using mixtures of oil pigment and water. The Cream's appearance in May packed the ballroom both nights. More great shows continued that year with Frank Zappa, Country Joe, Blue Cheer, John Mayall, and Steppenwolf. Tickets were $3 to $4.40. Local musician Peter Alt remembered: "The first time I went to the Scene, I was 14 years old. I stood against the back wall and watched hippie city, alone. I thought it was a really cool scene. It made me want to be more involved. Going to the Scene at such an early age made a huge impression on me and influenced my decision to become a rock musician."[15]

2 DAYS ONLY! Fri. & Sat.
THE CREAM
PLUS
The Invasion
Coming May 6-11
THE FOUR TOPS
Box Office Open
3 p.m. Daily
the SCENE
273-0968
624 N. 2nd

Courtesy of the Jean Cujé Collection

In early 1969 a projection room was added to the ballroom's balcony, allowing the Cream's "Farewell Concert" film to be featured alongside the Buddy Miles Express, and Pacific Gas and Electric performances. That summer, the ballroom quieted down and was billed as "Milwaukee's Newest Motion Picture Theater." [16] For a time, the ballroom ran old black and white movies for entertainment, featured burlesque shows, and a bit of country music. Eventually, the ballroom began featuring live concerts again with improved lighting.

Liban arrived back in Milwaukee in late 1969, and just happened to cross paths with musician friend Kenny Berdoll whose band, the Corporation, was a regular at the Scene and just completed a contract with Capitol Records. That day, they decided to form Short Stuff, featuring Junior Brantley. The band soon played the ballroom in 1970, and it helped launch their longstanding success. Jim still remembers: "Benny was a good friend and helped my career along." [17] In addition to local blues bands, the Scene hosted great blues artists such as, Paul Butterfield Blues Band, Junior Walker, Albert King, and Bobby Bland.

In 1970, the Scene's reputation rebounded, lightshows reappeared, and the music rocked again. Wisconsin, and regional, rock bands achieved top billing, including Soup, Oz, the SRC, OX, Rastus, Grease, and Short Stuff. The internationally known band, It's a Beautiful Day, appeared. Crowfoot opened for the Allman Brothers Band in September,

---

15 Peter Alt interview by Rob Lewis, 23 March 2003.

16 *Milwaukee Journal* advertisement, 3 July 1969.

17 Jim Liban interview by Rob Lewis, 29 March 2001.

despite headliner Arthur Lee's Love cancelling, reportedly, only 50 to 200 people made it to the ballroom to see the little-known southern blues/rock band from Georgia. Stemming from the British Invasion, Rod Stewart and the Faces played on the same bill with Haystacks Balboa and Fuse.

Teenager Mark Krueger took the bus downtown from Bayview with a friend. Mark heard the radio announce that the first 50 people would be admitted free and receive a copy of the Chicken Shack album *Accept*. It was August 1970, and they made it into the Scene for the special promotion. Scott Marshall's "Lite Effects" lightshow was featured. "There were more freaks than I would ever see on the south side," Mark said. "Bloomsbury People opened, with local musician Sigmund Snopek III [see Chapter 10]. British bands Chicken Shack and Savoy Brown played next and all three bands were great."[18]

Jazz contributed to the Scene's musical eclecticism on occasion. Gene Krupa and his Quartet played at the Scene back in 1965. Through the years Duke Ellington, Wes Montgomery, Jimmy Dorsey, Earl Hines, Frank Sinatra Jr. and Oscar Peterson performed in the ballroom. In March 1971, Miles Davis filled the theater with jazz-fusion music, for two nights. Judy Ramazzini, a ticketholder, remembered: "I was at the Miles concert. He didn't arrive until about 11 p.m. He came in wearing a floor length sheepskin coat, sunglasses, and had a beautiful skin bag with his horn in it. I was leaving because I thought he wasn't coming. I watched him seem to float up the big staircase to the venue." [19]

Unfortunately, the curtain went down on the Scene after losing money on Miles Davis. An article including Benny in the underground *Bugle American* explained:

> She says the concert business is very hard to judge…"Touch and go, up and down" is how she describes it. In the long run she may have broken even but, for her, it was time to vacate in 1971…. Small clubs, like the Scene, though ideal acoustically and comfortable for the concertgoer, could no longer feed the upper class needs of the superstar bands and the men who owned their careers…[In addition, there was] the lack of cooperation by the alternate press and progressive rock radio stations… All that has changed now, she says, but it came a little too late for her (Racine 1975, 155).

The new decade signaled change. After years of litigation, Frank Balistrieri served a short prison term for tax evasion. The family business replaced the Scene with the Centre Stage Playhouse Theatre in 1972. It closed in 1980 and the building was demolished in 1981. In the end, the Balistrieris left a legacy in musical entertainment that is too often overlooked. For Wisconsin, the Scene served as a Mecca for music in the late 1960s era.

---

18 Mark Krueger interview by Rob Lewis, 20 November 2013.

19 Judy Ramazzini email to Rob Lewis via http://www.milwaukeerockscene.com/, 3 January 2013.

Jazz Fusion's Social and Cultural Impact on Milwaukee
by Kevin Lynch

In his brilliant and widely acclaimed book, *A Long Way to Go: Black & White in America* (1997), Jonathan Coleman used Milwaukee as his test case in an exhaustive seven-year examination of race relations in America. He dubbed the city "the heartland of the Heartland." Coleman perceived Milwaukee as the archetypal Midwest American city afflicted by racism and neighborhood segregation and degradation compounded by the loss of manufacturing jobs, especially during the post-Civil Rights decades.

During the 1970s, local jazz fusion arose from this distressed environment and served as an influential conciliatory, integrative force. The genre incorporated modern jazz, rock, soul, funk, and even world music. Bands also had occasional lead vocalists. You could dance to some fusion music, which attracted a younger and a more racially diverse audience, which, concurrently immersed itself in the disco craze. One notable early Milwaukee fusion group, Side Street, included white and black men and women performers.

I learned first-hand how various jazz fusions were taking off while working as the jazz album buyer at Radio Doctors' "Soul Shop" on 3rd Street and North Avenue, in the early and mid-1970s. I saw how the funkier and more soulful side of fusion appealed to the city's African American community. The "Soul Shop"—also a regional wholesale outlet for jukebox owners, radio stations and record stores—throbbed with everything from soul-swelling gospel music to Grover Washington Jr.'s sinuous groove jams and even Miles Davis's challenging yet darkly funky fusion album *Bitches Brew* (featuring an all-star, multi-racial band including Chick Corea, John McLaughlin, Wayne Shorter, Dave Holland, Larry Young, and Lenny White, among others). From the late 1960s to the mid-1970s, the Soul Shop enhanced cultural vitality in an otherwise economically disadvantaged urban area.

When considering the actual live music that developed among the first Milwaukee jazz fusion groups, it's worth noting that this period just predated this rust belt city's major decline as a manufacturing center. There seemed to be more disposable income for live entertainment, buoying the city's social and cultural venues.

This was reflected in a revitalized city jazz scene and in fusion's popularity. The key group that hit the scene was Sweetbottom. Essential to the sound and drive of fusion was its jazz hybridization of rock and/or funk beats and use of electric solid-body guitar as a primary instrument. Sweetbottom centered on two preternatural virtuosos—guitarist Daryl Stuermer and saxophonist-flutist Warren Wiegratz. Stuermer had absorbed some of the technique of Jimi Hendrix and pioneer fusion guitarists Larry Coryell and John McLaughlin. Sweetbottom's two lead players introduced a repertoire of high-energy, imaginative music, which soon made them arguably the most popular jazz-related group in Milwaukee since the jazz heydays of the black neighborhood called Bronzeville, in the first half of the twentieth century.[20]

---

20 Listen to "The Whisperer" from Sweetbottom's *Live: The Reunion* http://www.youtube.com/watch?v=37ZOhqZm8g0 (recorded in Milwaukee's Shank Hall [December 2002]).

Guitarist Stuermer's spiraling musical intensity would earn him a job with leading French jazz and fusion violinist Jean-Luc Ponty (who also played with McLaughlin's Mahavishnu Orchestra) and with the popular progressive rock band Genesis, led by Phil Collins. Stuermer also backed an array of musicians, e.g., George Duke, Joan Armatrading, Tony Banks, Mike Rutherford, and Gino Vannelli. He also produced solo albums.

Warren Wiegratz contends that fusion's roots stem from when 1950s hard bop players "moved away from swing/bop rhythmic triplet feel and started writing and performing tunes" with "a straight eighth-note feel, which rock musicians were performing to ever-growing young audiences." In turn, younger musicians expanded "their musical horizons and challenged themselves with the new [jazz] style."

Furthermore, "audiences became more sophisticated in their tastes and started to appreciate the musical skills of the musicians, not just the lyrics, vocalists and something to dance to," Wiegratz explained. "Popular musical groups such as Emerson, Lake and Palmer, Yes, and others defined a fusion of rock and classical music with long, improvised solo sections. It was a short leap for audiences to assimilate…the power of rock with the freedom and intelligence of jazz. What's not to like?"[21]

Another Milwaukee group playing different strains of early fusion was Montage Project, led by Wisconsin Conservatory-trained guitarist John Zaffiro. Montage also featured the soul-drenched lead vocals of Marcia Cunningham. Zaffiro played a hollow-body electric guitar like straight-ahead jazz players, so the group had less of a sonic edge. But he developed a more spacious sound with synthesizer elements that anticipated some of jazz guitarist Pat Metheny's aural and improv-context innovations. Nevertheless, Montage Project could also play as funky as any band in town.[22]

Among the first Milwaukee groups to incorporate strains of fusion and soul-pop was Jasmine, fronted by guitarist Don Linke and electric keyboardist Frank Stemper. They traded on Linke's dual threat as a gritty-voiced singer, especially showcased in an oft-requested cover of Van Morrison's jazz-R&B hit, "Moondance." Jasmine had fairly sophisticated harmonies and deft arrangements; Stemper went on to a career as a composer, who headed the composition department at Southern Illinois University (and is now professor *emeritus*).

Opus, led by woodwind player Curt Hanrahan and guitarist Steve Lewandowski, also pioneered Milwaukee fusion, and had a longer existence than most city fusion groups, being still active today. Their 2015 album *Definition* documents the growth and depth of Opus, notably for its strong original compositions.

Matrix, a particularly innovative band (not to be confused with a better-known Appleton group of the same name) evoked Frank Zappa, given the band's experimental jazz influenced by rock, funk, and classical music.[23] Bassist Dave Phillips and saxophonist/flutist David Shostac were also members of the Milwaukee Symphony Orchestra. The group included guitarist Jack Grassel, pianist Denis Klopfer, and drummer Andy LoDuca

---

21 Warren Wiegratz interview with the author, March 2014.

22 Listen to the Latin-infused "Electric Rhumba" from Montage Project's album One. http://www.youtube.com/watch?v=HPaxge8Iu7E.

23 Sigmund Snopek III's music also complemented this "prog rock" period (see Chapter 10).

(who later drummed for What on Earth? See below), who was especially influenced by "world music" rhythms.

Inspired by Michael Brecker (1949-2007), the most influential saxophonist of his generation, Dave Matsen from Waukesha (schooled at the University of Wisconsin-Milwaukee) led Side Street. The band provided intriguing musical detours driven by Kim Zick's crackling, in-the-pocket drumming. Zick later teamed with keyboardist-singer Connie Grauer in the duo Mrs. Fun. They redefined fusion in high-spirited, quirky terms as a female duo, playing gender-blind jazz-pop-funk, and remain quite active.

Fusion also reflected Milwaukee's longstanding German tradition of *Gemütlichkeit*, or social good cheer. The group What on Earth?—an avant-jazz band—featured the unusual front line of trombone and solid-body electric guitar. Exploiting the talents of guitarist Jack Grassel, What on Earth? veered into the jazz-fusion realm with offbeat humor, which somewhat parodied the fusion genre and themselves, in tunes like "Eat My Shorts" and "Funkydiscohonkysuckinpunk." The band also influenced the renowned Milwaukee folk-punk band, the Violent Femmes (see Chapter 9).

Although they weren't a rock-jazz fusion band per se, the Latin jazz group La Chazz became one of the most important 1970s and 1980s Milwaukee music fusion bands by combining Afro-Cuban styles with modern jazz. The band was founded and led by Toty Ramos, who played a solid-body electric guitar. The band featured horn players and multiple percussionists (who included North African influences). La Chazz stayed largely true to the salsa dance sound and style, only pushing it further into improvisational jazz realms.

By the late 1970s, most of the city's first generation of fusion groups disbanded. Though proving very influential especially for rock jam bands, the first fusion era died of instrumental self-indulgence, and then from the comparative banalities of "smooth jazz," a radio-oriented development geared to aging baby-boomers.

Nevertheless, fusion remains an important legacy in the history of Milwaukee rock. Sweetbottom eventually released two albums with national label Elektra/Asylum.[24] On the cusp of national fame, fate intersected cruelly when Wiegratz suffered a severe gall bladder attack that required five hours of surgery. The group disbanded.

After Wiegratz's recovery, he formed Streetlife, which extended Sweetbottom's high-octane drive with a versatile repertoire. The new band caught the attention of the National Basketball Association's Milwaukee Bucks, who were looking for a house band akin to Paul Shaffer's Late Night with David Letterman Band. Streetlife became a fan favorite at Bucks games and gained some national visibility.

Jazz fusion's cross-cultural appeal helped Milwaukee contend with problems such as painful de-industrialization and enduring racial problems. The composition, musical and social, of groups showcased the diverse talents of the city's impressive musicians—a tradition that continues today.

---

24 *Angels of the Deep* (1978); *Turn me Loose* (1979). As mentioned above, the band reunited for *Live: The Reunion* (2003) (for Urban Island Music).

Photo by James Middleton

Photo by James Middleton

The Corporation, one of Milwaukee's most famous bands of the late 1960s

Courtesy of the Jean Cujé Collection

Thee Prophets

Courtesy of Gary Myers

The Mojo Men

Courtesy of Ken Adamany

The Van-tels

Courtesy of Jim Petersen

The Triumphs

Photo by Bob Cavallo

THE SKUNKS "GETTIN' STARTED"

TEEN TOWN
STEREO
TTLP-101

INCLUDING "ELVIRA" and "LITTLE ANGEL"

Courtesy of the Jean Cujé Collection

The Robbs

Rare Tracks

Courtesy of Bruce Robb

TONY'S

"LITTLE BY LITTLE"
INCLUDING "CAN'T BELIEVE"

Courtesy of Tony Dancy

Courtesy of Gordon Elliott

Courtesy of the Jean Cujé Collection

Photo by Rich Zimmermann

The Hound Dog Band featuring Fred Bliffert and Jon Paris (1972)

Fred Bliffert

Photo by Rich Zimmermann

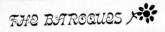

Courtesy of Dean Nimmer

Tom Green, a foremost Elvis tribute artist

Courtesy of the Jean Cujé Collection

Courtesy of the Jean Cujé Collection

The Legends reunite

Photo by Erwin Gebhard/Milwaukee Sentinel

Barry Ollman (background), the first performer at the Alternate Site (1971)

Photo by Rich Zimmermann

OX at the Alternate Site (1972)

Photo courtesy of the *Milwaukee Journal Sentinel*

**A Milwaukee super group (late 1970s): Tempus Fugit
(from left to right: Jeff Dagenhardt, Sam McCue,
Bruce Cole [front], P.T. Pedersen, John Tanner [front])**

Courtesy of the Jean Cujé Collection

**Mike Minikel (of
the Savoys) and
Sam McCue at
Nick's Nicabob**

Photo by Jennifer Dallman

Jack Grassel with his
"SuperAx" guitar

Warren Wiegratz
performing with
IN VIVO

Photo by Kevin Lynch

Photo by Jeff Dobbs ©

Warren Wiegratz performing at the tribute to Al Jarreau at The 37th annual WAMI Awards held at Turner Hall Ballroom, Milwaukee, WI on April 23, 2017

Photo by Erol Reyal

Rhino Entertainment, Warner Music Group

Daryl Stuermer

Blues legend Hubert Sumlin

CHAPTER 7

The Blues
in Milwaukee

For years Sonia Khatchadourian has hosted the Friday afternoon Blues Drive on WMSE (91.7 FM). Furthermore, she has interviewed and befriended scores of blues musicians including those featured in this chapter.[1] She provides a chronicle of local blues while providing blues musicians' biographies. The result is a history of blues and Milwaukee penned by a renowned "bluesologist." As Sonia recounts, Milwaukee was a familiar destination particularly for Chicago blues musicians. Milwaukee audiences as well as musicians especially appreciated the extraordinary accessibility to renowned Chicago blues performers in a variety of local venues such as the Avant Garde, the Scene, Teddy's, Century Hall, Zak's, and the Tamarack among others. In turn, Milwaukee musicians traveled to and performed in Chicago and elsewhere nationally and internationally earning respect and creating camaraderie. Bruce Cole ends the chapter by recalling and paying tribute to two Milwaukee performers: Terry Frank (d. 2009) and Kenny Arnold (d. 2010).

---

1   Quotations in this chapter are derived from "multiple, lengthy interviews" over time and place (Sonia Khatchadourian email to Phillip Naylor, 17 March 2018).

Milwaukee Blues Music:
A Brief History
by Sonia Khatchadourian

Introduction

Although soul music in the 1960s and disco in the 1970s became increasingly popular among young African Americans and many blues musicians were forced to find other lines of work to sustain themselves and their families, whites, who had already been exposed to blues music as a result of the "Folk Blues Boom" (see Chapter 2) that had pervaded coffeehouses and college campuses in the late 1950s and early to mid-1960s or through rock musicians acknowledging their influences in the mid to late 1960s, began to develop an interest in blues.

In Milwaukee, the Avant Garde Coffeehouse was especially important in fostering an interest in blues music during the mid-to-late 1960s. During the 1970s, there was a rise in local blues bands and young people had the opportunity to see live blues music at a variety of local venues ranging from small clubs like the East Village, which became Humpin' Hannah's, the Catacombs Coffeehouse, Teddy's, and The Scene to larger venues like Summerfest, the Performing Arts Center, the Milwaukee Arena, and the Milwaukee Auditorium.

Tony Machi, who owned Teddy's from 1968 until 1985, recalled that "Muddy Waters played at Teddy's and then played at the Kennedy Center immediately after that. That's the kind of place it was." Machi also mentioned that George Benson performed at Teddy's (in 1976) when Benson "had a number one record, *Breezin'*." Frank Habib, Vice-President of Development for the Milwaukee School of Engineering since 1997, came to Milwaukee from Detroit as a VISTA volunteer and managed the Catacombs Coffeehouse. Opened in the summer of 1970, the Catacombs was located in the basement of the Next Door Foundation on 31st Street and Wisconsin Avenue. At that time, it was a youth center and "now a model of youth centers across the country." Habib described the venue as "an intimate setting" sitting "audiences of 75 to 150 people, but "close to 200 [people] on big nights." He reminisced: "All of the good musicians in this town—I sought them out. I wanted to make it their place." Concerts took place on Fridays, Saturdays, Sundays, and Mondays, and admission was 50 cents to one dollar to make it "affordable for young kids and young adults to get exposed to a lot of really good music." Folk singers and groups or "local kids starting out" performed on Fridays; folk bands or blues bands performed on Saturdays; on Sundays, there was country/folk (like CSNY) or fusion/jazz; and, on Mondays, there was rock or blues. Bands and artists that performed at the Catacombs included Omaha, Woodbine with Bill Camplin (who recorded an album there), OX, the Hound Dog Band, Barry Ollman, and the Blue Ridge Ramblers, as well as national acts like Uncle Vinty and James and the Good Brothers. Nevertheless, it was mostly local, and this is where the Stone-Cohen band first performed, even though the band members were still in high school at the time. Habib said that it was a "personal environment where musicians could showcase their talents." Furthermore, "it was an environment to actually be heard." Habib added:

"Unbelievably phenomenal musicians played in that room." What made the venue so attractive was "'the vibe,'…the listener experience at a very personal level. People came to listen. They understood that they were getting something unique that they were never going to hear again."

Professional photographer Rich Zimmermann worked for the *Bugle American* newspaper from 1971 to 1974. Zimmermann photographed the Grateful Dead at the Performing Arts Center in 1971, David Bowie at the Milwaukee Arena in 1974, Frank Zappa at the same venue, the Rolling Stones at County Stadium in 1975, Pink Floyd at County Stadium in 1977, as well as many other national bands at large venues. However, as the newspaper's office was located only one and a half blocks west of Humpin' Hannah's on Locust Street and Humboldt Avenue, he was "shooting photos at least two nights a week at Humpin' Hannah's," a basement folk, rock, and blues club, run by Joe Balistreri and his brother, Dan. Zimmermann recalled: "The Hound Dog Band was very popular." In addition, "Waddy Wachtel was with everyone and played with the Everly Brothers here, including a performance at Pius X Grade School on April 22, 1972." He noted that "Omaha was very popular." To Zimmermann, "weeknights were great for music in Milwaukee."

Jim Liban

Many of the local blues musicians who began performing during that time are still performing today. The most notable is harmonica player, singer, songwriter Jim Liban, who has been playing music publicly since 1963. Liban was in two high school bands between 1963 and 1965, the Saxons and then the Avantis. At the time, Liban, who started as a drummer, attended Marquette High School, while guitarist Jeff Dagenhardt attended Waukesha Memorial. Bass player P.T. Pedersen and rhythm guitarist Jim Morris attended Brookfield East. They grew up listening to rock n' roll and English bands and learning where blues music started. They were thinking about putting together a blues rock band. They started making frequent trips to Chicago to Maxwell Street and some festivals where there was no age limit. Liban stated that, for him, being a musician "had already been decided by fate," adding, "we thought that we were indestructible. Every day was all about music. We were driven."

In 1966, Liban, Dagenhardt, and Pedersen, along with two classmates of Liban's, singer Chris Lorenz and drummer Augie Jurishica, formed the Unit, a blues rock band that had a light show. Harold Strohmeier, who owned and operated the Avant Garde Coffeehouse at that time, was their manager, and they regularly played at the Garde and recorded two songs, an instrumental entitled "Gooberdust," and Bo Diddley's, "Pretty Thing," at a studio in New York. Then, in 1967, New Blues, which changed its spelling at some point to Knu Bluz, was formed. According to Liban, Knu Bluz was closer to a blues band than the Unit had been. Other than Liban, the lineup included keyboard player Jimmy Peterman, who asked Liban to join the band, guitarist and vocalist Denny Geyer, bass player Jim Marcotte, and drummer Terry Andersen. According to Liban, his bandmates were older than him by three to four years and "were influenced by real blues musicians and Jazz musicians." Knu Bluz also played at the Avant Garde

Coffeehouse, but they decided to move to California in 1967. However, Peterman left to play with Steve Miller first and was replaced by Sam McCue on guitar. Then Liban, Andersen, Geyer, and Marcotte went to California in 1968 without McCue. Marcotte became the official manager of the band. Liban said: "Steve Miller put us up the first week. Then, Chet Helms of Family Dog took us under his wing, and we played up and down the coast: the Fillmore, the Avalon, the Whiskey a Go Go, from Portland to San Diego." Soon after they arrived, the band's name was changed to A.B. Skhy. Liban recollected that "San Francisco was the center of the hippie universe at that time. We played with Jefferson Airplane, Santana, Creedence Clearwater Revival, Taj Mahal...and hooked up with Howie (Howard) Wales from Milwaukee, on keyboards, who was in the Bonnevilles and the Green Men, which were big local Milwaukee bands. Everyone was cross-pollinating." Liban added: "The musicians knew that we were a good band." Jimi Hendrix sat in with them at the Whisky a Go Go. A.B. Skhy would play three-night stands, and Hendrix heard them when they were opening on a bill with Three Dog Night, who had just made their first album. A.B. Skhy recorded two albums for MGM on the strength of an interview with Jimi Hendrix in *Billboard* magazine. The band even opened for Pink Floyd in Sacramento in 1968.

Jim Liban of Short Stuff

Photo by Dennis Darmek

Liban was on one of the albums (*A. B. Skhy*, MGM Records, 1969), but he quit during the session in 1969. He had been with the band for one year. Liban explained: "The band was moving away from the blues." Also, he was "20 years old with a pregnant wife and 2,000 miles from home with no job." Liban returned to Milwaukee at the end of 1968 or the beginning of 1969 and, six months later, formed Short Stuff.

In addition to Liban, the original lineup for Short Stuff was Eric Epstein (guitar), Kenny Berdoll (bass), "who was in the Corporation shortly before that and was signed to a major [record] label," and Kenny Arnold (drums). Keyboard player Junior Brantley joined six months later, and the two performed together for 15 years, until 1984. Liban recounted: "Previously, Junior Brantley played the R&B circuit. One of our first shows together was the second Summerfest (1969)—a mud field, opening up for Sly Stone." Then "Jim Solberg joined in the late 1970s for not more than two years." During the 1970s, the band played at O'Brad's on Locust Street, the East Village/Humpin'Hannah's, Teddy's, the Stone Toad, Century Hall, and "a lot of festivals opening for a lot of touring acts." They played the after-party for the Who in the 1970s and opened for Johnny Cougar (John Mellencamp), Albert King, Albert Collins, Muddy Waters, George Thorogood, and Johnny Winter. They toured all over the Midwest, Canada, Colorado, New York, Boston, Washington, D.C., and other East Coast cities. Short Stuff had two official albums, *Short Stuff* (Third Coast Records, 1969) and *Talk Is Cheap* (Third Coast Records, 1981), "a handful of 45s, and Milwaukee compilations, like for WQFM."

About the era, Liban recalled that "the early to mid-1970s was Milwaukee's hippie era…which lasted until 1979. The East Side was where all of the artistic stuff was centralized. The East Side was the musical universe of Milwaukee." In that environment, "Short Stuff thrived as a blues band throughout the 1970s." However, when the disco era started, Liban "started tailoring some of the music towards R&B, Funk, and some disco rhythmic elements [and] we were packing the clubs."

Toward the tail end of Short Stuff and post-Short Stuff, from 1985 to 1986, Liban formed the Futuramics with Green Bay guitarist Billy Flynn and drummer Tom Wilson. According to Liban, they never released an album, but they recorded an album's worth of material shortly before Liban moved to Nashville in 1986, where he lived for two years and then returned to Milwaukee.

From 1988 to the present, there have been a series of Jim Liban Combos and three recordings under that name, *Live at Romie's*, *Blues for Shut-Ins*, and *Hot Tongue and Cold Shoulder*. Liban's most recent album, *I Say What I Mean*, was produced by Joel Paterson and is with the Joel Paterson Trio. In April of 2000, Jim Liban received a Milestone Award from the Wisconsin Area Music Industry (WAMI). In 2014, he received an M. Hohner Lifetime Achievement Award; and, in April of 2017, all the members of Short Stuff were inducted into the Wisconsin Area Music Industry (WAMI) Hall of Fame.

Reflecting on the decades since the 1970s, Liban said: "The mid to late 1980s was a blues renaissance period," and "the blues have never been more [a part] of the musical landscape than it is now. It will never go away—whatever form it takes." However, "the 70s was my era. That was when I really came of age musically." In particular, "I was influenced by the black musical forms that were developing and taking shape. There was a lot of revolutionizing of music in the 70s, and I was very much a product of that decade. I still am." Specifically, "Grover Washington, Eddie Harris, Les McCann, The Crusaders [and others] influenced my writing and Short Stuff's writing. They influenced everyone who was into music at that time."

Jeff Dagenhardt

Guitarist Jeff Dagenhardt "started playing [music] seriously in 1959, using his mother's guitar. His mom and sister wore a "cowgirl outfit" and played Western songs while their father sold "Lee Patent Medicine, a Snake Oil Medicine that was [actually] *Jagermeister*," in front of a wagon. Dagenhardt's first band was the Avantis, which included P.T. Pedersen, a bass player from Elm Grove, who was in his Spanish class freshman year in high school, vocalist Jim Kuiper, and drummer Jim Liban. Dagenhardt recalled: "We started doing CYO dances." At that time, "there were two versions of the band. First was the Avantis. A year or two into it, the band became the Night Shift [late 1963]. In that later version, Jim started playing harmonica and I would play drums." Liban suggested that they become a blues band and played them a Jimmy Reed song. Around this time, Kuiper left the band, was replaced by Chris Lorenz, and the other members became the Unit, with Liban changing instruments to harmonica. They played frequently at the Avant Garde Coffeehouse, Le Bistro and Gallagher's (both on Third and Wells Streets), and O'Brad's on Locust Street which became the East Village and, subsequently, Humpin' Hannah's. The Unit stayed together until the Fall 1966, at which time Dagenhardt went to California for a short while. When he returned, he began to perform with Johnny Young, Big Walter Horton, and others while Liban was with A.B. Skhy. "It was cool to hang out and become friends with all of those people, including Hubert [Sumlin]," with whom Dagenhardt renewed a friendship that began in the 1960s, when Sumlin and Howlin' Wolf performed at Teddy's in 1975.

In the early 1970s, Dagenhardt attended a performance at O'Brad's by the Last Fair Deal, a duo comprised of pianist Chuck Solberg and his younger brother, guitarist Jim Solberg. He learned that Chuck wanted to stay in Eau Claire, where their family resided, but that Jim wanted to move to Milwaukee. As a result, Dagenhardt and Jim Solberg formed Dynamite Duck, with Mark Lillis on bass and Jeff Hilgert on drums. Dagenhardt remembered, "There was a lot of blues in Dynamite Duck," even though the band's manager, Mike Kappus (see below), wanted them "to go more pop." The band was together for two years.

After Dynamite Duck, Dagenhardt joined Short Stuff while two of the members, Kenny Berdoll and Kenny Arnold, were on a world tour with harmonica great Charlie Musselwhite. Dagenhardt and drummer 'Hotdog' Bob Mueller were with Liban and Junior Brantley for 18 months until "the two Kennys returned and the band was [once again] the old Short Stuff." Also, Dagenhardt recalled that at some point, he was fired, and Jon Paris joined the band because "Liban wanted someone to share vocal responsibilities." In the meantime, they "did countless jobs around the state."

In the mid-1970s, Dagenhardt played guitar in Barry's Truckers, a "throw-back rock band" that played Chuck Berry, Buddy Holly, and the songs of other musicians who were popular in the 1950s and 1960s, along with P.T. Pedersen, who had just returned from playing bass with Charlie Musselwhite. The original drummer, Kenny Prili, "was a monster." At this time, Dagenhardt also was in the Shuffleaires—"I was a journeyman." After this point, he began to form bands under his own name and recalls that he performed at Sweetwater and other clubs located on Water Street.

In the late 1970s, Dagenhardt joined with Pedersen, along with guitarist Sam McCue, drummer Bruce Cole, and California keyboard player, John Tanner, to form Tempus Fugit, "a rock band with some originals that Sam and John had written." During the two years of the band's existence, one of the venues where they performed was Century Hall on Farwell Avenue.

One more collaboration that began in the late 1970s was with Minneapolis-based guitarist Dave "Snaker" Ray, who Dagenhardt knew since the mid-1960s. In the 1980s,

Dagenhardt and Ray performed together in Milwaukee, Minneapolis, and throughout the Midwest. By the late 1990s, along with bass player Dave Kasik, they formed 6L6, "the name of a power tube from an amplifier," and performed at the UW-Milwaukee Gasthaus, Thai Joe's on Prospect Avenue, and Ike's Pub in Pewaukee.

When Dagenhardt was considering who could join him to form a new band, Hubert Sumlin told him, "You've got the band at your house." Starting in 2001, Dagenhardt formed 3-D with his sons Dallas on guitar and Austin on drums and has performed with his sons ever since. Dallas and Austin also formed Super Custom Deluxe with bassist Dave Kasik. Dagenhardt's newest band is Idle Minds with his son Austin, Dave Kasik, Laury Katz (keyboards), and Gervis Myles (vocals).

Jon Paris

Multi-instrumentalist Jon Paris started performing in the summer of 1963 in the Squires, a rock n' roll band, which quickly became the Chevelles. According to Paris, "Blues and rock and Roll were so interconnected. The lines were even more blurred back then." Paris played drums while in the Chevelles. The other band members in the Chevelles were guitarist Mark Goetzinger, rhythm guitarist David Zucker, bassist Bob Schlaeger, and singer Mike Gatz. They played throughout high school at Bar Mitzvah and Sweet Sixteen parties, CYO dances, and teen clubs. Although drums were his first instrument, Paris was asked to play bass or rhythm guitar with other bands and began playing bass more seriously in the late 1960s when Jack Bruce (the renowned bass player of Cream) became a major influence for him. Starting in 1966-67, during his freshman year in college at the University of Wisconsin-Milwaukee, Paris played bass in the Walkers, a blues-based band, with guitarist Bob Metzger, keyboard player Jerry Harrison, drummer Bob Turner, and singer Tom Vonier. After Harrison, Turner, and Vonier left Milwaukee, Paris and Metzger started the blues rock band, the Ox, which became OX. The band performed from 1968 through 1972, during which time there were several drummers, including Scott Nelligan, Brad Seip, and Ed Sison. They played at the Catacombs Coffeehouse almost every week, as well as the Avant Garde Coffeehouse, Teddy's and O'Brad's (which, as stated earlier, became the East Village and then Humpin' Hannah's) and throughout Wisconsin and the Midwest. Paris said that the Avant Garde Coffeehouse "was the beginning of the blues scene in Milwaukee," and after the Avant Garde closed, "Teddy's was important and became [the center of] the blues scene." At various Milwaukee venues, OX opened for The Grateful Dead, Steve Miller, Ten Years After, Procol Harum, Siegel-Schwall, and other nationally-known bands.

In Fall 1972, Paris joined Short Stuff for a few months when Jim Liban went to Nashville. Later in 1972, Paris joined the blues band, Dynamite Duck when Jeff Dagenhardt left the band to join Short Stuff. The other band members were guitarist James Solberg, R&B singer Charlie Brooks, bassist Mark Lillis, and drummer Jeff Hilgert, who was replaced by Danny Shmitt. They performed "in a lot of bars, as well as all over the state, and even in Chicago" for most of 1973. Both Paris and Solberg played guitar and took turns singing and playing harmonica.

Paris moved to Greenwich Village in January of 1974 after Danny Shmitt's brother, singer-songwriter Stuffy Shmitt, invited Paris "to play some gigs with him in New York." They played in venues such as HOME, Folk City, the Bitter End, Kenny's Castaways, and other now-legendary New York clubs.

From 1978 to 1989, Paris played bass guitar and harmonica with Johnny Winter. Winter's albums that include Paris' playing are *Raisin' Cain*, *Serious Business*, and *The Winter of '88*. In the early 1980s and in the late 1990s, he toured with Bo Diddley. Paris has also toured and recorded with Robert Gordon and Link Wray. Paris appeared on Gordon's album, *All for The Love of Rock n' Roll*. In late July 1984, Paris recorded songs with Bob Dylan in New York City—"Driftin' Too Far from Shore" on *Knocked Out Loaded* and "Clean Cut Kid" on *Empire Burlesque*. Paris also played on albums by Lou Pallo, Edgar Winter, the James Solberg Band, Stuffy Shmitt, Joe Bonamassa, and others. Paris has two albums under his own name, *Rock the Universe* and *Blue Planet*. For years, Paris was a featured guest with the legendary Les Paul at Les's Monday night shows at the Iridium in New York City, and Paris appeared with Les in the PBS *American Masters* series DVD: *Les Paul—Chasing Sound*.

Paris still resides in New York, where he performs with his own band every Monday night at B.B. King's Blues Club and Grill in Times Square.[2] He has often returned to Milwaukee to play at Summerfest and major anniversary celebrations of Harley-Davidson Motorcycles. Paris was inducted into the Wisconsin Area Music Industry Hall of Fame in 2011 and the New York Blues Hall of Fame in 2012.

James Solberg

World-renowned, Grammy-nominated guitarist James Solberg developed an interest in music when he was very young. By the time he was 13 years old, in the early 1960s, Solberg played guitar, violin, and five-string banjo. He said that he "figured out stuff by ear." As a young teenager, he joined an established band called the Eliminators in northern Wisconsin as their guitarist and was with them in 1963 and 1964, as well as the band, All of The Days, in 1965 and 1966. He was interested in the bluegrass and folk scene and explained: "It took me awhile to discover electricity," in the songs of Muddy Waters and Howlin' Wolf. "Then, all hell broke loose." However, there were "Miles Davis, Coltrane and other Blue Note records around the house. Jazz has the same emotion to the music [as blues music]. It's like another language—how musicians communicate with each other. I have always brought that into the blues. We're having another conversation."

Solberg "stepped into Chicago Blues" spending time "as a teenager" at "Pepper's," "Theresa's" [and other] South Side joints." He "[was] invited backstage once in a while." Blues guitarist Eddie Taylor let him "sit in and later showed [him] some licks." Solberg explained, "I was the only white guy around."

In 1967 and 1968, Solberg was in Cold Turkey, "a bluesy band for the day." In 1969, he was in Whirlhouse: "The singer was Curtis A, who later became the Godfather of Punk in Minneapolis," but it was "as much of a blues band." In 1970, Solberg married,

---

2   The club closed in 2018.

lived in Chicago, and had a son, while playing with whomever he could. Then, he moved his family to Eau Claire, and joined his brother's blues band, Last Fair Deal. Chuck Solberg was ten years older than James and he went to school with Bob Dylan when they were kids. James recalled: "The Solbergs and Zimmermans shared a duplex together." In the 1950s, Chuck played cornet in dance bands in Eau Claire. (Note: Chuck Solberg also became an accomplished jazz and blues pianist and a ceramics artist whose works are in the permanent collections of several international art museums.) Mike Kappus, founder of the Rosebud Agency in San Francisco, who managed local bands while living in Wisconsin and who went on to manage many famous blues musicians at Rosebud during its forty years in business, "was from Eau Claire, and Last Fair Deal was the first blues band he booked."[3] With the help of Kappus, the band played all over Wisconsin, from "Milwaukee to Minneapolis, Green Bay, the Fox River towns, Madison," and elsewhere. The Solberg brothers played together in Last Fair Deal through 1971.

In 1972, Kappus put together a band for James Solberg, "along with some Rock guy friends of his," called Bacon Fat. Jeff Dagenhardt also joined the band, which evolved into Dynamite Duck. At that time, Solberg discovered that Luther Allison was living in the Cudahy Tower and played at Brothers Lounge, "the first street past the Park West on North Avenue. The Eldorado Room was part of the club, where you took your date." Solberg added that it was a "cheesy organ bar." Allison played there every Monday night, with Randy Joe Fullerton on bass and Bob Ritchie, "who played with [Howlin'] Wolf," on drums. "Jon Paris would also show up and jam." By this time, Solberg was 21 years old and Dynamite Duck opened for Allison in large college

Dynamite Duck at Ma Fischer's on Milwaukee's East Side (left to right) Jon Paris, Jim Solberg, Mark Lillis, Danny Shmitt

Courtesy of Jon Paris; photo by Tom Hayes

venues. They even served as the backing band for Chuck Berry and Bo Diddley when they were touring without a band. Solberg said that from 1972 to 1973, they played "the whole state university system, including Superior, Stevens Point, UW-Eau Claire, UW-Milwaukee, and Marquette." According to Solberg, "Jim Liban and Short Stuff were the heroes of the scene," and "we were trying to become our own Short Stuff."

---

3 Kappus moved to Milwaukee in 1971 and worked for Contemporary Talent booking performances by blues and rock artists and managing them. In 1976, he founded the Rosebud Agency in San Francisco, which particularly represented established blues artists (e.g., Muddy Waters, John Lee Hooker, Willie Dixon, Albert Collins) and booked performances. The Blues Foundation repeatedly recognized Kappus as Manager/Agent of the Year. Under the auspices of the Blues Foundation, Kappus also established the Handy Artists Relief Trust (HART) in 2000 to cover impoverished blues musicians' medical and funeral expenses. He also served as executive producer of notable albums such as John Lee Hooker's *The Healer*. See http://www.rosebudus.com/rosebud/founder.html and https://en.wikipedia.org/wiki/Mike_Kappus.

(Note: James Solberg performed with Short Stuff from 1979 to 1982 and played on their album, *Talk Is Cheap*.)

Then, in late 1973 through 1974, James and Chuck reunited as the Solberg Brothers and played at Teddy's and Humpin' Hannah's in Milwaukee, as well as "the rest of the state, Minnesota, and Illinois." Marquette University Music Librarian and local blues musician Bruce Cole was one of the drummers in the band for a short time.

However, James was "performing with Luther whenever I could," and in 1975, he became the full-time guitarist of the Luther Allison Band, along with drummer Jimi Schutte. (Schutte has also performed and recorded with many well-known blues musicians, including Jimmy Dawkins and Lonnie Brooks.) The other band members in the Luther Allison band were organist Skeeter Davis from Madison, who was "really a Country guy in Dr. Bop and the Headliners, who played piano and B-3," sax player Fat Richard, organist Larry Byrne, and bassist Jeff Aldridge, who was from Racine. Within a year, on 4 July 1976, they headlined the Montreux Jazz Festival, which was their first European performance, where they played a 45-minute encore. Solberg explained that they "had already played Coast to Coast and Canada the year before." In January 1976, they released a Motown album entitled, *Nightlife*, "under the contract of Berry Gordy." A few years later, they were recording for Alligator Records and then Ruf. Solberg's other albums with Allison include: *Motown Years 1972-1976*, *Live at Montreux, 1976-1994*, *Live in Paris*, *Luther Allison Live*, *Pay It Forward*, *Soul Fixin' Man*, *Blue Streak*, *Reckless*, and *Live in Chicago*.

For Solberg, "no matter where we were in the world, playing Madison and Milwaukee were highlights for us because that was home." He emphasized that "our Milwaukee, Madison camaraderie" between himself, Liban, Schutte, Paris, Junior Brantley, Dave Kasik, Jeff Dagenhardt, Sam McCue and others, "was an important part of our lives."

In the mid 1980s, Solberg joined the Nighthawks [based in Washington, D.C.] for several tours after Jimmy Thackery left the band, and they "played a lot of gigs as Elvin Bishop and the Nighthawks."

From 1986 to 1993, Solberg owned a club called Stone's Throw in Eau Claire. His band played every Wednesday night at his club, which he said was "Luther's biggest bragging rights." By this time, Allison had moved to France, but Allison would "sneak away," play at the club, and then the two "would go fishing for a couple of weeks."

Simultaneously, Solberg had the James Solberg Band, which consisted of "the guys from Luther's band": Mike Vlahakis (keyboards), Rob Stupka (drums), John Lindberg (bass) and Larry "Third Degree" Byrne on keyboards when Mike went with Luther's son," Bernard Allison. At one point, "for a year," also in the band were bassist P.T. Pedersen, drummer Kenny Arnold, and guitarist Charlie Bingham, "from Hoopsnakes." In 1993, shortly after Solberg sold his club, the mayor of Memphis gave him the keys to the city. The James Solberg Band won two W. C. Handy Awards for Best Blues Band, in 1996 and 1997. Around the same time, he produced one of the albums for the Nighthawks. In addition, Solberg has recorded five albums under his own name: *See That My Grave Is Kept Clean*, *One of These Days*, *L.A. Blues*, *The Hand You're Dealt*, and *Real Time*.

Nowadays, Solberg continues to perform with his own band and makes guest appearances with other musicians, including Walter Trout. Walter Trout's 2014 release, *Luther's Blues*, is comprised mostly of songs written by Solberg. He informed: "I still play two gigs a year with the Nighthawks. We play one night during Daytona Beach Bike Week in early March and one gig in late July in Dayton, Ohio at a big summer outdoor biker blues concert." He is also an arranger and producer for other blues musicians. In addition, Solberg owns Ace Motors, in which he "works on motors" and does "occasional total restorations for Indian motorcycles" in Middletown, Ohio. James Solberg returned to Milwaukee in 2011 for a reunion of Dynamite Duck at Summerfest.

Steve Cohen

Harmonica player Steve Cohen first encountered blues music at the house of his friend, classmate, and soon-to-be band mate, Bill Stone. Cohen recalled that he "hung out with Bill in 1968-69, eighth grade and freshman year [at Whitefish Bay High School]" recollecting that "Bill's parents [Bob and Shirley Stone] liked music: blues music, Country Blues, Lightnin' Hopkins, Sonny Terry and Brownie [McGhee]." Cohen also started hearing popular music of the psychedelic era, including musicians "who were captivated by Chess era music." Cohen said that he was "hearing Folk Blues at the same time, right after the Folk Blues Revival and at the beginning of the [British] Blues Invasion." All this, "to a 14-year old, it was cool."

Cohen explained that Shirley Stone nurtured the two teenagers by taking them to the Avant Garde Coffeehouse and The Scene, where they saw Magic Sam, Johnny Shines, Big Walter Horton, and New Blues. He recalled: "Jim Liban with New Blues was the first harmonica player that I saw play live." At this time, Cohen also read *On the Road* by Jack Kerouac, about the "Bohemian lifestyle that included Jazz music and that contributed to the culture that we were creating for ourselves."

Cohen's first instrument was violin. He said that because he did well, he began to pursue another instrument and bought a "cheap Stella guitar," and he and Stone "would write poems." Stone had a harmonica, and, "at some point, [they] switched roles." In 1970, during their freshman year, they started a band with bassist Dave Kasik and drummer Marc Wilson, who also attended Whitefish Bay High School. Cohen said that they also had another "very talented" drummer, Danny Shmitt, who attended Shorewood High School and is now deceased. They opened for Methyl Ethyl and the Keytones with Amy Madigan (see Chapter 8) at the high school auditorium, as well as dances in the gym on Saturday nights. "Bob Metzger, who played with OX and later played with Leonard Cohen," also played at the high school auditorium.

OX guitarist Jon Paris gave them their name, The Stone-Cohen Band, when "he came to Bill's parents' house basement" to visit them. Throughout high school, they "played at the Catacombs Coffeehouse. OX, Hound Dog band, and Woodbine, [which was] Bill Camplin's band, would also play there." Furthermore, "high school kids came to the Catacombs." In addition, The Stone-Cohen Band played at Finjan on Oakland Avenue, Pizzeria Uno on Oakland Avenue which also had folk music, the Living Room

Coffeehouse at the Brown Point Shopping Center, and occasional bar gigs at the Plaid Rabbit in Okauchee and Little Richard's in Sheboygan Falls. During his junior year in high school, Cohen moved to Oak Park, Illinois. He graduated a semester early, in January of 1972. While living in Illinois, he "took Greyhounds back on the weekends to play at the Catacombs."

After he and the others finished school, they "took five years off before reforming as Leroy Airmaster in 1978." The band at the time included Kasik and drummer Tom Wilson (Mark Wilson's younger brother), who is now internationally known for his decorative ironwork. As Stone was not initially in Leroy Airmaster, Cohen played both guitar and harmonica. "Our first steady gig work was at Dr. Feelgood's Blue Note on Brady [Street] and Warren, which later became Harp's, then Sherman's. We had a jam there." The band's "audience was our friends and others our age. It was our home base for a year." They also performed at The Kenwood Inn and at the Ballroom, both located in the UW-Milwaukee Student Union.

In 1979, six to eight months after the band was formed, Bill Stone joined the band as their guitarist. They played at "Klinger's on Locust [Street] every Sunday for a year and ran jam sessions at Woodrow's—a VFW Post on 10th and Mitchell [Streets], [which] filled up with neighborhood people." They also had another jam session at Copperfield's on Capitol Drive and Port Washington Road in 1981, "which took place before Woodrow's." At that time, club owner Joe Biezak decided that he wanted to manage a band but wanted a different drummer. Stone had been attending the Wisconsin Conservatory of Music's Jazz Department with Vodie Reinhardt, and Reinhardt became the band's drummer. In 1982, keyboard player Junior Brantley, who had been with Short Stuff, joined the band. Two months later, they started performing at the Up n' Under Pub, a rugby bar on Brady Street that started to have live music. Cohen reminisced: "Then, it was the happening East Side weekend group event. It was s subculture onto itself." Leroy Airmaster performed on Sundays from 3 to 7 p.m. and "later and later over the years."

Cohen said that by the late 1980s, "the market for blues bands in taverns was tailing off." In the meantime, Kasik left the band several times to perform with blues guitarist Bryan Lee, a native of Two Rivers, Wisconsin, who resided in New Orleans for several decades and toured internationally. In 1987, Leroy Airmaster disbanded. In 1991, Cohen and Reinhardt went to Lake Tahoe "to work a show…in a Blues Brothers act." After a year, they relocated to Reno. After two years, Cohen returned to Milwaukee and Reinhardt moved with the show to Biloxi, Mississippi, for an additional year.

After his return, Cohen "reinvented" himself as a duo with rotating partners, including guitarist Peter Roller, who performed and recorded with blues mandolinist, Yank Rachell. Cohen and Roller named themselves the Rolling Cohens. Cohen performed at Liquid Johnny's in West Allis "every Tuesday evening from 6 to 9 p.m. for 12 years," between 1993 and 2005. For Cohen, "The Up n' Under and Liquid Johnny's were a unique and organized musical environment that people enjoyed," and which he considers to be his legacy.

Leroy Airmaster reformed in 2009 and continues to perform as one of the premier blues bands in the Milwaukee area. Sadly, Vodie Reinhardt died suddenly in June 2014.

Marc Wilson, who performed with nationally known musicians such as Marcia Ball, Anson Funderburgh and the Rockets featuring Sam Myers, and Mike Morgan and the Crawl before returning to reside in Milwaukee, then took over as the band's drummer.

Junior Brantley

Junior Brantley grew up in Milwaukee but left in 1986 to tour with the Fabulous Thunderbirds. Then, he moved to Rhode Island to play with Roomful of Blues. Afterwards, he moved to Las Vegas to perform in a tribute to Little Richard, and he also recorded and toured with Jimmie Vaughan. He has resided in Las Vegas since 1992. According to Brantley, he has "never lost touch with Milwaukee" and "played with Short Stuff… right up until the death of Short Stuff's bass player, Jim "Big" Williquette, including a Short Stuff reunion CD and tour." He added, "I consider myself very local when it comes to staying and playing with bands. That's why I only played with a few." Junior Brantley played with Sonny Boy Williamson II (Rice Miller), the Junior Brantley Combo, Junior and the Classics, Pot Luck, Short Stuff, Leroy Airmaster, the Fabulous Thunderbirds, Roomful of Blues, Jimmie Vaughan and the Dell Vikings. (Note: Brantley said that Potluck "was a band led by Joe Miller, an incredible saxophone player who went on to play with people like Linda Ronstadt and many others. On harmonica was Jeff Karp, who played on the *Fathers and Sons* LP with Muddy Waters and others.")

Junior Brantley of Short Stuff

Photo by Dennis Darnek

Brantley cannot remember a time when he did not play piano. He explained that there was a "piano in the house" and that he "always played." The portability of keyboards gave Brantley the freedom to be able to perform in public. Brantley first saw the use of keyboards when Steve Allen played piano on *The Tonight Show*, which Allen hosted. Brantley also saw Ray Charles use the instrument in 1959 when performing "What'd I Say." Brantley said, "When the little piano came along, I had to have one."

When he was a teenager, Brantley played with Sonny Boy Williamson II at the Playboys Club on Walnut and 12th Street. After that, every time Sonny Boy was in Milwaukee, Brantley was able to play with him. Brantley said, "I had never played in a band before." In addition to Brantley, Sonny Boy Williamson's band included Arthur King (guitar), Roscoe Webb (drums), and Tom Burke (bass), "the late and great Michael Burke's father."

Brantley's first band of his own was formed in 1963 when he was in his twenties and called the Junior Brantley Combo. The line-up was Roscoe Webb (drums) from Sonny Boy Williamson's band, Jimmy Dice, "a great jazz upright bass player," Dempsey Lee "Kent" Ivey (saxophones) and Jules Brussard (saxophones). They "went out to California and got the opportunity to play with Earl 'Fatha' Hines on *The Ed Sullivan Show*, along with Carlos Santana and Linda Ronstadt. Then, the name of the band was changed to Junior and the Classics with Tom Fabre (saxophone), Bran Shank (bass), and Jerry Shwarski (drums). Junior recalled: "Tom Fabre left the band after a short stay and we hired Dennis Madigan and Kent Ivey. Those were the cats that signed with RCA and recorded "Do the Dog" and "Birmingham." Then "RCA changed the name of the band. We called ourselves the Classics, but there was a recording group with the same name already, so they added 'Junior' to the mix. So, when the record was released, it said we were Junior and the Classics and, at that point, we started using the name Junior and the Classics." According to Brantley, Junior and the Classics recorded three different versions of the Classics RCA Records, "Do the Dog" and "Birmingham" with Bran Shank, Jerry Shwarski, Dennis Madigan, and Kent Ivey. Other recordings included "Wise Up and Mixup a Go Go," "Kill the Pain" and "Stock Blues in D" with a few line-up changes. There were also line-up changes during the time when Brantley was in Short Stuff.

Brantley joined Short Stuff in 1970. The first time that he heard the band was at the Turning Point on 23rd Street and Fond du Lac Avenue. Brantley's cousin owned the bar and Brantley was living upstairs at the time. He thought that they "sounded like Sonny Boy." He sat in with the band and afterwards, their manager, Marty Leary, asked Brantley to join Short Stuff to be one of the singers. Brantley remained with Short Stuff for 14 years, until 1984. He recalled: "When you're young, you feel good. I was happy there. I loved all of them." Brantley played on all of Short Stuff's albums, as well as *Rock the Universe*, the first solo album of Jon Paris. Brantley recounted that sometime between 1984 and 1986, he joined Leroy Airmaster and recorded on their first album, *Taste and Compare* prior to performing with the Fabulous Thunderbirds.

Brantley also appeared as a piano player in two films in the late 1980s, *The Good Mother*, with Diane Keaton and Liam Neeson, and *Complex World*, which included Roomful of Blues and was filmed at Lupo's Heartbreak Hotel in Providence, Rhode Island. Brantley returns to Milwaukee occasionally during the summers to play with Leroy Airmaster at Summerfest, other festivals, and local venues.

Although a few musicians who performed in Milwaukee during the 1970s have passed or moved out of state, many continue to actively perform in the Milwaukee area. In April of 2017, surviving members of Short Stuff, which included Jim Liban, Junior Brantley, Jeff Dagenhardt, James Solberg, Kenny Berdoll, Eric Epstein, Jim Kirkpatrick, Mark Lamar, and 'Hotdog' Bob Mueller, were inducted into the Wisconsin Area Music Industry (WAMI) Hall of Fame.

Conclusion

It should be noted that all of these musicians have accomplished much more than what was recounted here, and that there are numerous musicians who were not discussed, such as Stokes, who deserve to be acknowledged for their contributions to Milwaukee music during that time period and for their substantial influence on other musicians.

Terry Frank:
"Terry Didn't Care about Money, He Just Wanted to 'Amp-up'"
by Bruce Cole[4]

I met Terry Frank around 1983. I joined his band Black Cat Bone. His wife Cheryl on bass, me on drums, and Terry playing loud—ZZ Top, Elmore James, and Buddy Guy stuff. He was somewhere in his early 30s at the time, I'd say, and already worn thin from very little sleep and a killer family and work schedule. He was 52 when he passed in 2009.

Terry was up early every morning working his day job and up late every night working on his slide—and keeping an eye on their small children. Gene Vincent always said: "I'll play anywhere, anytime." And that, for sure, was Terry in those early years. Murray Tap, Stockholders in West Allis, Mamie's on National, the Up 'n' Under on Brady, corner blues bars all over town, and not much over the bar at the end of the night. Terry didn't care about money; he just wanted to "amp-up" and rock.

Over the years Terry became a highly respected, major Miltown blues force. His bands worked Summerfest, for instance, every year, and only a handful of local blues acts can say that. As the decades rolled by, Terry would call me occasionally to play, and it would always be a pleasure—as well as a workout. He was never an arrogant player, and always a fun guy to be around.

When we started the Jean Cujé Milwaukee Music Collection at Marquette University libraries 10 years ago, Terry Frank was there with a generous donation—and he donated something every few months throughout the years.

Gary Huckleberry (see Chapter 10), a bandmate of Terry's over the years, called me from Florida a couple weeks ago and told me something that made me feel very good. He said he'd run into Terry Frank, who had recently moved down there and was living nearby. They talked about putting a duo together. Then Terry, out of the blue, said: "It'd be fun if Bruce Cole was down here to work with us."

Thanks Terry. We miss you and your wonderful playing.

---

4   Adapted with permission from Bobby Tanzilo and *OnMilwaukee*, 27 January 2009: https://onmilwaukee.com/music/articles/terryfrank.html.

Kenny Arnold:
"The Best Blues (Blues Rock) Drummer"
by Bruce Cole[5]

Just last week a friend told me that he had heard that Kenny Arnold was looking for a band. Arnie wanted to start playing again. Good news. I hadn't seen Kenny in half a decade. I missed hearing him play. We were good friends these past 45 years. (Kenny died in 2010. He was 61.)

We were close to the same age. I think we met at a Muskego Beach ballroom dance party in 1965 or 1966. We shared the stage; I was the drummer with the Grand Prix's (see Chapters 1 and 6) and Arnie was drumming with the Dynastys.

As young as he was, he steered and pushed that band with an old timer's feel and a rock solid groove. I didn't know the percussion terms, the drumming words, but my 17-year-old instincts told me that Kenny had that "precise beat," that strong, true "meter" that jazz drummers talked about in *Downbeat* (magazine). Of course, I for sure wasn't about to tell him that. Not for a few years anyway.

The obit I read this morning said he played with Short Stuff, the Rockin' Robins and the James Solberg Band. His Short Stuff years alone showed him to be, as I saw it, the best blues (or blues rock) drummer Milwaukee had ever come up with.

There were other, more famous names in his résumé. He played, in the 1970s, with the late, great, Grammy winning guitarist Luther Allison. He toured a couple years with Charlie Musselwhite (and, thanks in part to Arnie, I got that Musselwhite opportunity following his departure). And, he played with probably 20 or 30 other legendary Chicago blues icons and up-and- comers over the years, as well as all the local well-known types.

I don't know why he quit playing, or why he seemed to just disappear for maybe half a decade. I missed our occasional phone conversations. Now it's too late, too late for young drummers to hear and experience one of the best Milwaukee ever had to offer.

---

5   Adapted with permission from Bobby Tanzilo and *OnMilwaukee*, 9 June 2010: https://onmilwaukee.com/music/articles/kennyarnold.html.

Short Stuff playing at the Whitefish Bay High School Fieldhouse (1972)

Photo by James Middleton

Photo by Rich Zimmermann

Photograph by James Middleton

SHORT **S**TUFF

tGG
Post Office Box 5639
Milwaukee, Wis. 53211
Phone: (414)962-1500

THE
Jim Liban Blues Combo
Blues for Shut-ins

Photo by Francis Ford

Jon Paris
while with
OX (1973)

Photo by Rich Zimmermann

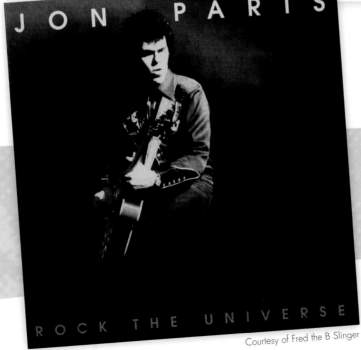

Courtesy of Fred the B Slinger

Photo by Francis Ford

Photo by Francis Ford; art and layout by Lindy Bostrom

Courtesy of Greg Koch

Photo by Jeff Dobbs

**Greg Koch performing
at the Les Paul 100th Anniversary
commemorative concert in Waukesha, WI**

Photo by Phillip Naylor

Muddy Waters
at Zak's (1976)

Courtesy of the Jean Cujé Collection

Zaks North Avenue

NORTH ave. AT HUMBOLDT ave.
264-1700

May 10-15

Muddy Waters

147

Koko Taylor at
Summerfest (1977)

Photo by Phillip Naylor

"Stokes," a popular
Milwaukee bluesman

Photo by James Brozek

**Willie Dixon at
Teddy's (1975)**

Photo by Phillip Naylor

**Jimmy Dawkins at
Century Hall (1977)**

Photo by Phillip Naylor

Photo by Rich Zimmermann

Omaha, performing in
Milwaukee in 1972

Courtesy of the Jean Cujé Collection

BLUES IN THE NIGHT

Terry Frank

Featuring:
Rick Holmes
Kenny Arnold
Jimmy Holsinger
Chuck Might

with Blues Harp Jimmy

WARREN ZIECH
Blues Band

Courtesy of the Jean Cujé Collection

Photo by Gary Porter

"Duet" by Blues great Hubert Sumlin
and Jeff Dagenhardt at Hubert's Milwaukee home

Jeff Dagenhardt
rock and blues
standout

Photo by Gary Porter

Photo by Maurice Seymour; courtesy of Ron Seymour

The G.T.O.'s, also known as Girls Take Over

CHAPTER 8

Milwaukee Women Rock Musicians

Rose Trupiano, an academic librarian at Marquette University and public radio DJ, biographically surveys some of the significant Milwaukee women's groups and individual artists, rich, albeit understudied subjects. An extended list of references enhances her essay and invites additional inquiry.

Milwaukee Women Rockers: A Survey
Rose Trupiano

This essay details some of the women who were a large part of the historical Milwaukee music scene. Although rock bands in the 1960s and the 1970s were predominantly male, there were some early, pioneering all-women and mixed gender bands.[1] In addition, the number of mixed gender bands has increased and is becoming much more common.

---

1 An early mixed gender band was Methyl Ethyl and the Keytones fronted by Amy Madigan, who later became a renowned actress and Oscar nominee (see http://sundayswithtodd.com/WebPages/MethylEthylAndTheKeTones/ MethylEthylAndTheKeTonesPhotoIndex.html). Significant duos have included Lightning & Thunder (Mike [d. 2006] and Claire Sardina; Claire still performs), Jack and Jill (Jensen) Grassel, and Paul Cebar and Claudia Schmidt.

With each new decade, more female singers, songwriters, and musicians have emerged to pursue careers in rock music.

The G.T.O.'s

In 1964, an all-female pop rock group was formed in Milwaukee called the G.T.O.'s (a.k.a. Girls Take Over/GTO/GTO's). The band was comprised of Cindy Lee Williams (vocals, guitar), Rinie Williams (vocals, drums), Wanda Williams (vocals, organ) and Gerri Gibson (vocals, guitar). The real last name of Cindy Lee, Rinie, and Wanda was Wilhelmi and Gibson's was Suskind. The G.T.O.'s played at a variety of clubs, bars, hotels and schools throughout the Midwest. In an interview with the *Milwaukee Journal*'s Divina Infusino, Cindy Lee commented on the audience's reaction to their music: "First they come to see us because we're all girls. Then they come because they like us" (Infusino 1997 [full citations are at the end of the chapter]).

The G.T.O.'s played a diverse set of music: rock and roll, R & B, Motown, folk rock, polka, country, and even novelty songs such as Cheech and Chong's "Basketball Jones." They covered many popular songs from the time period such as Melanie's "Candles in the Rain," Them's "Gloria" (in the G.T.O.s' rendition, the name was changed to "George"), Five Man Band Electrical Band's "Signs," the motion picture theme "Exodus," Jean Wright's "Mr. Bigstuff," Janis Joplin's "Me and Bobby McGee," and old country standards' such as the "Tennessee Waltz." In later years, the G.T.O.'s did some harder rock such as Black Sabbath's "Paranoid." The women took turns singing lead, and group was well-known for its tight three and four-part harmonies.

In 1965, the G.T.O.'s entered the *Milwaukee Sentinel*'s "Young America Rock 'N' Roll Revue" and were one of the local bands to make it to the semi-finals. The G.T.O.'s along with other local semi-finalists (predominately male) played to 6,000 audience members at the Milwaukee Auditorium on December 30, 1965. During this time period, the G.T.O.'s recorded a single, "Hi-Heel Sneakers" (originally recorded by Tommy Tucker) backed with a composition written by Cindy Lee, a slower number called "Stardust Come Back." The G.T.O.s' version of "Hi-Heel Sneakers" can be found on the CD compilation of Wisconsin artists, *Wisconsin Rocks Volume 9: 1964-1969*.

In 1970, the G.T.O.'s traveled overseas to entertain the American troops during the Vietnam War after a talent recruiter asked if they would be interested in playing at military clubs and bases in Southeast Asia. The women signed on for the venture not knowing what to expect. The tour would include two months in South Vietnam and two months in Guam and Thailand.

Once there, ferried by helicopters, the group performed three shows a night, seven days a week. In a personal interview, Cindy Lee Williams (now known as Cindy Wobst) spoke of the troubling conditions that the foursome encountered in war-torn Vietnam—the frightening sound of nearby gunfire; the constant fear of being attacked or ambushed; the heartbreaking poverty among the Vietnamese people; the crowded streets; and the irrepressible humidity and heat. However, the G.T.O.'s were very moved by the appreciative armed forces personnel they performed for during their tour. The group sensed the heartfelt and overwhelming gratitude of the servicemen and women. Their tour was dangerous, but the G.T.O.'s were happy to bring joy via their music.

A touching event happened after the G.T.O.'s returned to Milwaukee. While on their way to play a gig at a bar, they saw a man in a wheelchair going down the sidewalk on South Greenfield Avenue pulling another man on a hospital gurney. The girls wanted to stop and see if they could help, but their car was full of equipment and they were due to perform. Shortly later that evening, a commotion took place in the bar. People began getting up and moving tables and chairs around, making room for two new audience members—the man in the wheelchair and the other man on the hospital gurney. Both men were veterans and were being treated at the Milwaukee VA Hospital. They were in one of the audiences the G.T.O.'s performed before in Vietnam. When they heard that the same all-female rock band would be playing near them at a local bar, the men knew they just had to see them again. Between breaks, the G.T.O.'s had a very emotional visit with the men. The veterans told them how much they treasured the group's performance in Vietnam. To hear and see a live American band playing familiar music brought them a huge deal of comfort especially since the service men found themselves in the middle of a horrific war in a land so far from home.

After returning from Vietnam, the G.T.O.'s became a trio when Gibson left the group. In addition, the G.T.O.'s changed their name to Curtain Lace (because of a Frank Zappa-promoted group called the GTOs) and then to Lace. A year later, Loni James (vocals and guitar) joined the group and they continued to play gigs in the Midwest. Eventually, the band broke up in the mid-to-late 1970s as members started families.

As of 2015, two of the original members, Cindy Lee and Rinie, still live in Wisconsin. Gerri Gibson relocated to Florida and teaches guitar. Sadly, Wanda passed away at the age of 51 in 2004. In the years before Wanda's death, Lace would reunite and play for fundraisers or family parties (the last being for Wanda's 50th birthday.) Cindy continued to perform as a vocalist and bassist for the southeastern Wisconsin band, Cheap Date.[2]

Ruby Starr

During the early 1970s and 1980s, Milwaukee's most famous female rock performer undoubtedly was hard rocker Ruby Starr. She was a fiery, bold, bluesy, flamboyant, and sexy performer. Starr had a very powerful voice in the same vein as Janis Joplin but had her own style. She was small in stature, but her voice and her stage presence were huge.

Starr's original name was Constance Henrietta Mierzwiak and she was born in Toledo, Ohio in 1949. Connie Little, as she was known then, began singing at the age of eight belting out country and western songs. She had been known to sing "on flat-bed trucks in the parking lot of the local theater" and "near the concession stands at drive in theaters" (Yonke 2015).

Determined to be a singer, she dropped out of high school at the age of 16 and in her teens had several groups, including Connie and the Blu-Beats and the Blue Grange

---

2　With deep regret, I learned that Cindy passed away in 2018. She was a remarkable rocker who generously contributed to this essay.

Ramblers (BGR) (Muskovitz 2003?). In 1969 at the age of 20, Connie adopted the name of Ruby Jones and BGR morphed into the Ruby Jones Band. In 1971, her group was signed to the Curtom Record Label which was owned by Curtis Mayfield. They recorded the album *Ruby Jones* in the same year. In 1972, Ruby Jones released a single from the Ruby Jones LP—"You Better Run" (composed by Young Rascals members Felix Cavaliere and Eddie Brigati) with B-Side, Curtis Mayfield's composition, "Stone Junkie."

In 1972, Jim "Dandy" Magrum, the lead singer of the southern rock band Black Oak Arkansas (BOA) saw Ruby perform. He convinced her to leave the Ruby Jones group and join BOA as a back-up singer. It was at this time that she took on the stage name Ruby Starr. Starr was featured on the Black Oak Arkansas song "Jim Dandy," which became a top 30 hit in 1973. She toured with Black Oak Arkansas and sang backup on a handful of BOA albums.

In 1974, Ruby left BOA and BOA manager, Butch Stone became her manager. She began touring with Blackfoot, a band from Florida. On their tour, they played the Stardust in Los Angeles and *Variety* reviewer Todd described Starr as "potentially one of the most exciting rock acts around."

After her stint with Blackfoot, Starr met and began touring with the Wisconsin band, Grey Ghost which included Gary Levin (guitar), Marius Penczner (keyboards), David Mayo (bass) and Joel Williams (drums). They then became Ruby Starr and Grey Ghost and released a self-titled album on Capitol records in 1976. Four of the songs were co-written by Starr. In the same year, Starr also recorded her first solo album also on Capitol Records, also self-titled.

Her next recording was another solo LP, *Scene Stealer*, featuring Paul McCartney's "Maybe I'm Amazed." This song was also released as a single and was backed with the song, "Who's Who." On October 8, 1976, Starr (with backing from Black Oak Arkansas) performed "Maybe I'm Amazed" on the national television show, *The Midnight Special*.

Ruby Starr and Grey Ghost opened for Van Halen, Rod Stewart, Steppenwolf, Peter Frampton, Mahogany Rush, Bachman Turner Overdrive and J. Geils as well as Todd Rundgren, the Nitty Gritty Dirt Band, Black Sabbath and Black Oak Arkansas (Masino 2003).

In 1977, Starr recorded what was to be here final album on Capitol records, *Smoky Places*. Reviewed favorably by *Billboard*, this album contained a number of covers (Buddy Holly, Jackie DeShannon, etc.) and was a mixture of country, rock and pop.

Although Starr was from Ohio, by the end of the 1970s she had made Milwaukee her home. She played numerous gigs in the Midwest, packing the bars and clubs.

In 1979, Starr teamed with Lucy Grey, a band from Mayville, Wisconsin, resulting in a new group—Grey-Star (a.k.a. Grey Star.) Its members were Starr (lead vocals), Mike Findling (guitar, lead vocals), Robb Hanshaw (guitar, vocals), Freddie Hodnick (guitar, vocals), Steve "Pooh" Godfriarx (guitar), John Kerr (bass), and Dave Gruenwaldt—a.k.a. Mudslide (drums). Grey-Star issued two LPs both on Emotion records; the first was self-titled and released in 1981. The LP contained a number of originals and it received favorable reviews. The second Grey-Star album, *Telephone Sex*, came out in 1983; there were several cover songs, "Baby It's You" and "In Crowd," but a good number of the songs were originals.

In 1983, Grey-Star won a Wisconsin Area Music Industry award (WAMI) as Best Performers of the Year and Ruby Starr (of Grey-Star) won Best Female Vocalist (Cannariato 2015).

Grey-Star toured the country and during their tenure, opened for Van Halen, Allman Brothers, Cheap Trick, and Robin Trower. On December 7, 1982, the band had the honor of opening for the much anticipated Who concert in the Mecca Arena. This was the Who's first performance in Milwaukee and it drew 12,000 audience members. Grey-Star performed songs from their 1981 self-titled LP, including "Silhouette" and the Raganov/Bern song made popular by Janis Joplin and Big Brother and the Holding Company, "Piece of My Heart."

In 1983, Mike Gray (previous known as Mike Findling) left the group and the band was renamed the Ruby Star Band (Note: the second "r" of Starr was dropped in this new band name.) In 1984, their single was released on Emotion Records, "Under Your Spell" (side A) and "Pick up Speed" (side B). In 1985 they released a second single, "Secrets of the Heart" (side A) and "I'll Give You Everything" (side B). Mark Krueger, longtime friend and program director at Milwaukee's WQFM radio station, remembers that a music video of "Secrets of the Heart" was recorded at John Doe's Pub previously located at Vliet and 50th Street in Milwaukee.

Records & Reviews reported that two songs from Starr's group would be featured in the 1985 independent movie, *Pink Nights*: "Meet Me at the Same Time" and "You Don't Even Know"; film credits show they were performed by the Ruby Star Band. (*Pink Nights*).

In 1987, Starr was nominated for the Best Female Vocalist of the Year Award by WAMI and in 1988, again won the Best Female Vocalist of the Year award.

Ruby Starr at Humpin' Hannah's (1975)

Photo by Rich Zimmermann

157

In the early 1990s, Starr along with her drummer and long-time friend, Mudslide, moved to Las Vegas and played in clubs, casinos as well as hotels on the Strip such as the Riviera and Stardust (Jones 1995).

According to Mudslide, Starr was selected to perform in the Country Legends shows in Las Vegas. This would have been a great opportunity for a steady income and benefits. Unfortunately, before the contract was to be signed, Starr experienced a set of extremely severe headaches. Mudslide brought Starr to a doctor and after tests, learned the shocking and devastating news that Starr had lung cancer and a brain tumor. She had, perhaps, only six months to live. Mudslide moved Starr back to her home in Toledo to be with her family and helped her through hospice care. Starr died a year later, on January 14, 1995 at the age of 45. Starr was laid to rest in Toledo Memorial Cemetery.

Starr lives on through the Internet and YouTube where fans have posted numerous videos of her live performances from decades past. Starr continues to have a strong, loyal fan base. Raging Slab, a country rock group, wrote and recorded the tribute song, "Ruby (For Miss Ruby Starr)." Black Oak Arkansas also performs the Grand Funk Railroad song, "Heartbreaker" as a tribute to her.

After Starr's death, several of her albums have been reissued. The original 1971 *Ruby Jones* album has been renamed *Stone Junkie* and was re-released in 2000 and includes the bonus track, "You Better Run." The 1981 *Grey-Star* LP and the 1983 *Telephone Sex* LP were released as a single CD in 2003 by Mean Mountain Music and were re-titled *Grey-Star and the Great Ruby Starr*. In 1995, Ruby Starr was inducted into WAMI's Hall of Fame becoming the first female (albeit posthumously) to achieve this honor. For an excellent, detailed biography of Starr, see Susan Masino's chapter "Ruby Starr" in *Wisconsin Musicians* (source provided below).

The Shivvers

One of the best well-known and highly regarded Milwaukee bands in the late 1970s and early 1980s was the female-fronted Shivvers featuring Jill Kossoris (see also Chapter 9). The Shivvers were referred to as a power pop/new wave punk band and were described by OnMilwaukee.com music critic Bobby Tanzilo as "part Blondie, part Raspberries" (Tanzilo 2014).

Kossoris grew up in the Milwaukee area and studied classical piano for a number of years. As a teen, she joined several local rock bands. In the late 1970s, she sought to create a pop punk band which would become the Shivvers. The group featured Kossoris (lead vocalist, piano/keyboard player and songwriter); Jim Richardson (drums); Jim Eannelli (lead guitar); Mike Pyle (rhythm guitar/vocals) and Rich Bush (bass). Bassist-songwriter-vocalist Scott Krueger subsequently replaced Bush.

The Shivvers were massively popular in the Milwaukee area and played venues such as Zak's, Teddy's, the Palms and the Starship. They played numerous gigs in the Midwest especially Madison and Chicago. They opened for such acts as Iggy Pop and the Romantics (Ankeny) as well as for the Shoes and the Stooges (Warner 2006).

In 1980, the Shivvers recorded a single at Gold Star Studio in Milwaukee. Their 7-inch record contained two songs written by Kossoris, "Teen Line" (side A) and "When

I was Younger" (side B). The single was released on their own record label, Flip Top. The 45-recording brought favorable reviews from a number of music critics nationwide. "Teen Line" was a catchy, upbeat song while "When I was Younger" was an edgier rock number. Kossoris' voice was lively and upbeat. The Shivvers were excellent musicians and their music was high energy, fresh, fun and danceable.

It was the hope that the Shivvers would get a record label contract in the early 1980s. Recording artist Eric Carmen (front man of the 1970s group the Raspberries) expressed interest in them. Kossoris was a huge fan of Carmen whom she viewed as a large musical influence. Kossoris and Carmen's paths had crossed twice. In the late 1970s, Kossoris, a student at Brown Deer High School, entered and won a contest that brought the Raspberries to perform at her school (Warner 2006). In 1981, Kossoris, an Eric Carmen fan club member, sent him a copy of "Teen Line"/"When I was Younger" along with a videotape of the Shivvers performing "Teen Line." According to Divina Infusino in the *Milwaukee Journal*, Carmen saw the video, was impressed and telephoned Kossoris. Carmen produced a demo tape of the Shivvers that was sent to several record labels. He also expressed interest in producing their first album. Unfortunately, the Shivvers did not get the backing of a record label and no album was made.

Courtesy of Jill Kossoris

Although disappointed, Kossoris and Krueger continued to write songs and the band recorded a number of performances on video. In 1982, a *Milwaukee Journal* poll voted the Shivvers as Best Local Band. They were also getting known internationally. The Shivvers have been a "minor indie hit in Japan right from the earliest days" (Schultz 2006).

However, in the early summer of 1982, the Shivvers disbanded. Kossoris was in Nashville working as a songwriter and several other members moved to different states to pursue other music interests. In 1989, the band did get back together to record the single "Remember Tonight" (Gilvear 2012).

In 2001, Kossoris recorded an alt-country rock solo album, *Invisible*, which received very favorable reviews. The CD contained fourteen originals by Kossoris and was produced by Mike Hoffman and Kossoris. Kossoris was backed by ex-bandmates, Richardson (drums) and Krueger (guitar and bass). Joining them were fellow Milwaukee musicians, including Violent Femme Victor Joseph DeLorenzo (snare), Hoffman (guitar, bass, and vocals), and melaniejane (cello). Kossoris' CD contains mature, well-written songs including the beautiful "Rise" and "Beautiful Dream" and the haunting "Back to the Well" and "Invisible."

In 2003, a Shivvers' album was finally released *Til the Word Gets Out*. The album was released on the Hyped to Death label and contains 18 of the songs originally recorded by the Shivvers in the 1970s and 1980s. The album also contains six songs from the Orbits, a Milwaukee band in which Krueger and Richardson were in before they joined the Shivvers. *The Philadelphia Weekly* critic reviewed the work calling it "thrilling" and that the song, "Teen Line" is "arguably one of the most magnificent pop singles of its time" (Keyes 2017). *Victim of Time* calls the album "an essential piece of pop history" and that it had received "stellar reviews from *Bomp* and *NY Rocker*" (Cross). Hatch-Miller from *Dusted Magazine* wrote: "Best power pop band that you never heard in your life."

In 2009, Sing Sing Records re-mastered the Shivvers' originally recorded material from 1979-1981 to create released LP/CD, *The Shivvers: Lost Hits from Milwaukee's First Family of Power Pop: 1979-82*. It was also released in Japan as the Shivvers have a big following there (Noble). The album contains the 20 original Shivvers' songs plus five bonus videos of the band's 1980s performances. In 2014, a newer remixed and remastered version of the album came out containing 12 of their previously released songs and one newly released song.

Although it took decades for the Shivvers' songs to be released, their music and lyrics are timeless and just as original and captivating today as they were in the 1970s and 1980s. Their recordings are now being discovered by today's audiences worldwide.

Kossoris currently resides in the Milwaukee area and has a successful career as a songwriter for Mystery Train Publishing.

Julie Brandenburg/Julie Niedziejko

Julie Brandenburg (previously known as Julie Niedziejko) is a multi-talented composer, musician, singer and music instructor from Milwaukee. She is classically trained and earned a B.A. from the University of Wisconsin-Milwaukee (UWM) in music education/vocal studies and an M.A. from UWM in music theory and composition. Brandenburg has been a longtime member of the Milwaukee rock music scene.

Niedziejko performed with the psychedelic Milwaukee Liquid Pink band in the 1980s before founding in the early 1990s, True Heart Susie, a female-fronted progressive rock band, with herself on piano and vocals along with Tom Dougherty (drums), Jeff Hamilton (guitars), Steve Tyczkowski (bass), and Tom Hansen (violin). They released two CDs, *Three Sheets* (1994) and *Lately Story* (1997). Dave Luhrssen favorably reviewed *Lately Story* in *Billboard* noting that the "songs' chords have more in common with classical music than rock" and have "memorable melodies with rock energy."

Brandenburg also created a harder rock progressive band called Quark Quintet and later the Julie B Well whose music was described by *ExpressMilwaukee.com* as "intricate chamber rock infused with full-throttle metal dynamics." In 2006, she recorded a more pop-oriented solo CD – *Story So Far*. Brandenburg has opened for Green Day and Lowen & Navarro. She has also written music scores for feature films and teaches songwriting at her alma mater, UWM, as well as voice, piano, music appreciation, and songwriting at the Milwaukee Area Technical College. In addition, Brandenburg owns and operates Be Sound Music Studio offering voice and piano lessons, performance coaching, and group recording services. She continues to write, perform, and teach in the Milwaukee area.

Ronnie Nyles

Ronnie Nyles is a well-known female singer/songwriter/guitarist in the Milwaukee area and eight-time WAMI–winner. She has performed solo, as part of a duo, and with rock back-up bands. She has played numerous festivals, concerts, clubs, fairs and events all through the Midwest and had also gone on tour through Europe, Australia and Canada.

Nyles' has a distinctive, powerful voice and she is able to sing and play guitar in a number of genres, including rock, folk, blues, country and pop. Nyles won her first WAMI in 1989 when she was part of a country duo with fellow musician, Chris Gerard. Located in Green Bay, they were called Ladysmith and their WAMI was for Best Country Band.

LadySmith disbanded in 1990 and Ronnie joined the country group Sky Harbor Band, which played in Milwaukee and Chicago. Shortly afterwards, Nyles left to perform solo and start several new groups. She founded the Ronnie Nyles & Chix Mix band which included Tina Dimmer (drums, percussion), Mia Montenegro (guitar), and Melissa Beastrom (piano). The band disbanded in the early 2000s, however, Nyles continued as a solo act or with percussionist Dimmer. She has also worked with a number of backing bands including the group, Tallulah Who. Tallulah Who was comprised of Tommy Capponi (drums), Damon Landro (bass, vocals), Guy Crucianelli (guitar, vocals), and Dimmer (keyboards, synthesizer, percussion). In 2016, Nyles and Tallulah Who became the Ronnie Nyles Band, and they perform popular and harder rock songs.

Nyles has been nominated numerous times for WAMI Awards. In addition to the 1989 Best Country Band, Nyles has also won Best Country Artist (1990); Best Female Vocalist (2004, 2007 and 2009); Best Pop Adult Contemporary Artist (2008); and Best Pop Artist—Ronnie Nyles and Tallulah Who (2009.) She also received two Wisconsin People's Choice Awards in 2003 and 2008.

As of 2015, Nyles has released two CDs, one EP and a single. The CDs *Leaving Rome* (1990) and *January Weather* (2002) both contain original songs by Nyles and fellow musician Greg Girard. Girard also produced portions of both CDs with Nyles and fellow musician, Kevin Patrick. For the *It's Christmas* EP (2013), Nyles teamed up with local musician Greg Lathe to write and record five holiday songs including the "Let Freedom Ring" holiday tribute to the U.S. armed forces. In 2014, Nyles released a new single, "Movin' On" and in 2016, "Where does Love Go?" Nyles has shared the stage with Joan Jett and the Blackhearts, Melissa Etheridge, Lucinda Williams, The Indigo Girls, Night Ranger, Kansas, Death Cab for Cutie, Daryl Stuermer, and Cheap Trick.

As an activist, Nyles has supported a number of causes (including animal rescue groups and equestrian rights advocate groups) and has volunteered to play at numerous fund-raisers. In 2012, she founded SheRocks Wisconsin whose "goal is to support, connect, promote and recognize women in all music genres and all areas of Wisconsin's Music Industry." SheRocks Wisconsin also provides educational and developmental programs as well as opportunities for emerging talents to perform.

In addition to continuing to write, record and perform, Nyles is co-owner of a successful recording studio, Stella Productions / Stella Studios in Milwaukee.

Sue DaBaco

In 1998, Chicago native, blues/rock singer, songwriter and guitarist Sue DaBaco moved to Milwaukee. For seven years prior, DaBaco was part of Buzz Kilman (a regular on the Jonathon Brandmeir's WLUP 79.9 FM radio show) and the All Bubba Blues Band. DaBaco played lead and rhythm guitar as well as fronted some songs. The band played all the major festivals and venues in Chicago and opened for such headliners as Jefferson Starship, Koko Taylor, The Fabulous Thunderbirds, Dave Mason, Eddy Money and Lonnie Brooks. When the band dissolved, DaBaco moved to Milwaukee and started her own band.

In Milwaukee, DaBaco created the Sue DaBaco and Wise Fools band with local musicians, Scott Walters (bass), and Darrel Douglas (drums); they played many of the famous festivals in Milwaukee including Harley Fest, and have opened for major acts such as Lynyrd Skynyrd, Peter Frampton, Sharon Jones and the Dap Kings, Koko Taylor, Jeff Beck, .38 Special, Sue Foley, and Milwaukee blues guitarist Greg Koch. DaBaco continued playing lead and rhythm guitar and was the band's main vocalist and songwriter. She is an excellent lead guitar player. Her only formal education on guitar was tuning and chord structure. She learned everything else by ear and by watching other musicians.

DaBaco and Wise Fools were a very high-energy blues rock group. They played original songs by DaBaco and covered Hendrix, Muddy Waters and other rock and blues artists. In May 2008, they participated in the Grafton Blues Challenge held in Grafton, Wisconsin, and took first place. This success led to an invitation to compete with blues bands from all over the world in the 2009 International Blues Challenge held in Memphis, Tennessee. DaBaco's band won the Club Favorite honor and was ranked in the top 20 of over 200 competing bands. In 2010, DaBaco's band was nominated for a WAMI for Best Blues Band.

DaBaco has also traveled to Eastern Europe and has played with blues bands in clubs and festivals in Poland and Lithuania. While in Poland, DaBaco made a solemn visit to the Auschwitz death camp, inspiring her to write and record a very haunting beautiful instrumental called "Notes from the Underground." This song appears on Sue DaBaco and Wise Fools' CD titled *Voodoo Juice* released in 2007 on Happy Accident Records. The CD features 10 original songs penned by DaBaco and one cover, Jimi Hendrix's "Voodoo Chile."

In 2010, DaBaco released two news songs—"Crucify" and "Ten Feet Tall" (a beautiful slower rock and blues number with meaningful lyrics and excellent musicianship.) "Crucify" was recorded at Limelight Studio with WAMI nominated producer Joey Halbur, mixed by Steve Hamilton of Makin' Sausage Music, and produced by DaBaco and Steve Hamilton.

After Wise Fools disbanded, DaBaco formed Sue DaBaco and the Double Down Band which includes Craig Omick (percussion, drums, vocals), Darrel Douglas (drums, percussion), Randy Strumberger (bass, acoustic guitar, vocals), and Michael Caldwell (saxophone). In 2014 the band went on temporary hiatus. DaBaco was hoping to pursue a possible different path in music, focusing more on songwriting and production as well as progressive and acoustic guitar playing. Since then, DaBaco has created a number of excellent rock/blues originals including the psychedelic-tinged instrumental, "Hypnotique." In 2014, DaBaco earned an M.B.A. at Alverno College.

Currently Sue DaBaco and the Double Down Band continue to perform in the Milwaukee area, playing blues festivals and other venues.

Michelle Anthony

Originally from Kansas City Missouri, Michelle Anthony moved to Milwaukee in 1992 to attend Marquette University. She earned a bachelor's degree in English in 1996 and a Master of Physical Therapy degree in 1999. During that same year, Michelle, her husband, Scott Anthony, along with two other musicians formed Capital 8, a popular Milwaukee band. The group was comprised of Michelle (lead vocals, bass and keyboards), Scott (lead guitar), Mike Christiansen (lead vocals, rhythm guitar), and John Chipman (drums, percussion). Capital 8's music was primarily pop rock with some alt-country. They released two albums on Sparkler Records, *Reason* (2001) and *Payola* (2002). With the advent of the Internet, Capital 8 was able to get their music directly to the public. Capital 8's songs, "Love in the Title" and "100" both from the *Reason* CD were on MP3.com's pop/rock charts, reaching the top 50 of the national chart and topping the Milwaukee chart in the spring of 2001. The band's songs were well-crafted, catchy and melodious originals. Their recordings displayed excellent musicianship and there was variety with two lead singers. The band performed at many venues in the Milwaukee area including Shank Hall, Summerfest, the Globe, and Reed Street Station, and opened for national acts such as Shelby Lynne, k.d. lang, Ben Folds, Mindy Smith, Amy Rigby, Robbie Fulks, the Silos, Junior Brown, Bob Schneider, and Sophie B. Hawkins.

In 2004, Capital 8 disbanded and Anthony created another music group, Stick Pony comprised of Amy (lead vocals, piano, bass, organ), Scott Anthony (lead, rhythm guitar), Chris DeMay (guitar, harmonica), Ryan Stang (bass, organ), and Nick Verban (drums, percussion). Stick Pony backed Anthony on her successful, euphonious 2004 solo alt-country CD, *Stand Fall Repeat* released on Burn and Shiver Records. Anthony worked with the late former Wilco member, Jay Bennett, on the CD and it received very favorable reviews. In 2005, Anthony performed at the prestigious South by Southwest concert.

In 2011, Anthony moved to Austin, Texas and continues to write, record and perform. In 2006, she released *Frozenstarpalace* which received positive reviews from *Austin Chronicle*, *LA Daily*, *Milwaukee Journal Sentinel*, *Pop Matters*, and other sources. In 2010, she released the *Tornadoes* CD which also received positive reviews. In addition, Anthony's music has been featured in the "independent film Black Cloud as well in releases of the television series "The Wonderfalls" and "Roswell." Her songs have been heard in the MTV shows "Pimp My Ride", "Making the Band", and "Operation 17" (Musicxray).

As a solo artist, Michele has performed hundreds of shows around the country including in Los Angeles, Chicago, New York City, and West Virginia.

Other Significant Women Rockers

Other significant performers entered the music scene in Milwaukee in the 1990s including (Kelly Ann) Keedy and Marie Ulsberger of Wanda Chrome (Ulsberger) And the Leather Pharaohs. Dropmore Scarlet was formed in 2001 and was comprised of Kari Bloom (lead vocals), Kristen Kakatsch (guitars, drums and vocals), Laura Proeber (bass), and Ginny Wiskowski (drums, guitar, vocals). In 2004, the group released a self-titled CD on their independent label. Dropmore Scarlet later disbanded with three of the four members forming an all-female rockabilly band, Crazy Rocket Fuel (Snyder 2015). Crazy Rocket Fuel consists of Bloom (lead vocals, guitar), Ginny Wiskowski (lead guitar, vocals), Laura Proeber (stand-up bass), and Deb Bricault (drums and vocal). In 2010 the group released a CD filled with fun, hard-driving, original rockabilly numbers. As of 2015, Crazy Rocket Fuel was performing at numerous clubs, bars, and festivals in the Midwest.

Other recent female Milwaukee bands include The Barrettes, a punk rock band featuring JoAnn Riedl (vocals, guitar), Kari Lynn (bass, vocals), Joolz (drums) and Joey Zocher (vocals, guitar); the Addy Janes with Ashley Dolhun (vocals, keyboards), Carlan Johnson (guitars), Stacey Zwirlen (drums, vocals); and Vic and Gab, two sisters originally from Texas whose pop and rock is becoming known nationwide. There is also singer/songwriter/pianist Jayme Dawicki who has released three CDs and whose songs have been "licensed on television shows on MTV, NBC, the CW, the Style Network and the Lifetime Network" (Johns 2015). Peggy James released her fourth album in 2018. In addition, there are numerous mixed gender bands such as Annie B. and the Complication; the Whips; Red Knife Lottery; the Sugar Stems; GGOOLLD; Call Me Lightning; the Delphines; the Altos; Old Earth; Hello Death; Body Futures; the Twang Dragons; October Soul; Sin Bad; Rocket Paloma; Rocket Cat, and Heidi Spencer and the Rare Birds (a group getting international attention [recently featured on the BBC]). The number of female rockers continues to grow adding to the diversity of the Milwaukee rock music scene.

Conclusion

In addition to Nyles' SheRocks Wisconsin, there are several other Milwaukee organizations to help support the music careers of Milwaukee women--Milwaukee Chick Singer Night, providing opportunities for local female artists to perform and Ladies Rock Milwaukee, a three-day intensive music band camp for women musicians over 21 years of age. In addition, Girls Rock Milwaukee is a week-long day camp for girls aged 8-16. Girls

Rock Milwaukee was founded by businesswoman, Valerie Lucks, and local musician, Ashley Smith (the Whips and Red Knife Lottery) and its mission is to empower girls of all backgrounds through music education and performance. Organizations such as these will help to ensure a strong and vibrant future of female artists in the Milwaukee rock music scene.

Bibliography

Ankeny, Jason. Artist Biography – Jill Kossaris. http://www.allmusic.com/artist/shivvers-mn0000715297/biography. Web. Accessed 12 July 2017.

Anthony, Michelle. "Re: Interview." Message to the author. 3 February 2015. E-mail.

Borack, John M. "The Shivvers: Lost Hits from Milwaukee's First Family of Powerpop: 1972-82." *Shake Some Action: The Ultimate Power Pop Guide.* Not Lame Recording Company, 2007. 86–87. Print.

"Capital 8 Really Proud of New `Payola' - Modern-Rock Band with a Hint of Country Is at Shank Hall Tonight." *Milwaukee Journal Sentinel,* 31 January 2003, E16. *Google News.* Web. Accessed 15 February 2015.

Burns, Peter. Stone Junkie. Liner Notes. CD. Sequel Records. Np: 2002.

Cannariarto, Joe. "For Grey-Star No Room at Top." *Milwaukee Journal,* 11 June 1982, 4:14. *Google News.* Web. Accessed 20 January 2015.

_____. "Latest Albums Underscore Thriving Rock Scene." *Milwaukee Sentinel,* 12 February 1982, B7. *Google News.* Web. Accessed 20 January 2015.

Celine, Bonny. "Music Playing Together, Staying Together." *Milwaukee Journal,* 21 November 1981, Accent: 1. *Google News.* Web. Accessed 28 January 2015.

Cross, Brett. "EXHUMED: The Shivvers CD." *Victim of Time.com.* http://victimoftune,cin/articles/exhumed-shivvers/. 2 October 2006. Web. Accessed 7 July 2017,

DaBaco, Sue. "Re: Interview." Message to the author. 26 January 2015." E-mail.

Discogs. Ruby Starr Discography. https://www.discogs.com/artist/1234070-Ruby-Starr. Web. Accessed 10 July 2017.

Gilbertson, Jon. "Capital 8 Really Proud of New 'Payola.'" *Milwaukee Journal Sentinel* 31 January 2003, E16. *Google News.* Web. Accessed 2 February 2015.

Gilvear, Kevin. "Milwaukee on the Wild Side: An Interview with Jill Kossoris. *The Digital Fix Music.* 2 March 2012. Web. Accessed 14 January 2015.

"Girls Rock Milwaukee." *GIRLS ROCK MKE.* Web. Accessed 15 February 2015.

Hebert, Lou. "Ruby Starr....A Toledo Gem Remembered." *Toledo Gazzette.* 15 January 2014. Web. Accessed 14 February 2015.

Gruenewaldt, Dave (Mud Slide). Telephone Interview. 10 July 2017.

Hatch-Miller, Rob. CD Baby. https://store.cdbaby.com/cd/shivvers. Web. 12 July 2017.

Higgins, Terry. "True Heart Susie Songs Pack Punch." *Milwaukee Sentinel* 3 September 1993, D18. *Google News*. Accessed 20 January 2015.

Infusino, Divina. "A Fairy Tale in Real Life." *Milwaukee Journal*, 1 October 1982, sec. 3:1+. *Google News*. Web. Accessed 15 January 2015.

_____. "Female Band Rocks in a Man's World." *Milwaukee Journal* 28 December 1979, sec. 2: 1. *Google News*. Web. Accessed 10 January 2015.

Johns, Jamie. "Jayme Dawicki - Milwaukee Pianist." JJPlays.com. Web. 16 Feb. 2015.

Jones, Meg. "Ruby Starr, "Gutsy, Soulful' Rock Singer, Dies." *Milwaukee Sentinel*, 17 January 1995, A5. *Google News*. Web. Accessed 20 January 2015.

"The Julie B Well's Well-Composed Rock." *ExpressMilwaukee.com*. 2 March 2009. Web. Accessed 16 February 2015.

"Julie Brandenburg." *MATCMusic.com*. Web. 14 February 2015.

Koch, Bob. "Vinyl Cave: Milwaukee Is in the Reissue Spotlight with Vic Pitts & The Cheaters, The Shivvers, and Radio Ready Wisconsin - Isthmus." *TheDailyPage*. 3 August 2014. Web. Accessed 15 February 2015.

Keyes, J. Edward. "Records to Buy – Till the Word Gets Out by the Shivvers. *Philadelphia Weekly*. http://www.philadelphiaweekly.com/music/buy-these-records/article_8b48296b-2030-5c4c-ac76-ce6e56e226ca.html. Web. 12 July 2017.

Krueger, Mark. Personal Interview. 3 July 2017.

Larkin, Colin, ed. "Black Oak Arkansas." *Encyclopedia of Popular Music* 2011: 2006. Print.

Lisheron, Mark. "As Ruby Starr, Singer Had Big Voice on Local Scene." *Milwaukee Journal*, 17 January 1995, B1. *Google News*. Web. Accessed 2 February 2015.

Luhrssen, Dave. "Continental Drift - Milwaukee." *Billboard* 110.2 (10 January1998): 11. *Proquest ABI/Inform*. Web. Accessed 20 January 2015.

Maples, Tina. "Ruby Star Still Aims for the Top of the Rock Ladder." *Milwaukee Journal*, 23 August 1985, A5. *Google News*. Web. 20 January 2015.

Masino, Susan. "Ruby Starr" *Famous Wisconsin Musicians*. Pp. 43-48. Oregon, WI: Badger Books, 2003. Print.

"Musicians Donate Proceeds of Song to Help Ban Horse Slaughter." *Saving America's Horses*. 28 March 2010. Web. Accessed 15 February 2015.

McCormick, Moira and Karen O'Connor. "… Wisconsin Music Awards." *Billboard*, vol. 100, no. 49, Dec. 02, 1988, p. 64 Entertainment *Industry Archive*. Web. Accessed 10 July 2017.

"Music-Records: …Ruby Starr: Scene Stealer." Variety, vol. 284, no. 9, Oct. 06, 1976, pp. 62, 64, Entertainment Industry Magazine Archive. Web. Accessed 10 July 2017.

Musicxray. Michelle Anthony. http://www.musicxray.com/xrays/464502. Web. Accessed 10 July 2017.

Muskovitz, Mike. Liner notes. *Grey-Star and the Great Ruby Starr*. CD. Mean Mountain Music, 2003?

Noble, Tim. "Interview with the Shivvers." *Milwaukee Rock Posters*. WMSE, Milwaukee. 7 June 2014. http://www.wmse.org/archives/?time=572400. Radio.

Pink Nights Soundtrack. http://www.imdb.com/title/tt0089810/soundtrack?ref_=tt_trv_snd. Web. Accessed 10 July 2017.

Posniak, Alan. "Badger Beat: Wisconsin Bands and Combos." *Milwaukee Journal*, 22 November 1967, 3:1+. *Google News*. Web. Accessed 2 February 2015.

Roller, Peter. *Milwaukee Garage Bands: Generations of Grassroots Rock*. Charleston, SC: The History Press, 2013. Print.

Rombes, Nicholas. *A Cultural Dictionary of Punk: 1974-1982*. New York: Continuum, 2009. Print.

"Ronnie Nyles Is Back with Chix Mix." *Pride Guide*. Milwaukee, WI. 2001. 72. Web.

Samuels, Lennox. "Sound Ideas: Here's what's Spinning in Local Recordings." *Milwaukee Journal* 8 May 1981, sec. 3: 11. *Google News*. Web. Accessed 10 January 2015.

Schultz, Blaine. "Milwaukee's Pop Shivvers Get a New Lease on Life." *OnMilwaukee.com*. 19 May 2006. Web. Accessed 15 January 2015.

_____. "Unsung Heroes of Milwaukee Music: The Shivvers (Sing Sing Records)." *Scene Newspaper*, 1 August 2014. Web. Accessed 8 February 2015.

"SheRocks Wisconsin." *SheRocks Wisconsin*. Web. Accessed 14 February 2015.

Snyder, Molly. "Crazy Rocket Fuel Launches into New Year." *OnMilwaukee.com*. 7 January 2015. Web. Accessed 2 February 2015.

"Sounding Board-True Heart Susie in Category of Its Own."

Journal Times.com. 25 May 1995. Web. Accessed 20 January 2015.

Spletter, Mary. "A Report from Vietnam Volunteers." *Milwaukee Sentinel* 12 June 1971, sec: 2:7+. *Google News*. Web. Accessed 10 January 2015.

Tanzilo, Bobby. "What's Shakin' with The Shivvers?" *OnMilwaukee.com*. 17 June 2014. Web. Accessed 20 January 2015.

_____. "Anthony Does Double Duty with Stick Pony and Capital 8." *OnMilwaukee.com*. 12 January 2004. Web. Accessed 20 January 2015.

Todd. "Night Club Reviews: Starwood L.A., Ruby Starr, Blackfoot". Variety, vol. 290, no. 1, Feb. 08, 1978, p.67. *Entertainment Industry Magazine Archive*. Web. Accessed 10 July 2017.

"Top Album Picks: *Billboards's* Recommended LPs…Ruby Starr - Smokey Places." *Billboard*, vol. 89, no. 21, May 28, 1977, pp. 78, 80. *Entertainment Industry Magazine Archive*. Web. Accessed 10 July 2017.

"Top Album Picks: *Billboards's* Recommended LPs...Ruby Starr - Smokey Places." *Billboard*, vol. 89, no. 24, Jun. 18, 1977, pp.76, 78, *Entertainment Industry Magazine Archive*. Web. Accessed 10 July 2017.

"Vote for Your Favorite ROCK 'N' ROLL BAND to Appear at The Sentinel Young America Rock 'N' Roll Revue Finals, Dec. 30." *Milwaukee Sentinel*, 3 Dec. 1965, 1:10. *Google News*. Web. Accessed 12 February 2015.

Warner, Chuck. Liner Notes. *The Shivvers: Lost Hits from Milwaukee Powerpop*. CD. Hyped-2Death. Westminster, MA, 2006. Print.

"We Examine the Growing Presence of Women in Local Music in Episode 3 of On The Record." *Milwaukee Record*. Web. Accessed 16 February 2015.

Widen, Larry. *Milwaukee Rock and Roll*. Charleston, SC: Arcadia Pub, 2014. Print.

Wisconsin Association Music Industry. *A Powerful Lineup Descends Upon The Milwaukee Ale House* Milwaukee: Wisconsin Association Music Industry. 6 October 2003. Web. Accessed 10 January 2015.

Wobst, Cindy. Telephone Interview. 17 September 2014.

Wobst, Cindy. Re: Interview." Message to the author. E-mail. Accessed 16 February 2015.

Yonke, David. "Starr's Talent as a Singer, Friend Always Shone Bright." *Toledo Blade*, 18 January 1995, 2: 1. *Google News*. Web. Accessed 2 February 2015.

Photo by Maurice Seymour, courtesy of Ron Seymour

The G.T.O.'s

Photo by Rich Zimmermann

**Methyl Ethyl and the Keytones
(with Amy Madigan) at the UWM Union
(1972)**

The Shivvers, a Milwaukee powerpop
and punk group (1970s)

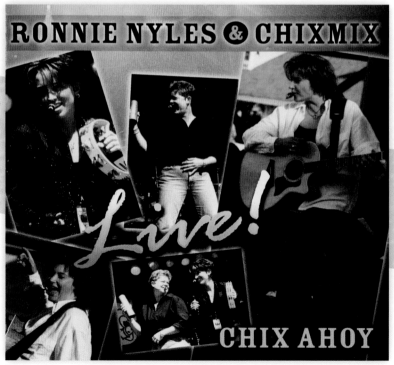

Photo by Rebecca Ornick

Blues/rocker Sue DaBaco at Summerfest 2012

Photo by Erol Reyal

Robyn (Robin) Pluer

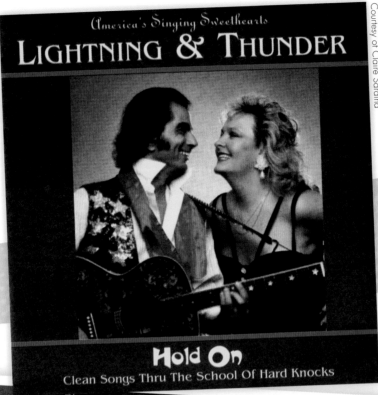

Courtesy of Claire Sardina

Photo by Erol Reyal

Jack and Jill Jazz (Jill Jensen and Jack Grassel) performing at The 35th annual WAMI Awards, held at Turner Hall Ballroom, Milwaukee, WI (2015)

Connie Grauer from Mrs. Fun performing at Bastille Days, Cathedral Square (2003)

Photo by Erol Reyal

Kim Zick from Mrs. Fun performing at Bastille Days, Cathedral Square, Milwaukee (2003)

Photo by Erol Reyal

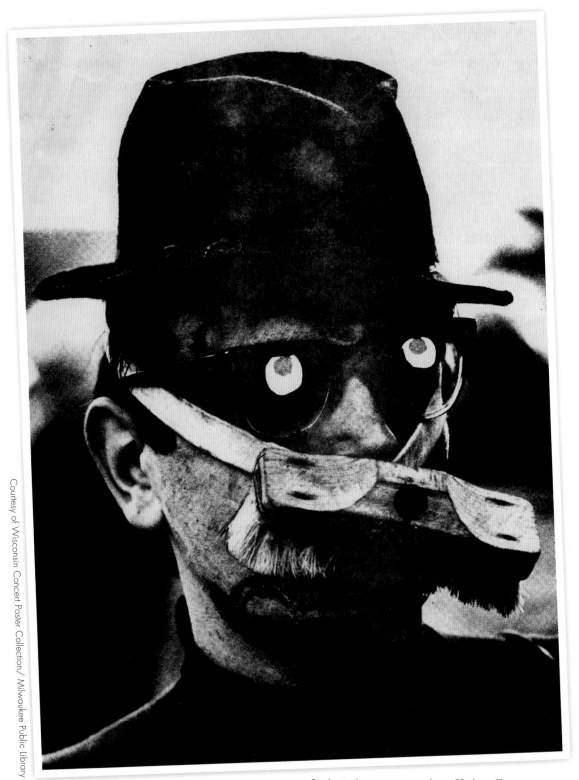

A photo from a poster for a Violent Femmes
performance at the Jazz Gallery on Center Street

CHAPTER 9

Punk and Post-Punk

David Luhrssen experienced most, if not all, of Milwaukee's punk and post-punk scene. He pulled an unpublished essay from his files and melded it with a piece he wrote for *Impulse*, a short-lived publication. He describes Milwaukee's vital punk and post-punk era, its groups, its clubs, and its social significance. Arguably Milwaukee's most famous rock band, the Violent Femmes, achieved remarkable notoriety with albums like *The Violent Femmes* (1983; certified platinum in 1991), *Hallowed Ground* (1984), and *The Blind Leading the Naked* (1986, produced by the Talking Heads' Jerry Harrison, a Milwaukee native). According to the *Rolling Stone Encyclopedia of Rock & Roll*: "Milwaukee's Violent Femmes cornered the market for frantic, angry acoustic post-punk folk rock" (George-Warren and Romanowski, eds. 2001, 1038). At that time, the group splintered rather than split. David Luhrssen recalls their subsequent brief 2013 reunion. Emerging from punk and post-punk, Evan Rytlewski surveys the alt-rock scene, particularly bands' rising and dashed aspirations regarding relations with major record labels. Putting aside alt-rock as a moniker, groups asserted their independence into the 2000s and perceived themselves as "indies."

The Punk and Post-Punk Era
by David Luhrssen

In 1981, a few years before succumbing to leukemia, Milwaukee musician David Wolf made a telling observation about his hometown. The keyboardist, who before his death founded the gothic techno-dance combo Dark Façade, was driving across the Hoan Harbor Bridge when he turned to me, his passenger, and remarked, "This city looks just like Prague."

The Warsaw Pact analogy did not seem at all farfetched. The winter sky was as gray as the sea of shuttered warehouses and padlocked factories that stretched across the horizon. A forest of dormant chimneys competed for air with church steeples. As in many an old Eastern European city, a parish rose from every block.

At that time the biggest musical news from Milwaukee concerned Wendy O. Williams. It seems that the vice squad spotted an article in the *Milwaukee Sentinel* about an upcoming Plasmatics concert and decided to crash the show. The evening ended as officers played racquetball with the singer against a curbstone in back of the Palms nightclub on State Street.[1]

Fast forward to the early 1990s. The Violent Femmes, forced to debut on Milwaukee sidewalks because Milwaukee clubs wouldn't have them, are a national phenomenon. The BoDeans are touching the charts. Plasticland are credited with launching neo-psychedelia; and Die Kreuzen sets the speed on the dirt track where hard core collides head-on with metal. Semi-Twang released an album on Warner Brothers, produced by homeboy-turned-Talking Head Jerry Harrison; and expatriate Kevn Kinney did two albums for Island with his Atlanta-based Drivin' n' Cryin.'

Although Milwaukee rockers had scored occasional national hits during previous decades, none of them were particularly eager to point out where they'd come from. Fact is, many of them lied and told the press that they hailed from Florida or anywhere but America's brewery capital.

When Milwaukee finally entered the consciousness of music fans worldwide during the 1980s, it wasn't through the carefully groomed acts maintained by the city's music industry. The bands that put Milwaukee on the pop map trace their artistic roots to a movement that not only began outside the industry, but also set out with the idea of destroying that industry. They called it "punk."

A hulking dinosaur by the mid-1970s, rock had become an entrenched, conservative institution sustained by fraying memories of the 1960s. Punk was a revolution against what rock had become. Forget about proletarian resentment. Milwaukee punk—and this was true throughout America—wasn't an assault on the class system as it was in Britain, but a revolt against the rock establishment. To put it another way, punk—whatever it later turned into—surfaced here as an art movement.

Milwaukee punk was more than emulations of London and New York. Sure, as the movement gained velocity, the Sex Pistols/Clash/Ramones copycat bands proliferated

---

1 See http://archive.jsonline.com/greensheet/punk-rocker-wendy-o-williams-has-her-days-in-court--in-1981-b9964800 2z1-365013521.html.

like ragweed. But they never dominated the stage. Unlike many metropolitan centers in heartland America, Milwaukee possessed a rich gene pool from which the nascent punks could draw life (see also Shurilla 1991). Underground musicians already lived here, before anyone had heard of the Sex Pistols. They were linked in their isolation from the mainstream more by a shared contempt for what rock had turned into than any common musical direction.

Milwaukee's precursors of punk quantum-jumped across the musical spectrum: Ruthless Acoustics (eventually called Trance and Dance Band) crossed the simplicity of folk with the simplicity of rock. Death—whose singer Brian Kaputnik lived the band's title by killing himself—mined the metallic claim staked by Iggy Pop in his sweat and blood-soaked performances, while In a Hot Coma (later the Haskels) combined the agitational political imagery of Maoism with the Stones-steeped rock of the New York Dolls. James Siegfried in his quartet upset the staid jazz community with his bent for noise and provocation before he left for New York and became "James White/Chance." Arousing Polaris (who evolved into Plasticland) dressed up space rock electronic assaults in high heeled, fishnet New York Dolls drag. The Uncle Vinty show and the Electric Assholes (later the Blackholes) pre-shadowed the Tubes with their outrageous, costumed, rock-based satire.

The Blackholes provided some memorable evenings of shock theater for Milwaukee-ans who sensed that the future of rock 'n' roll did not lie entirely with Bruce Springsteen. Their most unforgettable performance remains an Elvis Presley séance at Polish Falcons Hall, conducted within months of the singer's death (16 August 1977).

Lead vocalist Mark Shurilla, known in the 1970s by the stage name "Black Dog," recalled the Blackholes' "tribute" to the King:

> There wasn't really a punk scene in Milwaukee yet, but the night we brought Elvis back from the dead had that outrageousness. I got the idea of talking to Elvis Presley in a séance from the *National Enquirer*. We had a crystal ball on stage. I asked it questions and we had answers from actual Elvis interviews on tape, played through the PA. I said, "Is it true that you did drugs?" "Yes sir, but I didn't really mean to do it."
>
> Finally, we had Elvis pop out in a sequined white jump suit from a black coffin with "Return to Sender" on the side, do drugs and do a crazy set with twisted lyrics like "I'm on drugs, I'm all fucked up" to the tune of "All Shook Up.'"
>
> It seemed to hit people. Some guys from Tennessee, who were in the crowd threatened to blow us away with shotguns. "We're going to kill you for doing that to the King," they told us. Half the fans were laughing their heads off. The others were serious fans who thought we were disgracing the King. The manager of Polish Falcons was punched out by a punk in a leather jacket. The police were there. It was a riot.

At their best, the Blackholes walked on a tightrope stretched precariously between humor and seriousness. Their tune, "Warren Spahn," a tribute to the Milwaukee Braves'

WARREN SPAHN

THE BLACKHOLES

left-handed pitcher featuring a mid-1960s play-by-play local sportscaster Earl Gillespie, cracked the city's top-10 in 1979 with a charity fundraiser sponsored by the Brewers. They were the only Milwaukeeans to break into their hometown's singles chart during the 1970s. In September 1979, during "Warren Spahn Day," an event the band had blueprinted for a skeptical Brewers ball club, the Blackholes lip synched the record before 20,000 baseball fans in County Stadium as Spahn circled the outfield in a limo, waving to the stands.

In the years directly preceding punk, Milwaukee's scene was very much like Akron, Ohio, where Devo and Pere Ubu were working out a new aesthetic for a market that didn't yet exist—an aesthetic initially appreciated by a small vanguard who would soon shape the tastes of the marketplace. Milwaukee's underground bands were truly underground, just as Devo was before being signed to Warners. They had nowhere else to go, but underground.

The city was hardly a cultural cemetery during the 1970s. There was musical life for those who sought it. But Milwaukee waited for New York and London to give the discontent with mainstream rock a name, a look, a direction. Punk—an affront to the 1960s through its style and an assault on the 1970s through its sound—provided the context for cultural rebellion as news of the inspired primitivism of the Ramones and the shock rock of the Sex Pistols leaked in. Suddenly, Milwaukee's rock underground was submerged in an international movement.

"I can remember my first encounter with punk," said Peter Balestrieri, saxophonist for one of the city's first punk outfits, Buck Byron and the Little Seizures. He went on in the 1980s to play behind the Violent Femmes and to form the disarmingly quirky instrumental group called the Ghostly Trio. "I was watching TV and they were showing some footage of young kids slamming in England. I just burst out laughing and no one could figure out why. My friends said, 'This is scary and violent, how could you think this is funny?' At the time, I had long hair and wore jeans, but two weeks after seeing that I cut off all my hair, dyed it red, and bought all new black clothes. I was separated from my wife six months later."

"I remember listening to the Dolls in 1974 and everybody's talking like this stuff is new [i.e., punk in 1977] and I knew that it wasn't," said musician Voot Warnings. A crazed yet oddly sensitive wild man who began performing during the underground era preceding punk, Warnings went on in the 1980s to front a series of satirical, uncompromising bands as memorable for his insightful observation of American life as for his fright-wigged, open collared, gold medallioned persona. "I thought punk was okay because around that time, there'd be some bars opening up. Before that time everything was a drag. You'd have to like to do your own scene where you could go out and play at. That sort of changed with the punk thing with the bars opening up."

Isolated individuals who had been contemptuous of what was being sold as rock culture began to realize that they weren't alone. Jill Kossoris, pianist for In A Hot Coma and later on leader of the Shivvers (see Chapter 8), remembers the beginning of Hot Coma: "I advertised in the paper that I wanted to join a band when I was 16 [1977] and Richard LaValliere called me from Madison. 'What kind of stuff do you like?' He asked. And I said 'Patti Smith' and he said, 'Oh great! When can I come down and see you?' Whenever I mentioned her name to other callers, they went 'Oh God! What kind of girl is this?'"

At its inception, Milwaukee punk enjoyed greater intimacy with the city's art community than with the bar circuit. New music and new styles came together at the Rag Balls sponsored by the East Side resale clothes store Sweet Doomed Angel. The Water Street Arts Center brought the music together with visual art at "Dreva at 33 and One Third," a 1960s style happening with a decidedly punk twist hosted by Milwaukee artist Jerry Dreva (1978).

Though destined to become a bandwagon, punk wasn't an easy ride in the beginning. The border between it and mainstream rock was drawn as clearly as the wall separating East from West Berlin. Outsider was defined in 1978 by short hair, pre-1967 clothes, even the donning of a black leather jacket. In those days being an outsider was not a distinction worn casually—it carried the attendant dangers of taunts, violence even. This was several years before MTV would make a norm out of non-conformity.

When they ventured outside the tolerant East Side, the Haskels, the premier band of Milwaukee's emerging punk scene, were menaced by redneck rockers as much for the way they looked as the way they sounded. And the way they sounded was rock 'n' roll— three chords, no frills, no solos, no flash pods. They did the (Rolling) Stones' "Street Fighting Man" along with their originals. Acknowledging their hometown roots, they covered "Say Mama" by the Legends. Today it's hard to imagine how any of this could have been revolutionary. But it was.

As for the way they looked, it was a show without costumes. The Haskels wore their thrift store finds on stage and off. Jerome Brish a.k.a. Presley Haskel explained his roots in a July 1978 interview in *Impulse*, a local anarchist newspaper:

> I'm a high school dropout. I ran away from home at 16. Now I'm 26. I've been on the East Side all those years. I used to earn a living by panhandling. Eventually I picked up on music. The first bands I ever saw were the MC5, The Stooges and a Milwaukee outfit called Death. They did Velvet Underground, Stooges, MC5. They were so decadent that their singer, Brian Kaputnik, killed himself. They did everything like Iggy Pop. They wore tight fitting jeans, black leather jackets, leather boots, but they had long hair. They were punky and tough.
>
> I was a big fan of Brian's. He died about five years ago. I was invited to his wake. It was so solemn that I got sick of it, went to a bar to see Cheap Trick and transferred by fandom to them. They let me sing songs

with them on stage. Later on, [his band,] In a Hot Coma played on the same bill with them.

Bassist Richard LaValliere commented in the same *Impulse* interview:

> We once played at Sunset Bowl [in Waukesha]. We learned that people can get beat up because they've got short hair. It was really crazy, the way they stared at us as we walked into the bar...I guess we fell into a time warp and came out in 1968. The soundman was so belligerent that he cut off our monitors...
>
> What we're waiting for is the inevitable explosion of the Milwaukee music scene. It's stupid that musicians have to move out to one of the coasts. I don't want to move to California. Palm trees on the streets. Ridiculous![2]

Courtesy of Guy Hoffman

Scarcely less unfriendly than the city's rock fans were the club owners. A punk bar was needed as a rallying point and watering hole for the area's cultural rebels. The bar turned out to be Zak's, just a short ride from the East Side across the North Avenue bridge. One of the few clubs that welcomed punk money in the early days, it became Milwaukee's full-time new wave headquarters by the close of 1978.

At least for those who didn't run afoul the politics of a scene dominated by cults of personality surrounding club owner Damian Zak and Presley Haskel—at whose urging the Haskels played house band at Zak's—it was a party without rules. Outrageous dress and hair were prevalent on and off stage. Many of the bands consisted of fans in the process of learning their instruments. With the curtain dividing performer from audience torn aside, Zak's itself became the stage. The couple having a drink at the far end of the bar could be just as important as the top-billed group.

Peter Balestrieri remembered:

> It was a very magic time. Whenever you first discover music it becomes a magic time. People were looking for something new and once you found that was there, it was like you were on to a secret. I remember

---

2   Luhrssen, "The Haskels," *Impulse*, July 1978, 11.

everyone smiling. There really were not any attitudes. You didn't care who was playing. You just went out every night, and if you didn't care for the band, you just went to the bar.

I think what made those early days so amazing was learning that there were so many just like yourself in the world, and you could get together whenever you wanted.

Music, though, remained the cornerstone. The bands provided the excuse for the party, and the soundtrack varied considerably from night to night. The Haskels balanced the rock classicism of Presley Haskel with the witty eclecticism of Richard LaValliere. The Orbits updated the look and sound of the mod rock popularized on these shores by the "My Generation" era Who. The Shivvers performed songs steeped in the female pop performers of the mid-1960s revved–up to a punk tempo.

Some of the performers tried to rekindle the lost fire of rock 'n' roll. "I wanted to create music that made other people as excited as some songs had made me. I wanted to write songs that would last," Presley Haskel said.

Others wanted to throw away all the old rules and just do it. "It soon became a reality to get a band together and open up for a national act. You didn't have to be extra special or overly talented," Peter Balistrieri said, commenting on the inspired amateurism characterizing those years.

Still others wanted to reclaim rock 'n' roll from the prevalent attitudes of the 1960s and 1970s. "A lot of people assumed that if you were a woman and a rock 'n' roll singer, then you're some kind of beer swilling hussy. That you have loose morals," Kossoris said. "They feel they have the right to walk right up to you and call you honey. So, in a lot of ways, I really did worry about what people thought about me because I'm a pretty private person." She recalled:

> I used to think, my God, I'm in this so-called punk/new wave band and people would come up to me, expecting me to do all these drugs. It's too bad that women, especially, have this sort of image. When you're in a band, people keep telling you sex sells. Sex sells. Take off the jacket. Why don't you take off the jacket? I didn't want people to look at my body. I wanted them to look at my face. I wanted them to hear my voice. I wanted them to listen to the songs. It was almost a rebellious thing for me because all the other rock women were dressing in hot pants—the Ruby Starr look. I was trying to change that image.

What to label these new directions soon became confusing. "This was an extremely conservative city," Kossoris said. "Anything that wasn't a hard rock band was considered new wave. Under those circumstances, I thought the label was a compliment for the Shivvers."

Video's first entry into Milwaukee club land occurred at Zak's on special evenings organized by DJ Downstairs Dan (1979). It would be several years until video screens were standard equipment in the area's night spots. Shown along with Devo's pioneering vids was work by Little Seizures singer Buck Byron, who was on the cutting edge of wedding performance rock to video.

The punks—no one ever said the new wavers, although conventional rock fans termed them punkers – also congregated at a larger hall called the Palms. Situated in a combat zone of strip joints and a plasma bank, the former hard rock roadhouse opened its doors to the Ramones, the Police, the Boomtown Rats, the Talking Heads, U2 and any British and American new music band that toured the Midwest.

The Palms was also the staging point for Milwaukee's biggest new wave band in terms of overall popularity—Yipes. The witty power pop combo fronted by showman and songster Pat McCurdy was accepted by all but the most radical wing of the Zak's scene, and crossed over into the mainstream public also. The pair of tuneful albums they recorded for RCA (1979, 1980) received air play around the country, and the band toured the US as the opening act for a number of groups but were quickly dropped by their label.

An important venue for national acts for many years, the Palms was sold in 1985. It became a topless sports bar, Hoops. It burned down in February 2017.

At Zak's, the party was already ending by 1980. Chalk some of it up to over-familiarity. The bands and the audience tired of frequenting the same public house night after night.

More importantly, the once amicable alliance between club owner Damian Zak and scene kingpin Presley Haskel was souring. When semi-formal meetings were held in the early months of 1980 by the city's new music performers, the order of business was to find a new club.

The music scene became a turf worth warring over. A Zak's bartender freelancing as a new music promoter was beat up outside Landmark Lanes, which he intended to use as a venue. A car belonging to Suzette, Presley's wife, was bombed outside Haskel Hotel, the band's living quarters and rehearsal space and the setting for the city's biggest music crowd parties. Many musicians were running scared.

LaValliere and drummer Guy Hoffman (later of the BoDeans) had already left the Haskels to form the Oil Tasters, a guitarless, saxophone-driven trio. Their debut that spring at the Skylight Comic Opera Company left no doubt that new sounds were brewing at the start of the new decade. The rhythm was funky and sinuous; the sax steeped in both James Brown and Ornette Coleman. LaValliere's songs spoke of dead girlfriends appearing on fuzzy TV screens, of vengeful bricks hurled through midnight windows, of the prospect of life as an encyclopedia salesman.

The Oil Tasters album, recorded for California's cutting-edge Thermidor Records (1982), remains one of the strongest discs released by a Milwaukee band, ever. But lacking the will to tour extensively, the group never pursued its national cult potential and broke up the following year.

Presley continued to front the Haskels in various lineups for a couple of years after the departure of LaValliere and Hoffman. But even a Haskels disc featuring a tour of Presley's crisply written rockers (198?) didn't shore up the band's sagging popularity.

Although Zak's remained in the new music business for several years after the demise of the understanding between Presley and Damien Zak, the torch had clearly passed. Zak's became Kilroy's, a college bar. (Today it is closed.)

A new era dawned when the scene shifted from Zak's to the Starship (1980). Owned by drummer Kenny Baldwin, the downtown club fast became home to the Oil Tasters and an exciting new breed of bands.

"Club owners don't seem to care as much anymore," Balestrieri said. "I remember that Kenny Baldwin would say he hoped people would have enough money to see a particular show at the end of the month that he thought was really cool. He really wanted them to come see a band he truly liked. That caring is gone."

A few of the young groups who grew up at the Starship outlasted the club. Among them, the Stupid Frogs, who've long since abbreviated their name to the Frogs.

A snare drum and guitar duo who performed wearing giant bat wings, the stage flanked with washing machines for props, the Frogs were eventually known as much for their ambitious, ambiguous songwriting as their wacky antics. The Frogs a.k.a brothers Dennis and Jimmy Flemion finally put out an LP in 1988 featuring such numbers as "I'm a Jesus Child." Song of praise or song of spoof? Neither the lyrics nor the performance revealed any clues. Another strange record, this one a largely acoustic collection of gay-oriented material, followed in 1989 on New York's Homestead Records.

Many groups who didn't survive the era nonetheless left deep memories. Among them are the rhythmically fractured, abrasive guitar and rhythm ensembles like the Ama-Dots and Volume Unit and the rootsy punk of the Prosecutors.

Volume Unit emigrated (1982) to the thriving youth culture mecca of West Berlin. After the Ama-Dots broke up, bassist Lisa Wickland played in the G-Spots and later, Dark Façade. Impressed when Dark Façade gigged in the divided city at the start of 1986, she ventured to Berlin later that year and formed the F. Spoons. Another graduate of Dark Façade, guitarist Michael Ford, joined the West Berlin band Sprung Aus Den Wolken.

At the time of the Starship's demise when Volume Unit left town, the prognosis for Milwaukee's music scene was not favorable. Volume Unit chose Berlin after careful deliberation. Said guitarist Tim Foran: "L.A. is very commercially oriented. New York seemed like too ordinary a place to go. We wanted to see Europe. Paris isn't a good town for music. London's a tough town to survive in. Berlin's a haven for young people. The bars are open 24 hours a day. The clubs are packed at 4 in the morning. You have to fight your way in."

Prosecutors guitarist Kevn Kinney performed post-Starship with Richard LaValliere before departing for a clime less distant than Berlin, Atlanta, GA. His eclectic, historically informed, but never retrospective approach to rock 'n' roll, finally came to fruition in his adopted home with Drivin' n' Cryin'. Drivin' was signed to Island Records in 1987 on the basis of their live reputation in the South and an album—equal parts punk, country and metal—released on Atlanta's 688 label.

"Milwaukee surrounded me with respect because it was a close community. Back when I started (1980) there were the Ama-Dots, the Oil Tasters —there was more security. Those people were always there," Kinney said, recalling the closely-knit scene of that time.

But before its closing, the mood characterizing the Starship grew increasingly darker than that of the old Zak's scene. Black became the uniform, and the hair was butched boot camp short. For a time, any music having audible ties to the past was suspect.

History was worse than bunk; and history included not only the post-Woodstock era rejected by the original punk wave, but also often those original punks too. Supplanting the Haskel Hotel as the music scene's social center was a flop known as Heroin Hotel.

The soundtrack for a typical Starship night was the dirgey music of the Tense Experts. The thrashing slam dance of hardcore found a home there too.

Die Kreuzen sprang from the gathering hardcore sub-culture. By decade's end they had gained an international reputation for their dynamic brand of metallic punk, expounded on an early independent EP, three tracks on the US hardcore sampler LP "Master Tape Compilation" (they appeared alongside Toxic Reasons and Articles of Faith), their three albums for Michigan's Touch and Go Records, and in concert.

Die Kreuzen came out of the Stellas, an early hardcore band (1981) centered around three refugee musicians from Rockford, Illinois. Singer Danny Kubinski routinely provoked barrages of beer cans, glasses and drinks from the Starship audience. "I thought it was fun," Kubinski told the local fanzine *Electric Frontier* (1985). "That's the way the Stellas would respond to it. Get drunk and fuck you!"[3]

They changed their name at the start of 1982, but not their brutal live presence. Slam dancing, a form of body language characterized by ballistic action on the dance floor, got so out of bounds at their shows that the band was obliged to book themselves under the name Demon into the hard rock bar Rock City and the more middle-of-the-road downtown Toad Club.

Beginning in 1983, Die Kreuzen embarked by van on a series of nation-wide tours. Later, they played in Europe. Die Kreuzen tour stories became legendary. While marooned for a month in San Francisco, they lived on potatoes—mashed, fried, baked, made into soup. Sometimes they literally pushed their death trap van to the next destination.

"If I had done what my parents had wanted, "bassist Keith Brammer said, "Go to school for four years and get a job, it would have been the same thing over and over—school, work, more work all day every day. Hell no, I have had so much fun. There is nothing you can compare it to."

"We always had a strong sense of direction," added drummer Erik Tunison, speaking on the band's decision to build their name on independent labels. "A lot of bands are willing to be led. They think, 'Well, this label has a lot of hits,' but what they don't realize is that the label has a lot of non-hits that you will never hear. Yours could easily be one of them."

Last call for the Starship's was during the summer of 1982. After standing empty for years, the building was torn down to make way for a vacant lot.

Around that time, new music was undergoing subtle transformations deeper than fashion. New sources of musical information had arrived, changing forever the composition of the new music audience.

Punk taste had been shaped by national magazines *Trouser Press* and *New York Rocker* and locally by the *Express*, a monthly publication launched in '78 by Kevn Kinney and myself as a punk fanzine, *X-Press*.

---

3   Die Kreuzen members were also responsible for a series of fanzines reflecting the mood of the Starship, *Fall from Grace* and *End of the World*.

Because commercial radio's intransigence, music had become a reader's medium. "Radio is in the hands of people who don't respond to the art of music," Downstairs Dan told *X-Press* in 1979. Downstairs had worked for the recently defunct WZMF, a station that began as early 1970s free-form radio, only to go under by decade's end as a prisoner of playlists. "It's in the hands of people who respect the ability of records to make money," he concluded.

It was easier for a long time to read about records then to hear them. Aside from sporadic programs hosted by Downstairs on local radio stations, it was hard to form firsthand opinions on much of the "new wave" because of FM rock radio's hostility to the new sounds.

The advent of WMSE changed everything.

The Milwaukee School of Engineering had been broadcasting for some time like an underground Radio Free Europe to neighborhoods abutting the downtown campus. After the station's signal was boosted city-wide (1981), a steady river of local and national new music flooded across Milwaukee. No more the preserve of a private club, the music was thrown open to a wider, some thought less discriminating public.

WMSE was part of a national trend toward college radio, which created a kind of musical farm club for the major labels. It would contribute to the success of R.E.M. and closer to home, the Violent Femmes, by giving bands a means to reach the growing audience for new music while insulating them from the commercial pressures of competing with mega-selling Michael Jacksons and Bruce Springsteens.

College radio wasn't the only new medium. First the suburbs and then the city of Milwaukee were wired to cable.

Said drummer Ron Ford of Couch Flambeau, a band who reached a wide local audience in the days after the Starship's demise: "The first thing that helped us was a cartridge of two songs that we gave to WMSE. It got heavy airplay. The second thing that helped was a spot-on Viacom Cable in West Allis. It exposed us to a bigger audience of people, of people who didn't even listen to WMSE."

Local musicians were appearing on suburban cable regularly, through the offices of Milwaukee comic and WMSE morning jock Pete Christensen. Christensen's weekly cable show brought live performances and interviews into homes throughout the area until its demise (1987).

Milwaukee had no unified scene after the Starship.

Enter the age of fragmentation. "The casual fan is so confused by what he perceives as new music – that's such a dumb term – to be," said Rob McCuen, who drummed at various times for the Red Ball Jets, Plasticland, Liquid Pink, Trance and Dance Band and numerous Voot Warning ensembles. "Nobody knows what the fuck new music is anymore. Maybe that's good for musicians, that so many styles can coexist. But for the fan, it probably confuses him."

Chronicling the clubs after 1982 becomes an exhausting and not entirely illuminating effort. Big East Side venues like Century Hall and Teddy's and the downtown nightclub the Toad were neutral venues rather than scenes. More reflective of cutting edge ambiance were the Landing on the East Side and the Gordon Park Pub in River West. Bars and halls catering to hardcore came and went, often under police pressure. Top of the Hill, Lincoln Arcade, Irene J's, Yano's, Lost Dutchman's Mine (later the Unicorn) and especially Niko's (1982-83), a southside bar, formed a network for Couch Flambeau, Die Kreuzen, Sacred Order, the Shemps and, later, a younger generation of brash hardcore bands spearheaded by NRK and the Crusties. The latter group are remembered for featuring trumpet in their lineup, as well as the creaking, rust-eaten van sporting the band's logo that became a fixture on the streets of town.

For a time, the hardcore scene preserved the close knot essence of the Starship and Zak's. "I think a lot of the bands had a lot to do with putting us together," Crustie Tim Cole said. "From when I used to not play in a band at all and used to go out and see Die Kreuzen and Sacred Order, that really put the bug in me. I never really thought about being in a band until I was getting close to the guys in town here. It just kind of fell together that way, and that was my first main influence."

Niko's owner Nick Stathas was peerless. As Channel 10 filmed a live program on punk from his bar, featuring Die Kreuzen, Stathas elbowed his way into the discussion to announce his candidacy for mayor. Niko's became La Cage Aux Folles (La Cage), a gay bar.

"By 1984 the hardcore scene was on its way out," Ford said. "As MTV was getting a greater hold on United States culture. It became more of a young kids' thing. The all-ages shows did great but the drinking crowd didn't care about hardcore anymore. And the bands changed. Die Kreuzen changed. We changed."

Club life enjoyed a brief renaissance with Tony Selig's graffiti-covered downtown cellar, the Underground (1984-85) and Scott Schanke's arty, garden furniture decorated Café Voltaire (1985-87). While Café Voltaire was noted for showcasing ensembles on the razor's edge between performance art and industrial noise (PMT, Boy Dirt Car), the format changed after it became Jack Kosshek's all-purpose Odd Rock Café. The Odd Rock was the site of several police raids (the Social Distortions riot of 1988, GG Allin's nationally noted arrest for public scatology) as well as blues and oldies show.

Video and disco lit dance clubs competed successfully for the new music audiences as the 1980s wound down. Live music was no longer the story of clubs coming and going. By the middle of the 1980s, the news was being made by the bands themselves. Milwaukee started becoming a city to talk about on the coasts and around the globe.

Couch Flambeau bounced between the Toad and Niko's during their formative years. "The crowd that came to see us at the Toad weren't people we knew personally," Ford said. "That used to bother me. We'd play out and unless it was a big show with a lot of other hardcore bands, you wouldn't see too many of your friends. We were a safe band to see for south side and west side people. Sacred Order got violent and scared people. Danny from Die Kreuzen was sort of intimidating. He could scare a lot of people away. Couch Flambeau were a band that college students could enjoy. We were on the zany side of hardcore."

Like Die Kreuzen and the Frogs, Flambeau's national reputation was built outside the major labels. Their eccentric sound simultaneously honored and spoofed the expectations of hard rock. Steeped in the folkways of his hometown, guitarist Jay Tiller authored such off-beat local color pieces as "Santa Claus Skips Cudahy," a humorous dig at the denizens of Milwaukee's blue color suburb, and a satire of teen cruising with a Milwaukee setting, "Hwy 100."

The first new music album from Milwaukee belonged to neither Die Kreuzen nor Couch Flambeau but Einstein's Riceboys. "Milk of Amnesia," a 1982 release recorded in a six-day marathon, netted the band a deal (1983) with Florida's QL Records. "Civil Rice," recorded in Miami, was the first live digital recording by a Milwaukee group.

"We wanted to be different. To stand out." Said Riceboy Steve Whalon—who later fronted his own bands, Cherry Cake and Monkey Bar—in a 1982 interview with *Express*. "When we got together, everybody called themselves the this or the that. We didn't want to be the Einstein's Riceboys.

"New wave got me back into listening to rock. But once we started to form the band, our music went beyond that. We didn't want to be another '60s-ish band. We wanted a futuristic approach, pointing to the new."

Those X-Cleavers were the most popular new music band in Milwaukee after Yipes and before the rise of the Violent Femmes. Packing large clubs across the state with dancers, the Cleavers drew their college-aged audience with flawlessly executed, relentlessly melodic, electronically enhanced modern pop. Those X-Cleavers' first album, released at the close of 1982 by Mainstream Records, a subsidiary of the local record store chain, featured "Skip a Beat," a song popularized on commercial radio. A coldly erotic dance floor drama with an unforgettably catchy chorus, "Skip a Beat" kept company on Milwaukee's airwaves with moody hits by Human League and other techno-pop contenders.

"Techno-pop displaced hardcore," Ford noted. "Dark Façade and the Bon Ton Society became the big groups. The bar owners weren't selling alcohol at all-ages hardcore shows. There was no money in it."

those X-Cleavers

SAT. JULY 21

10¢ BEER 8–9

Century Hall 2340 (n.) Farwell

Courtesy of Clancy Carroll

Although huge in the dance clubs, Dark Façade and the Bon Tons got no further than locally-released records. Colour Radio, backed to the hilt by FM rock station WQFM and its programming director, Lee Arnold, were able to ink an album deal with A&M subsidiary Gold Mountain. However, they weren't able to sell any albums.

"The whole idea of the group," Dark Façade, keyboardist David Wolf stated in an interview with *Express* (1983), "is influenced by the decadent art movements that began in the late 19th Century and continued through Expressionism and Surrealism into the early '30s. It is that mystique that we draw our inspiration from."

"The audience can take it in intellectually," added Steve Nodine during that interview. "But the strong beat is there to make people dance and move around."

Colour Radio also began as a two-man synthesizer outfit. Unlike Dark Façade, bandmates Patrick Nedobeck and Stephan Schneider were groomed for pop and were compared to Duran Duran. Their sensibility gained them support from commercial FM radio in the Milwaukee area. One of their tracks appeared on the otherwise entirely mainstream *93QFM Hometown Album Project*. As their popularity increased Colour Radio added a pair of crack local musicians to their lineup: Shivvers' guitarist Jim Eannelli and drummer Kenny Baldwin, owner of the Starship nightclub. Signed to Gold Mountain Records, they released an album produced by Rick Derringer but were soon dropped by the label and disbanded.

Clad in the stripes and paisleys of Carnaby Street, London's fashion center in the swinging Sixties, Plasticland became prophets of the global psychedelic resurgence of the Eighties. A series of self-made singles and, later, albums for Lolita Records (France), Bam-Caruso (UK) and Enigma (USA) opened the minds of music fans to psychedelia, a musical form widely reviled in new music circles at the start of the 1980s.

While few of the band's numerous recordings equaled the power of their live shows, Plasticland's plastic grants access to the visionary world suggested by the lyrics of guitarist Glenn Rehse. Darker in mood than the original psychedelic pranksters, Plasticland songs substitute the lurking paranoia of 1980s cutting edge for the giddy optimism of the 1960s.

For all of their impact—artists as diverse as Prince and R.E.M. have cited their influence—Plasticland seldom ventured from their hometown for extended tours. During daylight hours, its members traded paisley scarves for blue collars. Commented Rehse on the reaction he receives from co-workers at his courier company: "It's exciting for them to see someone involved with the arts, very visibly getting press and recognized around the world, being involved in their personal lives in this capacity. They're very entertained. Some of them think I'm a celebrity. Some of them probably just wonder why I have funny hair."

August 23, 1981 has gone down as a turning point for Milwaukee rock.

I know where I was on that evening: helping babysit the children of Trance and Dance's leader Jerry 4TA (Jerry Fortier). Violent Femmes bassist Brian Ritchie, an ex-Trance and Dance member who was sleeping in a spare bedroom of the 4TA's East Side flat, hurried up the stairs and into the living room. His normally impassive features registered something resembling excitement. "The Femmes are opening for the Pretenders tonight," he said in a winded voice. All mouths fell as he disappeared into his room to change.

Earlier that afternoon the Violent Femmes—an acoustic trio who had been entertaining crowds on sidewalks and in jazz dens—were discovered on the curb outside the Oriental Theatre by Pretenders singer Chrissie Hynde. Although the Femmes never heard from the Pretenders again, the exposure gained that night as the unannounced opening act for the Pretenders concert at the Oriental forged the first link in the chain leading to a national recording contract with Slash Records.

Arguably, Milwaukee's most famous
rock band—the Violent Femmes

The Femmes music—always low in decibels but high in energy—uniquely blended the direct simplicity of early rock n' roll with the spontaneity of jazz. Although they ventured onto folk, gospel and country tangents, their fascinating music took the back seat for teenage fans nationwide to the impassioned lyrics of singer Gordan Gano, who clambered a high-tension wire between his Christian faith and his fleshy nature.

Ritchie and Gano's first performance together, at an assembly at Rufus King High School auditorium, resulted in Gano's expulsion from the National Honor Society. His crime was to perform a hungry tale of teenage sexuality, "Gimme the Car." The offending song would later be released by Britain's Rough Trade Records on a Violent Femmes single on a 12-inch 45.

Bassist Brian Ritchie reflected:

> The 70s were bogus until punk rock came around and that turned my head around. My two favorite bands back then were the Jam and Television. The music had been so bland and ridiculous up till then I thought hey, I play guitar better than most of those guys. Maybe I should form a band.
>
> I was also getting into free jazz: Albert Ayler, Ornette Coleman, John Coltrane. I thought hey, this is a really great approach to music. They were playing whatever came into their minds. I would never say that what I'm playing is jazz. Jazz is an influence at most. Jazz is a highly evolved musical form I don't even read music.

In Milwaukee there was nothing happening [1978]. There were boogie bands. Country Western bands. Then there was Arousing Polaris —pre-Plasticland. They were pretty underground. They played a lot of weird shit. I identified with them a lot. I met them on the street and they took me under their wing. We'd hang out, listen to records, talk about music. Right after I met them the whole punk thing started happening in town. I was part of that scene, but younger than most of the other participants. The Femmes were not the first generation of punk rock in Milwaukee. We were the ones that benefitted from the fact that a few years had passed, and people were willing to listen to something different instead of being afraid of it. Now it seems they're getting afraid of it again.

As they climbed to the height of their popularity with the ascent of their third album, *The Blind Leading the Naked* (1986), into the Billboard's Top 100, the Femmes abruptly called time out. Mounting tensions made the recess imperative, but rumors of a breakup were greatly exaggerated.

"I was entertained in this whole period just by what I read in the papers," drummer Victor DeLorenzo said. "And then Brian would call up saying, 'you won't believe what I just heard now.' And we would all laugh about it because by this time we had divorced ourselves from being entirely serious. We always planned to make more albums[;] the channels were always open."

The Femmes returned from vacation with an all-acoustic album, *3* (1989).

With members living in Milwaukee, Madison and Rockford, Illinois, EIEIO logged a good many nights in this city's clubs. One of the first bands in the area to discover the neo-country rock resurgence, EIEIO recorded a Steve Berlin-produced album in that vein for Britain's Demon Records, *Land of Opportunity* (1985), before jettisoning the heartland approach on a second LP, *That Love Thang* (1988).

Originally called DaBodeans, the BoDeans began as a low-tech duo playing rock 'n' roll in the bars of the neighboring city of Waukesha. They picked up a rhythm section as they went on, graduating to acclaim as a hot live act on Milwaukee's fragmented club scene.

The twosome got together to play Kurt "Beau" BoDean's 19th birthday party. Guitarist Kurt recounted the affair in a 1986 interview in *WAM*, a monthly Wisconsin music magazine. "I called up Sam (BoDean) and said, 'You want to come over to my house for a birthday party, act like we're playing and pick up chicks?'"

The BoDeans' manager, high school mate Mark McGraw, is credited for pushing the deal that found the band signed to the Femmes' label, Slash.

If the BoDeans became identified nationally with the roots rock trend on their debut album for Slash, *Love & Hope & Sex & Dreams* (1985), their follow-up, *Outside Looking In* (1987), brought them a greater measure of mainstream chart acceptance.

Several other bands mining the roots of American music brushed against national attention during the 1980s. The R&B Cadets, fronted by Paul Cebar and Robin Pluer and enhanced by the songwriting of Semi-Twang's John Sieger, toured extensively but disbanded shortly after the release of their album, *Top Happy* (1986). Ian and Tom Spanic, a father-and-son team, performed as Those Spanic Boys and produced an extensive discography for Rounder Records and other labels. They reached the height of attention when they performed on *Saturday Night Live* (1990).

As the 1980s shut down, Milwaukee had no lack of musical talent. As ever, Milwaukee bands worked across the spectrum. A typical week on the live music calendar included the compact, insightful writing of Ward and his Troubles; the brassy dynamics of Wild Kingdom; the club rock of 3 On Fire; the punk pop energy of Wobble Test; the Buddy Holly-ish yet totally modern Dellman Trio; the fractured early 1980s assaults of Blue Room; the multi-ethnic folk and rock of Trance and Dance; the solo jaunts of Brian Ritchie, who did two albums for California's SST Records.

A co-op of Milwaukee musicians published their own editorially independent monthly, *The Newsletter*. The Wisconsin Area Music Industry's (WAMI) Awards have grown from an industry clique to a more broadly-based effort to gain recognition for Wisconsin musicians. The Alternative Concert Group has turned the city's biggest campus, UW-Milwaukee, into a regular venue.

The most characteristic Milwaukee band might have been Liquid Pink, with an album on Atomic Records, a subsidiary of the East Side record store (now closed). "Part of our charm is we don't know who we are," drummer Rob McCuen said. "We started as a punk/pop band but we're in a constant state of transition. It's a controlled free-for-all."

The ties between new music and the punk explosion that conceived it grew increasingly unrecognizable as the decade progressed. Not only was there no common music, but scene-makers were no longer united in a common look. Short hair was joined by moussed hair, or just plain long hair. Augmenting the 1950s retro look favored by the original punks was the flotsam of every recent decade.

The primary legacy of punk was the idea that anything is possible.

"This is a great place to live," said Pat McCurdy, still fronting pop-rock bands as well as performing his songs as a soloist. "You don't have people going, 'you gotta do this, you gotta do that.' Think of the music that comes out of here. There are no preconceptions. Anything goes."

"The Return of The Violent Femmes"[4]
by David Luhrssen

No one was more surprised than Violent Femmes' drummer Victor DeLorenzo when the play button was pressed and the band's six-year pause ended. "Gordon [Gano] called me last October, on John Lennon's birthday," he recalls. The unexpected message from the Femmes' singer-songwriter was simple: Their manager had the opportunity to book the band at the annual Coachella Festival in Indio, California, and wondered if the Femmes would want to play.

---

4   Originally published in the *Shepherd Express*, 20 June 2013. Printed with permission.

Then again, as DeLorenzo adds, "It was a surprise for all three of us that we caught on." The Milwaukee band's self-titled 1983 debut album didn't sell well initially but soon became a unique touchstone for restless adolescents everywhere. By now it's been the soundtrack—maybe even the light in the darkness—for two or three generations troubled by that unpleasant rite of passage called high school and the unsettled emotions of teenage life.

And then again, DeLorenzo and bassist Brian Ritchie originally had no intention of sticking with Gano long enough to cut a single, much less an enduring album. "We were going to move to Minneapolis and form a band," DeLorenzo says. "But Brian and I never made it up there." Something clicked quickly and a small local following encouraged the trio to continue hanging around Milwaukee's East Side. Famously "discovered" by The Pretenders on the corner of Farwell and North, they were added to the British band's show at the Oriental Theatre—but those moments in the spotlight were more a morale booster than a deal maker.

Even after DeLorenzo's dad lent the band money to record that first album, the odds were against a band that sounded like no one else in the world. "I have drawers of rejection letters," DeLorenzo says, but the demo finally caught the ears of Slash Records in Los Angeles. It became that true rarity, an epochal album in the increasingly long, drawn-out history of rock 'n' roll.

Little wonder The Violent Femmes performed that first album in its entirety—and in the tracking order of its 10 songs—for their first two reunion shows at Coachella and the follow-up at Napa's BottleRock festival. They plan the same format for their upcoming return to Summerfest.

"Swarming might be a good description of the Coachella response," Ritchie says of their first concert. "After we kicked off the set with 'Blister in the Sun' it looked like insects around spilt honey as they descended from other stages. It was a mixed demographic, but as usual there was a whole new group of teenagers familiar with the songs and singing along. This regeneration of the fan base has been the most remarkable thing about the band over the decades."

Not everyone would be as cruel as the editors of *Spin* magazine's *Alternative Record Guide*, who dismissed everything the Femmes recorded after their debut as "beyond marginal" and "fairly silly." And yet, nothing released since then has had the impact of those starkly recorded first songs with their deceptive simplicity and naked emotions, and an undercurrent of free jazz propelling them beyond the narrow boundaries of folk or punk. Looking like Sal Mineo and sounding like a teenage Lou Reed, Gano shifted from defiance to suicide in a heartbeat.

"There was not a lot of dust to shake off," Ritchie says of the Femmes' rehearsal in Los Angeles to prepare for their short summer tour. "The Femmes' sound works within pretty well-defined parameters and it's simple, so it's like riding a bike."

In addition to the first album, the Femmes will perform portions of their second LP, *Hallowed Ground*, and a smattering of later songs. For the Milwaukee show, the Horns of Dilemma, a free-floating lineup that will probably include local musicians Jeff Hamilton and John Sparrow, will join the trio.

As for Ritchie's 2007 lawsuit against Gano, a *Bleak House* affair during which the former accused the latter of "greed, insensitivity and poor taste" for licensing their signature song, "Blister in the Sun," for a Wendy's commercial, Ritchie says: "We've gotten over it."

All of the original Femmes have been busy without the band, producing, playing sessions, releasing solo albums. DeLorenzo's new album features Gano on one selection, "Dr. Um." An expatriate in Australia for many years, Ritchie is music curator for Tasmania's Museum of Old and New Art and tours with the Break, a space-surf band he formed with members of Midnight Oil.

"For me, the Femmes function as another project I'm working on, albeit one that means a lot to the other musicians and the public," Ritchie says. "At this point in my musical life I only work on things if they're fun. These gigs have been, and if that continues, we'll go on."[5]

The 1990s Alt-Rock Explosion and New Rock Opportunities
by Evan Rytlewski

Nirvana's 1991 hit "Smells Like Teen Spirit" was the big bang that essentially created an entire alternative nation, dethroning the hair-metal bands that had previously ruled MTV, spurring a brand-new radio format and opening the door for a generation of bands with baggy flannels, distorted guitars and indifferent stage presences. That's an oversimplification, of course, that downplays at least a decade's worth of underground bands that laid the groundwork for alternative's ascent to the mainstream, yet it's hard to overstate Nirvana's impact. The band's breakthrough album *Nevermind* sent major labels into a signing spree, racing against each other to gobble up any band that might sell in this new alternative economy, and the ripple effects were felt in music scenes across the country, Milwaukee's included.

"The change in the air was unmistakable," recalls Jeff Castelaz, who managed some of Milwaukee's most successful bands of the 1990s, including Citizen King, The Promise Ring and the Gufs, before co-founding Dangerbird Records and becoming president of Elektra Records. Like their peers around the country, Milwaukee's underground rock bands had operated under the assumption that there was a ceiling hanging over everything they did, that they most they could realistically hope for was a home on an independent label and the opportunity to tour here and there. When bands like Nirvana and the Smashing Pumpkins began topping the charts, however, suddenly anything seemed within reach. Jeff recounted:

---

5   After performing at Summerfest 2013, drummer Victor DeLorenzo left the band. Gordon Gano and Brian Ritchie continued (with Brian Viglione replacing DeLorenzo). The Violent Femmes released *We Can Do Anything* in 2016. Viglione departed that same year and John Sparrow joined the band.

It made all of us in the music scene stand up and go, "We could actually do this." The problem with the music industry before all this was you had to be such a complete douchebag to make it. You had to be a heavy metal person, and you had to have the hairdo, and the weird sunken cheeks. You had to have the whole getup going on, and you had to be able to play *arpeggio* guitar solos. It was all so specific and lame, and there was something so L.A. about it all, but suddenly you had these bands blowing up, selling millions of records, and they were from these other cities. You had all these bands from Seattle, and the Smashing Pumpkins, right down the street from us in Chicago. They were close to Milwaukee, so we were there when they put out there when Sub Pop Records put out their first single, and we were there when their first album *Gish* came out, and we were there when they sold 40 million records, too.

If you would have told me in 1991 that the Smashing Pumpkins would sell out arenas all over the world, I would have punched you in the face, so to see that happen cast an incredible array of sunlight all over the Milwaukee scene. Suddenly there were these opportunities for bands that didn't care about heavy metal or Whitney Houston or whatever MTV's idea of pop was.

Despite its helpful proximity to both Chicago and Madison, home of Smart Studios and the most in-demand producer in alternative rock, Butch Vig, Milwaukee's alternative scene never managed to carve out a distinguishing identity the way more unified scenes in Seattle, Boston, and Minneapolis did. So instead the era was more of a free-for-all, with Milwaukee bands fitfully capitalizing on the scattered opportunities that trickled their way.

The Gufs typified the modest success stories of the day. Formed on the city's East Side, the group built up enough steam on college radio to land a deal with Atlantic Records, which released their self-titled album in 1996. The band was an easy sell—telegenic, with a clean, melodic, lightly distorted sound that hinted at grunge while sanding away its roughest edges. They might have become bigger stars if labels at the time hadn't been overstocked with so many other bands that sounded just like them. Unlike many one-and-done major label alternative bands from the era, though, they did manage a second album for Atlantic, 1999's *Holiday From You*, an even cleaner record that filtered any remaining grunge from their sound.

The Frogs, meanwhile, were everything the Gufs weren't—crude, unpolished and contentious. The brainchild of brothers Jimmy and Dennis Flemion, the comedic acoustic pop group had been kicking around Milwaukee's underground scene since the 1980s, releasing a cult album for the indie label Homestead Records, but in the 1990s their social circles grew a lot more famous. They joined Pearl Jam and the Smashing Pumpkins on big tours, confounding audiences with their ambiguously satirical songs about race, homosexuality and fornicating grandparents. That exposure was enough to land them a short-lived deal with Matador Records, but even with famous friends like Eddie Vedder and Billy Corgan singing the Frogs' praises, the band behind songs like "God Is Gay" and

"I Had a Second Change Done at the Shop (Now I've Added Animal Cocks)" was never long for the masses.

Two other established Milwaukee bands with 1980s roots enjoyed far more lucrative career bounces. The Violent Femmes' jittery folk-punk finally found the home on radio that it never had during the 1980s, with several singles from the group's 1983 self-titled debut receiving regular rotation on alternative stations around the country. Rather than trying to capitalize on the belated exposure with a zeitgeist-chasing album along the lines of R.E.M.'s *Monster*, instead, in 1994, the Femmes released one of their trickiest albums, *New Times*, a prickly, world-inspired record that had little to do with the guitar-drenched rock of the time.

The Waukesha roots-rock band BoDeans, meanwhile, scored their biggest hit when the TV series *Party of Five* adopted their track "Closer to Free" as the show's theme. The show has been mostly forgotten, but "Closer to Free" remains the band's signature song.

Perhaps Milwaukee's greatest casualty of the alt-rock era was Citizen King. Formed from the remnants of the locally popular ska-rock band Wild Kingdom, they honed a sound like little else at the time, filtering soul, jazz, and hip-hop through the prism of punk. Produced in part by Milwaukee rapper Speech (see Chapter 5), who was fresh off a couple of Grammy wins with his group Arrested Development, Citizen King's sharp 1995 debut *Brown Bag LP* and spirited live shows caught the attention of Warner Brothers Records, which signed the group then put them on the back burner. By the time Citizen King's Warner Brothers debut, *Mobile Estates*, finally arrived in 1999, their sound wasn't nearly so fresh. The raw soul of the *Brown Bag LP* had been replaced by the instantly dated slacker hop of Sugar Ray and Sublime, and though the band scored a big hit with the dopey "Better Days (And The Bottom Drops Out)," the song was so desperately of the moment that it felt like a thin victory. Even Milwaukee, a city usually eager to trumpet anything resembling a homegrown success story, couldn't find much nice to say about the band's major-label makeover. Citizen King quietly disbanded in 2002.

By the turn of the century alternative had fallen out of favor, and most of the bands who had landed fluke label deals in the wake of grunge had either broken up or been dropped by their labels. Most would say they weren't much better off for the experience. For decades, career-minded artists had romanticized major label deals as a kind of silver bullet, the most likely ticket to real success, but the 1990s alternative boom killed that perception. By the 2000s, the new dream for bands was no longer to make it big on a major label, but rather to carve out a career without one, a value shift that was reflected in how artists classified themselves. Bands no longer wanted to be tagged "alternative"—that term now had ugly commercial connotations and was too associated with the broken promises of the post-Nirvana era—so instead they took to the term "indie," a word that celebrated their freedom from the commercial music complex. They re-calibrated their expectations accordingly, letting go of whatever dreams of arena tours and platinum sales that alternative had planted in their heads, but their fates were in their own hands, and after a decade spent at the whims of fickle major labels and shifting public tastes, that felt like a victory in and of itself.

Jerry Harrison,
performer, producer,
member of the
Talking Heads

Photo by Erol Reyal

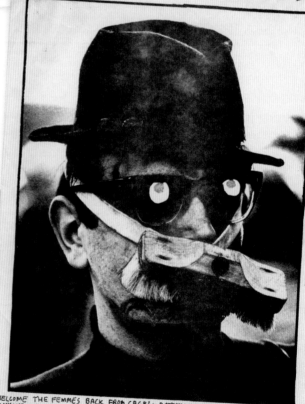

VIOLENT FEMMES

WELCOME THE FEMMES BACK FROM CBGB'+ BOTTOMLINE IN NEW YORK CITY!!!!
ANYONE NAMED CHARLES ADMITTED FREE WITH ID!! VOMIT DEATH WARTS!!!!

TUES
AUG 17 MILWAUKEE jazz gallery
932 E. CENTER
SP@T

Courtesy of Wisconsin Concert Poster Collection/ Milwaukee Public Library

THE MILWAUKEE BLACKHOLES PRESENT

1) THE RETURN OF THE KING (ELVIS SEANCE)
and 2) RISE AND FALL OF MILWAUKEE

ULTIMATE CHRISTMAS CONCERT
from your MASTERS OF REALITY

801 E. CLARKE
POLISH FALCONS NEST
$1.75
FRI. DEC. 16 8 PM
<u>FREE BEER</u> 8 - 9 PM

Courtesy of Clancy Carroll

NOTED SCIENTIST SAYS:

"These Blackholes may have just discovered the secret of the universe!"

"God help us if they have!"

THE BLACKHOLES
TO UNVEIL NEW
POWER POLKA
BLITZ RAY
AT zak's

HUMBOLDT AT NORTH AVENUE
FRI. and SAT NIGHT
OCTOBER 12th and 13th
9p.m. is POLKA TIME!

Courtesy of Clancy Carroll

Photo by Erol Reyal

Mark Shurilla, irreverent yet sentimental proto-punk

197

Photo by James Brozek

**The Oil Tasters, a premier punk group with from left to right:
Caleb Alexander, Richard LaValliere, and Guy Hoffman**

Courtesy of Guy Hoffman

Courtesy of Clancy Carroll

Courtesy of Guy Hoffman

Courtesy of Guy Hoffman

Courtesy of Clancy Carroll

Word Of The Week
SHEET!

THE SHEET

Edited by Larry Mondello and Dave Luhrssen

January 8th, 1979

CITY PARALYZED BY BLIZZARD –HASKELS, LUBRICANTS ROCK ON

Bad Boy didn't bother showing for their Sugar Mountain gig on New Years Eve. Too much snow for the starboys. Someplace Else closed down. But rock'n'roll warmed up Zac's North Avenue till four 0'clock January 1st.

The Lubricants performed for the first time since around July. No one was disapointed. They still haven't found a full time replacement on drums since Jeff split for LA, but Rob of M____ ___ __ ____ for the night. Bass Craig Crabbe actually played guitar on a co____ _____ ___ _ position filled by Leroy's wife Patti. The bigge__ _____ ____ was when they covered a Haskels song – "Eve_____ ____

The Haskels finally had ___ ____ cert. "Liberace,"Dead Man's ___ The Bomb","Calling Idi Amin"__ ___ the Stones,Iggy Pop,The Bea____ ___ Yardbirks. The Haskels also ___ ___ Smile" and "Brick Through ___ ___

Inspite of the weathe_ ___ ___ included Jerry Dreva,Downs____ ___ and Arousing Polaris,the ___ _____ (except a couple of burno___ ____ riped-off by the $5 cove__ ___

Many people ___ ____ called ...AN____ ___ of KALEIDOSCO__ ____ should have ___ ___ of the mont___ _____

Damien Zac__ ___ What's wi__ ____ Eve? How ___ ____ two stori__ ____ gangbust__ ___ They de___ ___

Sid Vicious
R.I.P.

THE SHEET

QUOTE OF THE WEEK
"Rock'n'roll will never die. Too many people like it."
—George Thorogood

February 10,1979

Edited by Dave Luhrssen and Larry Mondello

HASKELS,CHICAGO G. THOROGOOD

Monday,January 29 and Sunday, January 28,The Haskels told Chicago who was the fairest of them all.

First,it was Mothers. The Haskels backed a lousy New York band called The Past. That band was definitely going nowhere. [FAST]

Haskels originals like "Every Night","Baby,Let's French," and "Liberace" proved that Milwaukee is not the polka cowtown Chicago thinks it is. Milwaukee is the home of the best.

On the 28th, The Haskels backed Immune System. The Haskels popped the question "who's backing who?" There wasn't much of an audience that night, but The Haskels definite style and tight sets kept them more than interested.

In short,they were great. The Haskels have a great show. Check our calendar and write their next gig on your's. Now take $2 out of your pocket and sit tight.
- Larry the M.

Rumors of George Thorogood's magnificient abilities as a performer and showman traveled ahead of him. The capacity audience at The Palms, February 4th,was not disapointed by his show.

Thorogood physically resembles Mick Jagger but,to his credit,he doesn't try to mimic Jagger as Steve Tyler does. His stage presence was natural - no put ons. But most impressive was Thorogood's prowess on guitar. Thorogood is a genius in the same sense as Hendrix or Segovia. He can use rock'n'roll,blues and country swing as fodder to create something new - to push across new musical horizons.

Songs performed during his set included "Cocaine Blues," "It Wasn't Me," "Johnny B. Goode," "Move It On Over," and "Who Do You Love". The roots were represented: Hank Williams,Chuck Berry,Johnny Cash and Bo Diddley.

The Destroyers are one of the best rhythm sections in music today,providing a solid framework for Thorogood's guitar genius.

Short Stuff opened and disapointed most of their fans with a lustreless performance. Maybe it was a bad night for them?

Downstairs Dan (where is he now?) MC'd the show,leading the crowd in chants of "disco sucks" and passing out disco albums with instructions that they be destroyed. Broken pieces of vinyl littered the floor of The Palms.
—D.L.

Courtesy of Clancy Carroll

Locate Your Lips promotional photo by James McCarter featuring from left to right Jim Eannelli, Andy Cavaluzzi, and Kenny Baldwin (owner and punk/new wave impresario of the Starship Club)

LUBRICANTS

SEPT. 14

STARSHIP

634 NORTH 5th ST.   MILWAUKEE, WISC.

½ BLOCK SOUTH OF WISCONSIN AVE. ON 5th STREET

278-9780 $2.00 cover

THE WIGS

AT ZAK'S
Humboldt and North

Tuesday - Wednesday - Thursday
September 25 - 26 - 27

THE
STRANGS
WITH GUESTS
THE GIRL SCOUTS
APPEARING AT
9:30 P.M. IN
CHARLIE'S
SKYROOM
PLANKINTON
HOTEL
609 N. PLANKINTON
FRI MAY 11TH AND SAT MAY 12TH

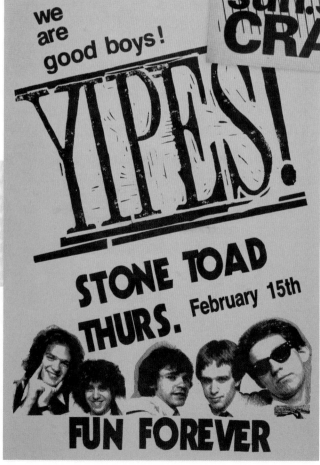

Die Kreuzen's
Dan Kubinski
performing
after the band
reunited in 2013

Photo by Dennis Darmek

James Siegfried
also known as James White
and James Chance

Photo by Erol Reyale

The Bodeans, from Waukesha, performing at
the "Big Brew Ha Ha" at the Miller Brewing Company
150th Birthday Celebration at Miller Park (2005)

Photo by Erol Reyal

**The Violent Femmes performing
at the Pabst Theatre (2005)**

Photoy by Erol Reyal

**Mayor Tom Barrett declared "Patti Smith Day" on her visit
to Milwaukee in 2017. From left to right: Lenny Kaye, Patti Smith,
Peter Jest (owner of Shank Hall), and Tony Shanahan**

Pale Moon's Grin

Gary Huckleberry with guitar along with Bruce Cole (top)
and Gary Huckleberry's "Conqueroo" van (bottom)

CHAPTER 10

Milwaukee
Sonic Explorers

Gary Huckleberry, Paul Cebar, and Sigmund Snopek III are among Milwaukee's most interesting rock musicians. Their initiative and individuality distinguish their lives and their music. Although, this book has featured other musicians who also share musical exploration and longevity, Bruce Cole and Phillip Naylor offer these exemplars.

Gary Huckleberry: A One and Only
by Bruce Cole

I met Gary Huckleberry somewhere in the 1980s while playing with super good blues guitarist Terry Frank in his band Black Cat Bone (a.k.a. Bone Deluxe) (see Chapter 7). Gary was his harmonica player. "Huck" went on to start "John the Conqueroo" in the early 1990s, and rode that bizarre, crazy, and highly entertaining show band into the aughts. I joined late—the last lineup.[1] The "Conqueroo" was a "Cajun porch band"—that was Huckleberry's description—and a one-of-a-kind in Miltown. Tuba, "Roo-tar," gut bucket

---

1   See: http://www.milwaukeerocks.com/showbanddetail.asp?bandID=5696.

bass, a pots and pans drum set, fiddle, lead guitar and sax were what you usually got, but things changed from week to week, and lots of musicians went through the group over the years. Huckleberry was hands down one of the best, most entertaining front men Milwaukee ever produced. He was a fine, fine harp player with great tone, a cool slide player on his homemade (metal sink body) guitar, and he would pick up his accordion and dance and sing and put big smiles on everyone in the joint until way past when the band was supposed to quit.

A multifaceted artist, Gary also produced and directed a movie, *Truth Beauty* (2004) and composed the soundtrack for the film, which the Cujé Collection possesses. He also wrote a novel, *The Doozie* (2008).

Above all, Gary is a performer. Halfway into a gig, while dancing and singing, in the middle of a song, he'd turn to me and say: "Can you believe it? They even *pay* us to do this! Hah!" Nobody enjoys entertaining more than Gary Huckleberry—it was all about having fun, period.

It still is.

Gary now performs in Florida.

Paul Cebar's Revelatory Rhythms
by Phillip Naylor

Paul Cebar is a great explorer. I perceived that when we lunched at Gil's on Downer Avenue (now the Café Hollander) decades ago and most recently at Buckley's on Cass and Wells Streets. He grew up on 44th Street between Capitol and Hope, attended Pius XI High School, and graduated from the New College of Florida (Sarasota). His "musical journey" began at the age of eleven (or probably later as he recently recounted) at the Lakefront Festival of the Arts when he heard the Wild Magnolias (from New Orleans), Art Blakely and the Jazz Messengers, and Nigerian drummer Babatunde Olatunji.[2] He remembers that occasion as a "pivotal moment."

Paul spoke of "happy accidents" in his lifetime, such as the variety of popular music (rock, R&B, Soul) played by AM stations WOKY, WRIT, WNLV, WAWA and Chicago's WLS and WCFL. Ron Cuzner's *The Dark Side* jazz program also aired from midnight to dawn on WFMR-FM. The neighboring Murphy family inherited R&B records that once belonged to the renowned Milwaukee artist, Karl J. Priebe (1914-76). Daughter Chrysa Murphy introduced Paul to country/delta blues (e.g., the music of Bukka White, Skip James, Mississippi John Hurt, Son House)[3] and deepened his appreciation for jump blues (e.g., Louis Jordan and Buddy Johnson) as well as the extraordinary R&B performer Screamin' Jay Hawkins. Cebar later opened for a variety of blues artists including

---

2   Cebar recalled that he first played the bongos and then guitar during Masses at St. Stephen's Catholic Church on 51st and Hope. Singing in the choir helped him learn how to sing in a group.

3   Not surprisingly, Taj Mahal would also become an important musical influence.

Brownie McGhee and Sonny Terry, Willie Dixon, Buddy Guy, and B.B. King. He is still thrilled remembering B.B. King's complimentary recognition: "And how about that Paul Cebar!?!"

New Orleans, a musical cauldron melding sounds and cultures, especially fascinated Cebar, who began annually attending the New Orleans Jazz & Heritage Festival.[4] Paul's expeditions to the Crescent City included trolling record store stacks and discovering music and musicians of years past who deserved more than b-side notoriety. They needed to be heard again, shared, and appreciated. He sought "records that sounded like they came from Mars." He refers to New Orleans as "a prism," since it has historically diffused so many musical styles—blues, R&B, and Caribbean.

Cebar's music career began in Milwaukee coffeehouses in the 1970s, e.g., the Blue River Café, the 19th Street Coffeehouse, and the Eighth Note. He also performed in New York. Back in Milwaukee, Cebar joined the fledgling R&B Cadets in the late 1970s, which featured original songs by John Sieger as well as music discovered and recovered by Paul's exploratory forays. Concurrently, he played with the Milwaukeeans featuring Rip Tenor ("Art Kumbalek") on saxophone, Robin (Robyn) Pluer on keys and vocals, and Alan Anderson on upright bass. After the R&B Cadets broke up in the mid-1980s, Paul devoted more time to the Milwaukeeans, which added Randy Baugher and Juli Wood to the band.[5] Cebar continued his sonic quests and immersed himself in Cuban, Caribbean, and African rhythms, which included a visit to Cuba. Already an admirer of Ry Cooder's musicianship, Cebar appreciated Cooder's service as an impresario gathering renowned Cuban musicians that director Wim Wenders's filmed in the *Buena Vista Social Club* (1999). Paul has also performed with Peter Mulvey and Willy Porter while performing with his latest band, Tomorrow Sound. Given Cebar's wide array of musical interests and influences, it was only appropriate that Marquette University invited him to perform during the celebration formally inaugurating the Jean Cujé Milwaukee Music Collection in 1999.

Music to Paul is meant to be exploratory and existential as well as transformational. He embodies this ethos and invites his audience to extend its musical awareness and appreciation; and it has learned as it listened. (He also serves as a DJ for WMSE.) As we left Buckley's, a patron dining there recognized him: "Hi Paul. Keep up the good work." That's exactly what he intends to do.

Sources and Additional Readings

Interview, 17 July 2018

David Luhrssen, "Mr. Milwaukee: The Rhythm of Paul Cebar," Shepherd Express, 23 November 2006, 1, 18-19.

https://en.wikipedia.org/wiki/Paul_Cebar

http://www.paulcebar.com/bios/home_files/paul.html

---

4   As of this interview/writing, Cebar has attended 38 straight New Orleans Jazz & Heritage Festivals.

5   Paul and the Milwaukeeans received WAMI song of the year honors in 1997 for "Didn't Leave Me No Ladder" and Paul earned another WAMI song of the year accolade for "Clap for the Couple Down the Hall" in 1998.

https://www.google.com/search?q=babatunde+olatunji&oq=babtunde+ola&aqs=chrome.1.69i57j0l5.12145j0j7&sourceid=chrome&ie=UTF-8

https://www.youtube.com/watch?v=QXxtqXnUFoQ

http://www.chicagotribune.com/entertainment/music/ct-paul-cebar-ott-0115-20160111-story.html

http://articles.chicagotribune.com/2014-04-10/entertainment/ct-paul-cebar-tomorrow-sound-milwaukeeans-20140410_1_beach-music-country-music-nick-lowe

http://paulcebar.com/reviews/

Sigmund Snopek III:
Discovering "New Mysteries"
by Phillip Naylor

When I first heard the name "Sigmund Snopek," I thought it was a made-up appellation for a rock group. I later learned that this was a gifted musician's real name who eventually earned induction into the Wisconsin Area Music Industry (WAMI) Hall of Fame (2015).[6] Snopek's manifold musical interests distinguish his work. His hundreds of compositions range from symphonic to popular music. "Prog (Progressive) Rock" is usually associated with Snopek, who pioneered the genre locally, nationally, and internationally. Nevertheless, placing Snopek in a specific musical genre is problematic. "Sig"/"Siggy" defies categorization. Consequently, listeners are compelled to engage a musical mélange comparing Snopek with a wide variety of influences such as Frédéric Chopin, Claude Debussy, Erik Satie, Edgard Varèse, Frank Zappa, Sun Ra, Randy Newman, Procol Harum, and Pink Floyd—to name a few! Like Paul Cebar, Sigmund Snopak is a sonic searcher.[7] He concisely explains on his website:

> It was the late 1960s, long before the phrase "prog rock" was coined. I began a quest to find a new musical voice. At the heart was a desire to combine classical music with rock music, electronic music and theater, to explore new ways to share ideas and images. In part, my journey was launched by my musician's disdain for "commercial" pop music. More importantly, my natural inclination to search outside traditional music genres fueled my explorations into unusual chord progressions, distinctive rhythms and unexpected melodies. I felt certain that there were new depths to be found in modern music, new mysteries to be discovered.[8]

---

6   Snopek" became the name of his group after Bloomsbury People.

7   Cebar recalled buying a Snopek album while attending rock performances at the "Alternate Site" (concert space along the lakefront). He realized: "I'm in touch with something here" (Interview with Paul Cebar, 17 July 2018).

8   https://www.sigmundsnopek.com/prog-rock/.

Snopek's musical career began as a teenager in his native Waukesha where he organized his first band, Bloomsbury People, that recorded an eponymous album. According to Bob Mielke: "Their somewhat pretentious title no doubt reflected a sense that they represented an elite, oppositional culture in contrast to what passed then for the Milwaukee music scene (a lot of psychedelic jam bands…) (Mielke 2013, 450).[9] *Bloomsbury People* (released in 1970) has its psychedelic, rocking moments but also meditative ones on "Demian" (inspired by Hermann Hesse's novel) and "Suite: Classical #II. "Greensleeves" also is heard. Snopek plays keyboards and trombone on the album. (A multi-instrumentalist, he also plays the flute, woodwinds [clarinet, oboe], and various horns.). The album is important since it foreshadowed Snopek's distinctive prog rock period. As for Bloomsbury People, the group played at Milwaukee's Midwest Rock Festival (see Chapter 6) and, notably, at the Atlanta International Pop Festival (July 1970) sharing a stage with Jimi Hendrix, Procol Harum, and Spirit, among others.

Sigmund Snopek III

Photo by Philip Naylor

Snopek's quest for "new mysteries" led him to the University of Wisconsin-Milwaukee (UWM) and the tutelage of John W. Downey (1927-2004), the internationally renowned composer and composition and musical theory professor. Professor Downey helped score Snopek's first symphony, *Orange/Blue*, that the Milwaukee Symphony Orchestra (MSO) performed in 1971.[10] His *Talking Symphony*, played by the MSO in 1975, bookended his principal prog rock period, which included albums Virginia *Wolfe* (1972), *Trinity Seasseizesans* ([an opera] 1974-99), and *Nobody to Dream* (1975-1997).[11] Mielke considers *Nobody to Dream* as Snopek's masterpiece (Mielke 2013, 462).

Exploring more commercial routes, Snopek's music, "fluctuating between prog rock and new wave," resulted in albums such as *Thinking Out Loud* (1978); *First Band on the Moon* (1980), and *Voodoo Dishes* (1982) (ibid., 449). Mielke calls the next group of albums

---

9   Bob Mielke, a professor at Truman State University (Missouri), is also involved in a documentary on Snopek's life and music. In his book, *Adventures in Avant-Pop* (see Bibliography), he includes Snopek with other "avant-pop" exemplars: Yoko Ono, Frank Zappa, Neil Young, Joni Mitchell, Sun Ra, and James Brown.

10 While visiting Sig in his East Side apartment/studio (September 2018), he pulled out the original score (for orchestra and rock band) that he inked and followed along as a recording of the symphony played. It was obvious that this music still moved him. He also showed me the original score for the *Talking Symphony*. Sig also created a jazz symphony commemorating the 150th anniversary of the founding of Waukesha and composed for the experimental award-winning Theatre X.

11 Mielke writes: "Like Pete Townshend, Sigmund Snopek likes to revisit and polish his progressive projects" (Mielke, 456).

"stand-alone collections of sundry compositions," e.g., *Roy Rogers Meets Albert Einstein* (1982), *Miasma Fragments: New Music for Pipe Organ* (2001), and *Jade* (2003) (Mielke 2013, 449) (ibid.). The holidays are important to Sig as evinced by *Christmas* (2001); *Ornaments* (2010) and *The Easter Bunny's Christmas* (2011).[12]

What makes Snopek particularly relevant to this book are his references to Milwaukee. This is where he particularly exercises his sense of humor (e.g., "Cookin' with a Wok in Milwaukee [1983], a 45) while taking us on "moveable feasts" of the city and its history.[13] Milwaukee is described as "the land of a thousand bars" in "Thank God This Isn't Cleveland" in *WisconsInsane* (1986).[14] Sig is well known as a fervent baseball fan. The Braves' World Series championship (1957) is celebrated in "Baseball in Outer Space" in *Elephant* (1989). "The Kid" recounts Robin Yount's stellar career in *Baseball* (2006), an album with 70 tracks.[15] *Beer* (1998) includes polkas but also "Locust Street Blues" and "Brady Street Shuffle." His "Balad of Walter Busterkeys" is a tribute to Milwaukee-born Liberace.

Besides being a prolific composer, Snopek is a consummate sideman. He has toured the world backing the Violent Femmes. His friendship with the Femmes and other Milwaukee musicians, e.g., Jim Liban, has led to their participation on Snopek's works.

Sig's instrumental exploration is complemented by his melodic lyricism and his fine voice. His music is often sentimental, e.g., "Sing for Me" on *WisconsInsane*. Although Snopek's music has occasionally been categorized as commercial, who else would add bagpipes to "Thank God This Isn't Cleveland"? Or be lyrically and musically inspired by the news that "diamonds are raining on Saturn"?

Prog rock remains an essential, enduring influence. Snopek reflects:

> Old loves are deepest loves. My adolescent desire for a music that could synthesize diverse musical traditions into something new has matured into a need to refine, record and perform this complex music for audiences everywhere. As a journeyman musician, I have had to write, play and record in all different styles to make a living. But prog rock, along with classical music, is the music I have always come home to, the music that continues to challenge and inspire me.

> Who knows where the next circle will take me?

And us?

---

12 Sig's apartment features lighted ceramic holiday villages.

13 He defines himself as "musician-composer-humorist" on his home page.

14 Sig's "top ten list of favorite gigs" includes playing "Thank God This Isn't Cleveland" in Cleveland (Mielke 2013, 501-2).

15 "The Kid" also evokes Mark Shurilla's "Warren Spahn" (see Chapter 9).

Sources and Additional Readings

https://en.wikipedia.org/wiki/Sigmund_Snopek_III

https://onmilwaukee.com/music/articles/snopek07.html?viewall=1

https://www.allmusic.com/artist/sigmund-snopek-iii-mn0000753003/biography

https://www.sigmundsnopek.com/?p=565

https://www.sigmundsnopek.com/?page_id=83

https://www.sigmundsnopek.com/?page_id=112

https://www.sigmundsnopek.com/?page_id=87

https://www.sigmundsnopek.com/?page_id=581

http://bigbangmag.com/csnopek2.php

http://gepr.net/sh.html

https://www.sigmundsnopek.com/prog-rock/

Paul Cebar

Photo by Dan Johnson

**Paul Cebar during an interview
with Phillip Naylor in 2018**

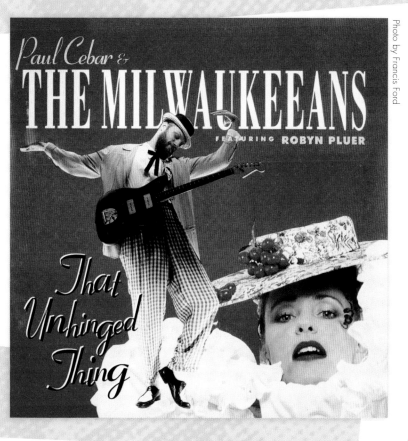

Photo by Francis Ford

Courtesy of Sigmund Snopek

Photo by Phillip Naylor

Sigmund Snopek III with keyboards at his home (2018)

Photo by Phillip Naylor

**Sigmund Snopek III sharing a
composition at one of his pianos at home (2018)**

Epilogue

Chicago has always been bigger and Madison more bohemian, yet Milwaukee nourished a flourishing music scene with its own character from the arrival of rock and roll through the end of the twentieth century and beyond. The city's extensive bar culture, regardless of the ills of excessive alcohol consumption, provided a plenitude of venues for bands—a fact that drew many musicians from neighboring states to Milwaukee, occasionally to live but more often as regulars in the city's barrooms and back halls. During the 1970s, for example, Milwaukeeans embraced Cheap Trick as a hometown band since they played the city's clubs with such regularity.

Through at least the first half of the period covered in this book, Milwaukee was predominantly an industrial city and the musicians brought that work ethic with them into the clubs. Until the disco era, when the number of venues for live music began to diminish, many musicians made a good living playing a circuit in the Milwaukee area. At the same time, the city's heritage of Central European high culture provided sufficient encouragement for creativity. Music instruction was common, whether in schools, private homes, instrument stores or at the Wisconsin Conservatory of Music. Milwaukee musicians such as Sam McCue and Daryl Stuermer played supporting roles in the careers of internationally known stars (e.g., the Everly Brothers and Genesis). And Milwaukee gave rise to many superb songwriters in many styles, including Jim Spencer, Harvey Scales, Sigmund Snopek III, Paul Cebar, Gordon Gano, Terry Tanger (X-Cleavers), Richard LaValliere (Oil Tasters), Jerome Brish (Presley Haskel), and Glen Rehse (Plasticland).

Rock music did not originate in Milwaukee, but by the end of the 1950s to the present, virtually every genre was represented here from rockabilly to hip-hop, psychedelia to heavy metal, progressive rock to punk, soul music to surf and folk to blues rock. Milwaukee was always a year or two behind New York—at least until the 1980s when bands such as the Violent Femmes, Die Kreuzen and Plasticland played leading roles in emerging forms of rock.

We have extolled Milwaukee's accessibility for listeners and musicians. For the latter, as Jim Liban once related to Bruce Cole, the many opportunities offered (often six-nights-a-week) by bars and nightclubs locally and statewide in the 1960s and 1970s, and the stiff competition led to, if not insisted upon, the development of excellent musicianship. Our book commemorates and celebrates an understudied legacy. While not intended to be definitive but reflective and informative, this publication serves as an invitation to readers and listeners to explore and engage in greater breadth and depth Milwaukee's rock and roll history.

Admittedly, this is no longer Sam McCue's Milwaukee nor Harvey Scales's, nor Gordon Gano's. A lot has changed here—stagflation, de-industrialization, a rising skyline, a return of street cars. Nevertheless, Milwaukee continues to evoke and inspire. Somewhere in this great city a nervous band musters conviction besides courage and steps on a stage like so many in the past. The guitarist "amps up"; the singer glances at lyrics scribbled an hour ago; the bass player twists a peg and bottoms out; and the drummer anxiously stretches his skins. When they start playing, it's now their time, their city, and their sound and story. And we thank them for it.

Bruce Cole
David Luhrssen
Phillip Naylor

Selective and Suggested Bibliography

Note: Additional sources (particularly digital), can be found in the narratives as parenthetical citations, footnotes, or attached to the essays as references.

The Jean Cujé Milwaukee Music Collection. Marquette University, Milwaukee, Wisconsin.

Bugle American.

Express.

Kaleidoscope.

Milwaukee Journal.

Milwaukee Journal Sentinel.

Milwaukee Sentinel.

Shepherd Express.

X-Press.

Angeli, Mike, and Mark Goff. 1975. "The Avant Garde: Magic in the Mid-sixties." *Bugle American*, 5 November, vol. 6, no. 38 (no. 223), 20-21, 23.

Barry, Bob. 1991. "Beatle Bob's Bandstand: The Golden Age of Wisconsin Rock and Roll." In *The Illustrated History of Wisconsin Music*, 1840-1999, edited by Michael G. Corenthal. Milwaukee, WI: MGC Publications, 416-433.

_____. 2018. *Rock 'n' Roll Radio Milwaukee: Stories from the Fifth Beatle*. Charleston, SC: The History Press.

The Beatles Invade Milwaukee. 2014. Directed by Raul Galvan. Milwaukee, WI: Milwaukee Public Television, DVD, 27 mins.

Bruckner, Bill. 1975. "Milwaukee's Music & Musicians: Selected Highs, Lows, and In-Betweens." *Bugle American*, 5 November, vol. 6, no 38 (no. 223), 137, 139-141, 143, 145-46, 148-49, 151-53.

Bugle American. 1975. "A History of the Counterculture in Milwaukee (1960-75)." (Special issue) 6, no. 38 (no. 223), 5 November.

Cole, Bruce (interview and Steven Vickers, 10 April 2017). http://mkemelodiesandmemories.weebly.com/storytime-with-bruce-cole.html

Coleman, Jonathan. 1997. *A Long Way to Go: Black and White in America*. New York: Atlantic Monthly Press.

Corenthal, Michael, ed. 1991. *The Illustrated History of Wisconsin Music 1840-1990: 150 Years of Melodies and Memories*. Milwaukee: MGC Publications.

Flessas, Peter A. 2007. *Kids, Soda & Punk Rock: The Story Behind Milwaukee's All-Ages Music Club Yano's*. Milwaukee. Self-published.

Freck, Ken and Joel Kiedrowski. 2017. *Milwaukee Radio Chart Hits: WRIT Radio Surveys 1960-1974*. Milwaukee.

George-Warren, Holly, and Patricia Romanowski, eds. 2001. *The Rolling Stone Encyclopedia of Rock & Roll*. 3d ed. New York: Fireside.

Gurda, John. 1999. *The Making of Milwaukee*. Milwaukee: Milwaukee County Historical Society.

March, Rick. 2015. *Polka Heartland: Why the Midwest Loves to Polka*. Madison, WI: Wisconsin Historical Society Press.

Mielke, Bob. 2013. *Adventures in Avant-Pop*. Kirksville, MO: Naciketas Press.

Myers, Gary E. 1994. *Do You Hear That Beat: Wisconsin Pop/Rock in the 50's and 60's* Downey, CA: Hummingbird Publications.

_____. 2006. *On That Wisconsin Beat: More Pop/Rock/Soul/Country in the 50's and 60's*. Downey, CA: MusicGem, 2006.

Nodine, Steven Willard. *The Cease Is Increase: An Oral History of Milwaukee's Punk and Alternative Music Secene*. 2013. Milwaukee: Steve Nodine.

Nodine, Steve, Eric Beaumont, Clancy Carroll, and David Luhrssen. 2017. *Brick Through the Window: The Oral History of Punk, New Wave & Noise in Milwaukee, 1964-1984*. Milwaukee: Splunge Communications.

Pinkham, Derek J. 2010. *Milwaukee Jazz Profiles: Lives & Lessons of Musicians from the Cream City*. Milwaukee: Marquette University Press.

Racine, Marty. 1975. "From Beatles '64 to Stones '75: Milwaukee Makes It on the Music Map." *Bugle American*, vol. 6, no 38 (no. 223), 5 November, 154-59, 163.

Roller, Peter. 2013. *Milwaukee Garage Bands: Generations of Grassroots Rock*. Charleston, SC: The History Press.

Shurilla, Mark. 1991. "The Progressive Rock Explosion in Wisconsin, 1970-Present." In *The Illustrated History of Wisconsin Music, 1840-1999*, edited by Michael G. Corenthal. Milwaukee, WI: MGC Publications, 434-48.

Spielmann, Peter. 1975. "The 8-year Odyssey of 'Underground' FM." *Bugle American*, no, 6, no 38 (no. 223), 5 November: 160, 163.

Starks, Mark. 2006. *Johnny Green and the Greenmen: The Incredible True Story of the Green-Haired Entertainer and His Top-Rated Show Band*. Copyright Mark Starks.

Szatmary, David P. 2014. *Rockin' in Time: A Social History of Rock-and-Roll*. 8th ed. Boston: Pearson.

Widen, Larry. 2014. *Milwaukee Rock and Roll*. Charleston, S.C.: Arcadia Publishing.

Essay
Contributors

Diana L. Belscamper is a historian who has taught humanities and cultural studies courses at Concordia University Wisconsin, Marian University, Marquette University, Milwaukee Area Technical College, and the University of Wisconsin-Milwaukee (where she received her doctorate). Her published works include articles in the *Journal of Girlhood Studies*, the *Encyclopedia of American Women's History*, and the *Encyclopedia of Milwaukee*. Diana is currently revising her dissertation, *"Your Ticket to Dreamsville": The Functions of 16 Magazine in American Girl Culture of the 1960s*, for publication.

Bruce Cole is a librarian at Marquette University and curator of the Jean Cujé Milwaukee Music Collection, the archive showcased in this book. A legendary drummer, renowned locally, nationally, and internationally. Bruce currently plays with the Doo-Wop Daddies, keeping him in direct contact with Milwaukee's rich and diverse music scene. He is often consulted and has collaborated with the Milwaukee Historical Society.

Gordon Elliott is a singer/songwriter/guitarist. He lived in Milwaukee from 1959 to 1968. He played in numerous Milwaukee bands including the Outlaws, 4MOR, the Notations, the Saints Five, Poor Richard's Almanac, and, in particular, Shag.

Stephen K. Hauser is a lifelong Wisconsin resident and a fifth generation Badger, his great-great grandfather having operated one of the earliest blacksmith shops in Milwaukee. He has been a college history professor for 36 years, teaching at Marquette University, University of Wisconsin-Milwaukee, Lakeland College, Milwaukee Area Technical College, Mount Senario College and the University of St. Francis. He is the author of books and articles about local history and has delivered hundreds of lectures on Wisconsin history to local historical societies and various community organizations. Since 2010 he has authored the "Past Times" history column for the *Elm Grove Times-Independent* newspaper. A confirmed Luddite, he navigates the 21st century without cell phones, palm pilots or computers. "I'm living the dream," he says. "For me, it's still 1964."

Sonia Khatchadourian has taught 15 different courses on blues music through the University of Wisconsin-Milwaukee (UWM) School of Continuing Education, including a course on "Women and the Blues," a semester-long course on the subject of blues at Justus Liebig Universitat in Giessen, Germany, and a freshman seminar at UWM on blues music as cultural studies. She also hosts the *Blues Drive* on WMSE (91.7 FM) on Friday afternoons.

Rob Lewis lives in the Milwaukee area and, since 1996, has conducted extensive research on Jimi Hendrix in Milwaukee and Madison. He has contributed writing to many books and magazines in the United States and Europe, notably, the article "Cream at The Scene" for the British magazine *Where's Eric!* For more on his research, go to milwaukeerockscene.com.

Lil Rev is a Wisconsin-based, award-winning author, entertainer, and educator who travels North America performing and teaching ukulele. His one man shows celebrate: Stephen Foster, Tin Pan Alley, Yiddish, quilting, and blues history. He won the 1996 National Blues Harmonica Championship (at Avoca, Iowa) and in 2004, WAMI (Wisconsin Area Music Industry) named him Best Folksinger in Wisconsin. Pete Seeger once exclaimed: "Listen to this! Lil Rev is great!"

David Luhrssen is Managing Editor of the Shepherd Express, Milwaukee's weekly newspaper. He is author or co-author of several books, including *The Encyclopedia of Classic Rock, Brick Through the Window: An Oral History of Punk Rock, New Wave and Noise in Milwaukee, Secret Societies and Clubs in American History*, and *Elvis Presley: Reluctant Rebel*.

Kevin Lynch is author of the forthcoming book, *Voices in the River: The Jazz Message to Democracy*, and an award-winning arts journalist who was nominated for a Pulitzer as lead writer for *Just Jazz*, a *Milwaukee Journal* Newspapers in Education project. He has also written for *Down Beat, The Chicago Tribune, No Depression: The Quarterly of Roots Music, The Antioch Review* blog, *New Art Examiner, Graven Images: Studies in Culture, Law, and the Sacred,* and other publications.

Phillip Naylor is a professor of history at Marquette University. Although his departmental specialty is Middle East and North Africa (MENA), he introduced a popular rock and roll course with Bruce Cole occasionally "sitting in" and team-teaching.

Barry Ollman was born in Milwaukee and as a son of Benn Ollman, a Midwest correspondent for *Billboard* Magazine (1950-75), music became a principal interest and influence. Barry emerged as a singer-songwriter often performing at the Catacombs and other venues and was the first act to play at the Alternate Site in 1971. He has jammed with John Prine and written and recorded with Graham Nash. He moved to Colorado in 1972 and occasionally returns to Milwaukee. He is a lifelong collector of rare letters and autograph material of musicians and authors with a notable focus on Woody Guthrie, Lead Belly, Bob Dylan, Pete Seeger, the Weavers, and the Beatles.

Jamie Lee Rake was among the first writers to give Milwaukee's contributions to the hip-hop genre coverage in Los Angeles's *Op*; *Ojai, CA's Sound Choice*; and England's *Soul Underground*. He has been a regular contributor to Milwaukee's *Shepherd Express* newspaper and writes for the online gospel music magazine the *Phantom Tollbooth*.

Martin Jack Rosenblum (1947-2014) created the Rock and Roll Certificate Program at the University of Wisconsin-Milwaukee. He was a recording artist for Rounder Records, the archivist at Harley-Davidson, an artist endorsee for Gibson Guitars, a recipient of an Academy of American Poetry award, and co-author (with David Luhrssen) of *Searching for Rock and Roll*.

Evan Rytlewski is the web editor at Radio Milwaukee (88.9 FM). He was music editor for the *Shepherd Express*. He also co-hosted the Milwaukee talk program, *The Disclaimer*, on WMSE (91.7 FM). A former reporter for the *Wisconsin State Journal*, he has contributed writings on music and pop culture to *Pitchfork*, the *A.V. Club*, *Paste Magazine*, and *American Songwriter*.

Rose Trupiano is an academic librarian at Marquette University. She is also a public radio DJ and hosts a bi-monthly radio program which highlights American and international women performing rock, folk, blues, jazz, and dance music.

Index

Note: *Page numbers in italics refer to images*